Made in Scotland

An anthology of new Scottish plays

The Cut by Mike Cullen, **The Life of Stuff** by Simon Donald, **Bondagers** by Sue Glover, **Julie Allardyce** by Duncan McLean

The Life of Stuff: 'This is such stuff as the greatest nightmares are made of . . . The writing is fuelled by heavy Caledonian humour, and a monstrous eloquence, like tigers reciting Blake, or like someone carving arabesques on your skin with a meat cleaver.' John Peter, *Sunday Times*

The Cut: 'A first-rate new play from Scotland . . . a tough moral thriller with a firm narrative spine. Cullen offers a bleak, unsentimental picture of division, rancour and manic obsession with status.' Michael Billington, *Guardian*

Bondagers: 'A subtle and powerful myth about human connectedness; with the earth, with each other and with ourselves. Glover's bondagers may have been haunted by their own future but they also haunt us, unforgettably.' Richard Loup-Nolan, *Independent*

Julie Allardyce: 'Julie Allardyce rushes into the theatre like a fresh breeze off the North Sea . . . Here is a play which makes us feel and see what it is like to work offshore on those strange iron prisons with their unsettling combination of five-star services and social deprivation.' Julie Morrice, *Scotland on Sunday*

Ian Brown has been artistic director of the Traverse Theatre, Edinburgh, since 1988. He trained at the Central School of Speech and Drama and taught drama for two years before becoming a community arts worker at the Cockpit Theatre. He was appointed associate director of Theatre Royal, Stratford East, for two years and then became artistic director of TAG Theatre Company, Glasgow. He has directed new plays, almost exclusively.

Mark Fisher is a freelance writer and critic. He is managing editor of *Theatre Scotland* magazine and theatre editor of *The List*. He writes for *The Herald*, *The Scotsman*, *The Guardian*, *The Observer* and the *Daily Telegraph*.

also available

Black Plays: Three (ed. Yvonne Brewster)
Paul Boakye, *Boy With Beer*; Fred D'Aguiar, *A Jamaican Airman Foresees His Death*; Bonnie Greer, *Munda Negra*; Tunde Ikoli, *Scrape Off The Black*; Winsome Pinnock, *Talking in Tongues*

Frontline Intelligence 1 – New Plays for the Nineties (ed. Pamela Edwardes)
April De Angelis, *Hush*; Declan Hughes, *Digging for Fire*; Judith Johnson, *Somewhere*; Edward Thomas, *East from the Gantry*

Frontline Intelligence 2 – New Plays for the Nineties (ed. Pamela Edwardes)
Karen Hope, *Foreign Lands*; Sarah Kane, *Blasted*; David Spencer, *Hurricane Roses*; Rod Williams, *The Life Of The World To Come*

Gay Plays: Four (ed. Michael Wilcox)
Neil Bartlett, *A Vision of Love Revealed in Sleep*; Eric Bentley, *Round 2*; Gerald Killingworth, *Days of Cavafy*; Joe Pintauro, *Wild Blue*

Gay Plays: Five (ed. Michael Wilcox)
Rod Dungate, *Playing by the Rules*; Noel Greig, *Plague of Innocence*; Jonathan Harvey, *Beautiful Thing*; Joe Pintauro, *Snow Orchid*

New Woman Plays (eds. Linda Fitzsimmons & Viv Gardner)
Elizabeth Robins, *Alan's Wife*; Cicely Hamilton, *Diana of Dobson's*; Elizabeth Baker, *Chains*; Githa Sowerby, *Rutherford and Son*

Plays by Women: Seven (ed. Mary Remnant)
Kay Adshead, *Thatcher's Women*; Claire Dowie, *Adult Child/Dead Child*; Lisa Evans, *Stamping, Shouting and Singing Home*; Marie Laberge, *Night*; Valerie Windsor, *Effie's Burning*

Plays by Women: Nine (ed. Annie Castledine)
Marieluise Fleisser, *Purgatory in Ingolstadt, Pioneers in Ingolstadt, Avant-Garde, Early Encounter* and *I Wasn't Aware of the Explosive*; Maureen Lawrence, *Tokens of Affection*; Sheila Yeger, *Variations on a Theme by Clara Schumann*

Plays by Women: Ten (ed. Annie Castledine)
Simone de Beauvoir, *The Woman Destroyed* (adapted by Diana Quick); Elfriede Jelinek, *What Happened After Nora Left Her Husband*; Claire Luckham, *The Choice*; Phyllis Nagy, *Weldon Rising*

Walks on Water – an anthology of work by leading experimental artists (ed. Deborah Levy)
Rose English, *Walks on Water*; David Gale, *Slips*; Guillermo Gómez-Peña, *1992*; Claire MacDonald, *Storm from Paradise*; Deborah Levy, *The B File*

Made in Scotland

An anthology of new Scottish plays

The Cut
Mike Cullen

The Life of Stuff
Simon Donald

Bondagers
Sue Glover

Julie Allardyce
Duncan McLean

Selected and introduced by Ian Brown and Mark Fisher

Methuen Drama

Methuen New Theatrescripts

This collection first published in Great Britain in 1995
by Methuen Drama
an imprint of Reed Consumer Books Ltd
Michelin House, 81 Fulham Road, London SW3 6RB
and Auckland, Melbourne, Singapore and Toronto
and distributed in the United States of America
by Heinemann, a division of Reed Elsevier Inc.
361 Hanover Street, Portsmouth, New Hampshire NH 03801 3959

Reprinted 1995 (twice)

ISBN 0–413–69180–2

A CIP catalogue record for this book is available at the British Library

Front cover photograph of *Bondagers* at the Traverse Theatre by Sean Hudson

Typeset by Wilmaset Ltd, Birkenhead, Wirral
Printed in Great Britain by Clays Ltd, St Ives plc

Contents

In memory of Alasdair Cameron

Introduction

What's so special about Scottish theatre? If it is special, how special? If it is outstanding, what stands out? It is easy, perhaps too easy, to point to the many admirable qualities in the acting, writing, directing and stage-craft in Scotland's contemporary theatre, but try and pin down the characteristics that make it unique or even clearly distinguishable from any other nation's theatre and you quickly start to sound imprecise. In Scotland we like to talk about the energy, the openness, the willingness to collaborate, the direct and democratic relationship with the audience, the ability to be sentimental, hard-nosed and undercuttingly comical all at the same time, but it is hard to argue that any one of these characteristics is exclusively Scottish.

A brisk look over the four plays in this collection makes any attempt at blanket categorisation seem particularly spurious: what connection could there possibly be between the bucolic poetry of *Bondagers*, the drug-dazed irreverence of *The Life of Stuff*, the coal-face politics of *The Cut* or the oil-rig drama of *Julie Allardyce*? As plays, they represent the diversity of a nation that embraces people on the land, at sea, underground and at play, yet a nation that, for all their contrasting experience, calls every one of them Scottish. Whatever it means, that sense of Scottishness is important and, in itself, might be seen as a defining quality of much Scottish drama. Scotland is a country almost obsessively aware of itself, aware of its history, its social and political make-up, its geographical and linguistic variety, aware of its relationship with the wider world outside. And like any nation, it looks to its artists to define and redefine what is by necessity a complex and contradictory identity.

Each of the playwrights brought together here presents a picture that undermines, challenges or broadens our understanding. Sue Glover in *Bondagers* not only draws our attention to the little-known practice of 'bonding' female farmhands to their male counter-parts, an exploitative system of cheap labour that flourished in the Borders farms of the last century, but also creates an evocation of what such lives were like in all their drudgery and joy, solidarity and loneliness. Simon Donald in *The Life of Stuff* shocks and surprises by reflecting a marginalised urban experience that is rarely made articulate, a world of ravers, wasters and chancers, hedonists, hardmen and head-cases, out for what they can get, whenever they can get it. Mike Cullen in *The Cut* draws on his own experience in mining to upturn our conventional idea of working-class solidarity with a vision of a post-strike coal industry beset by division, cynicism and a bitter every-man-for-himself mentality. And Duncan McLean in *Julie Allardyce* is one of few playwrights to respond to the contemporary experience of the north-east where the oil industry has brought tremendous wealth even as it has upset the established pattern of social relationships.

In as much as these are their distinguishing characteristics, the plays have little in common beyond being produced in the same country. Collectively they might provide a snapshot of Scotland, but individually none would claim to be *about* Scotland. They are, however, the products of a period of sustained health in Scottish theatre which, unlike its English cousin, has managed to stay buoyant despite the relative decline in state subsidy over the past decade. It is a healthiness dependent on the hard work and commitment of theatre workers and as such is a fragile thing, but it has brought about an optimistic and open-minded atmosphere conducive to creativity.

The Cut for example, would not have been produced were it not for a theatre company – Wiseguise – being prepared to stage work it believed in, using trained actors but paying next to no money. The other three plays originated in the subsidised sector – *Bondagers* and *The Life of Stuff* at the Traverse, Edinburgh, and *Julie Allardyce* a co-production between Boilerhouse Theatre Company and the Lemon Tree, Aberdeen – but they too reaped rewards from the creative ferment of the Scottish arts scene. Sue Glover's brief when she was commissioned to write *Bondagers* was to produce something that would give the director lots of work to do. Thus she was liberated to write a fluid, often impressionistic piece, safe in the knowledge that movement and music would become an integral part of the final production.

In a small country it is easy for writers to meet directors to meet painters to meet musicians to exchange ideas and to collaborate, and such cross-fertilisation is a characteristic that gives contemporary Scottish theatre much of its energy and edge. There is a freedom also that allows a novelist and short-story writer such as Duncan McLean or an actor such as Simon Donald to be accepted equally as a playwright. Neither *Julie Allardyce* nor *The Life of Stuff* was a first play, but both were produced after their respective writers had earned a reputation in other fields. Again, this does not make them unique, but it does reflect promisingly on the conditions for creativity.

So if the answer to what's so special about Scottish theatre lies in this book, it is that it thrives on diversity. From a playwright's point of view, there is space to push forward into his or her own imaginative world, be that the exclusively male experience of *The Cut* or the exclusively female experience of *Bondagers*, a play which in its chorus-like sharing of several lead roles even seems to be 'female' in structure. Linguistically, the spiky word-play of *The Life of Stuff* is as successful as the lyricism of *Bondagers*, the Doric lilt of *Julie Allardyce* or the scatological machismo of *The Cut*, distinct registers all and celebrated lovingly by each of the writers. This book does not claim to be a definitive selection, but it does present a cross-section of voices from four corners of the country and, as such, gives a taste of the vigour and variety that has sustained Scottish theatre through an especially dynamic period.

Mark Fisher and Ian Brown
September 1994

The Cut

Mike Cullen

This play is dedicated to my wife Lesley, for her tireless support, and her crucial ideas

The Cut was first produced at the Tron Theatre, Glasgow, on 15 June 1993 by Wiseguise Productions and transferred to the Bush Theatre, London, on 18 January 1994. The cast was as follows:

McGee	Jim Twaddale
Salter	Frank Gallagher
Sandy	Billy Riddoch
Hessel	Kenneth Glenaan
Conch	Martin Ledwith/Allan Henderson

Directed by Martin McCardie
Designed by Martin Ledwith (Glasgow) and Suzanne Field (London)
Lighting by Stewart Steele

Characters

McGee, *the undermanager, fifties*
Salter, *ex-union rep, ex-convict, thirties*
Sandy, *workman, sixties*
Hessel, *oversman, second-in-command, thirties*
Voices of **Conch**, *and a workman*

The play takes place in the present day. Various underground locations: the electrician's howf, roadways, outbye the faceline, faceline.

Act One

Scene One

The howf. There is a wooden bench, next to which is a recessed seat, higher than the rest of the seating. A wire-brush. A hailer on the wall. Two exits, one up, the other down the pit.

Enter **Sandy**, *coughing. He sits on the higher seat, takes out a sandwich and a small whisky bottle. He can't face the sandwich, but has a slug of whisky, which doubles him up with pain. He has a bad coughing fit. There is a beep from the hailer.*

Voice on hailer Calling Wullie McGee, Wullie McGee to the hailer.

Sandy And you can go fuck yoursel.

Sound of man-riding bogies, a bell rings, the bogies come to a halt. **Sandy** *quickly vacates the high seat, sits on the bench.*

Workman (*offstage*) Haw Wullie, Simmy says you said the maingate.

McGee (*offstage*) Fucking tailgate, I said, how in fuck's name you get a weekend shift . . . watch my lips . . . you take the bastard supplies in the bastard tailgate, now MOVE IT.

Enter **McGee**, *in a rush. He carries a cable coupling, which he places in a vice, and proceeds to clean, during the following dialogue.*

Sandy Wullie.

McGee So, you're here.

Sandy Aye, I was early.

McGee Thought you'd maybe seen sense and went on the panel.

Sandy Like fuck, I'm fine. You said yesterday to come right . . .

McGee (*on 'come'*) I ken what I said, dinnae tell me what I said.

Sandy Is there something wrong?

McGee Been any messages?

Sandy Naw, no no since I come down . . . what's up?

McGee Never you mind. (*He takes out a pocket watch.*) Piece-time already?

Sandy It was only a wee slice.

McGee You'll be working piece-time, then?

Sandy What?

McGee Or does the company hae to subsidise your wee slice?

Sandy It's only . . . I was putting it away. (*Starts to put it away.*)

McGee You might as well hae it now.

Sandy I'm no hungry now.

McGee You'll no have time later on.

Sandy I'm no hungry, I said. I *want* to put it away.

Pause.

McGee So why were you eating it?

Sandy I wasnae eating it.

McGee So you were just looking at it.

Sandy I was gonnae eat it.

McGee Well eat it.

Sandy I dinnae fucking want it.

McGee What for no?

Sandy Cos I'm no . . . I dinnae ken.

Pause.

McGee So you're sitting here, haeing a slice, you dinnae even ken why?

Sandy Naw. I dinnae . . . it's what you dae, s'what every cunt does.

McGee S'no what I dae.

Sandy I've *seen* you dae it.

McGee Cos I was under the mistaken impression I came here to bastard work.

Pause. **Sandy** *coughs.*

McGee So you're no haeing a slice, get doon the bastard pumphoose.

Sandy Pumphoose?

McGee Fucked float . . . you watch the water level, switch on the pump it hits the bastard mark, else the general manager's surfin doon the brae, and you and me's signin on the broo.

Sandy Fuck . . . the hail shift?

McGee Na, you could hae a wee break, go and get your P45.

Sandy Aw Wullie . . .

McGee Dinnae bastard Wullie me . . . get yoursel doon that bloody pumphoose, else you'll be sitting in the square wi' the ten o'clock tipplers. (*Pause.*) I mean, what is it wi' you? Pumphoose is a cushie job, nae hassle, nae bastard *work* for fuck's sake.

Sandy I ken that . . . it's just . . .

McGee What?

Sandy (*coughs*) Nothing. It's nothing. (*Bigger cough.*)

McGee Are you okay?

Sandy I'm fine.

McGee Maybe you'd be better up the pit.

Sandy Like fuck . . . I'm fine.

McGee You're looking a wee bit . . .

Sandy (*on 'wee'*) I'm fine, I said. It's only a wee cough.

McGee Fuck Sandy . . . it's the general manager . . . I cannae afford fucking . . . it's the bastard board of directors . . . I mean, this cut's my fucking neck . . . we dinnae get this faceline up and running, it's P45s for the lot of us. I could send you on a message . . .

Sandy I'm no gaun up nae fucking pit, and that's final. You *ken* what would happen the doctors get their hands on me.

McGee You can still catch the bogies.

Sandy I mean, you *ken* . . . you said, you said I wouldnae hae to . . . you said.

McGee But it's the general fucking manager, Sandy, it's my job on the line here.

Sandy It's maybe your job, it's my fucking . . . (*Coughing fit. Pause.*) Still, I wouldnae want you risking your job, son, no for a useless auld bastard like me.

Sandy *rises slowly, and begins to put away his things.*

McGee Look . . . it's only for the day, that's all I'm saying . . . go hame the day, come back the morn.

Sandy Aye, that's fine, son.

Sandy *heads for the exit.*

I'll be fine, dinnae go worrying aboot me . . . I'll go get my wee bit stuff fae the doctor, he'll put me in one of they nursing hame places, I'll be awright.

Stops at the door and turns.

I just want you to ken, son, you've done me proud.

Exits.

McGee Sandy, SANDY!

Crosses the stage.

Auld bastard! (*Exits.*)

Pause.

Enter **Sandy**, *followed by* **McGee**.

Sandy Cos the last thing I want to be's a burden to anybody.

McGee Dinnae worry aboot it. Just . . . just keep oot the bastard road.

Voice on hailer Wullie McGee to the hailer, calling Wullie McGee.

McGee (*into hailer*) What?

Voice Zat you Wullie?

McGee   Naw, it's Arthur Bastard Scargill. What is it?

Pause.

Voice   Is Wullie McGee there, Arthur?

McGee   This is Wullie McGee, ya stupid . . .what is it?

Voice   I thought you'd want to ken, that's Salter past me, Salter on the way. (*Lower.*) Crabbit auld bastard.

McGee   I heard that, Conch, you're on a bastard warning.

Sandy   Salter?

McGee   Now, Sandy . . .

Sandy   Salter Salter? Murdering bastard Salter?

McGee   Dinnae start, right?

Sandy   You mean, he's back here, the day? Away to fuck, I dinnae . . . Salter?

McGee   You just keep oot the road like I said.

Sandy   But . . . they gied him life.

McGee   Life disnae mean life, Sandy, it means ten year tops.

Sandy   But they widnae gie him his job back, no efter what he done.

McGee   D'you think they bastards upstairs gie a fuck aboot a man's past? Christ, you could be a fucking cannibal, wouldnae matter a fuck, when they're looking at a profit. Cos Salter might be a murdering bastard, but he's still the best shotfirer this place has ever seen, so it's fuck the criminal record, here's your lamp.

Sandy   Aw fucking hell, he's coming for me.

Sandy *paces up and down.*

McGee   I kent it, look, calm doon . . .

Sandy   Vicious wee bastard and he's coming for me.

McGee   He's coming for naibdy.

Sandy   He used to kick fuck oot all the scabs, during the strike.

McGee   Sandy, will you listen?

Sandy   Once broke a cunt's thumbs wi' his bare hands, his bare hands.

McGee   He's coming back here to work, he's no gonnae try nothing stupid.

Sandy   He's gonnae kick fuck oot me.

McGee   He's no gonnae kick fuck oot an auld man.

Sandy How no? We're talking aboot a man chucked a boulder off a motorway bridge, for fuck's sake, he's no gonnae stop and ask me my age.

McGee He's no even gonnae come near you.

Sandy Murdering bastard. He's gonnae break my thumbs, Wullie, and I'm telling him, I am.

McGee What? What are you telling him?

Sandy Everything, whatever he wants.

McGee Look, for the last time, he's no interested in you . . . if he's gonnae dae anything, it'll be me he wants to fuck up, no you. All you have to dae is lie low till he's past . . .

Sandy Here? I'm no staying here.

McGee It's the best place.

Sandy You said the pumphoose.

McGee You're staying here oot the road.

Sandy Like fuck.

Sandy *rises and heads for the exit.*

McGee Sandy, you step through that door, and that's it fucked, you're up the pit, and forget the stuff.

Sandy *halts.*

McGee Listen to me, Salter's no gonnae come in here, he's gonnae head straight for the face, he's nae reason to come in here.

Sandy He comes in here, I'm telling him, Wullie.

McGee You open that stupid fuckin trap of yours, and it's needles . . . and tubes . . . and bastard machines, and months and months and bastard months of nothing but waiting, watching the paint flake off the ceiling . . . and they'll keep you there as long as they need you . . . and that's as long as they can find a place they havnae shoved a bastard needle . . . so you just keep it shut. I'm away the pumphoose . . . I get back, want to see my pus in that fucking coupling.

McGee *heads for the door.*

Sandy Wullie wait . . .

McGee (*stopping in doorway, but not turning*) What is it, Sandy?

Sandy You'll . . . you'll come back up?

McGee I said, didn't I?

Sandy And you'll bring some . . . some . . .

McGee Fuck, Sandy.

Sandy I . . . I widnae ask, you *ken* that, but . . . well, it's a wee bit worse. Fuck, it's a lot worse, son. A wee bit stuff . . . helps me breathe.

McGee Look . . . I'll try . . . I cannae promise.

Exit **McGee**. **Sandy** *has another coughing fit.*

Scene Two

A roadway, on the way to the howf. Enter **Hessel***, followed by* **Salter**. **Salter** *is holding his cap lamp in his hand, continually turning it on and off.*

Hessel . . . see, what I'm saying, what I'm trying to say, your pits, right, your pits are basically fucked, ken what I mean, they're F.U.C. kayed, boy . . . cos your gaffers . . . your gaffers are fucking away wi' it, boy, cos there's nae stopping . . . there's nae frigging *union* . . . well, no what you'd cry a union, I mean, a union needs power, a union needs *clout* . . . fucking *drive*, boy . . . nane of this broon-tongue brigade wi' their secret ballots, and their frigging democracy, see your secret ballot, it's just so the cowards can hide away, so's naibdy sees them putting the bit in . . . see what I'm saying, here, so . . . so, I says to myself, efter the strike, I says, how, I says, how can you represent the men now, eh? How can you look efter their frigging interests? And then it dawns . . . you get on the fucking INSIDE, boy, you get yoursel a bit of CLOUT! And then, and only then, can you look efter the interests of the men . . . see? So, I packs in the union, and frigging . . . one mair step, and I'm under-frigging-manager . . . and then, right, then . . . I dae things MY way, and I can put the men first. D'you see what I'm getting at here? You dinnae actually *need* a union, just the right men in chairge, men wi' convictions . . . I mean, no they kind of convictions, like, I didnae mean . . . what I meant . . . men wi' the right sympathies . . . see? D'you get it?

Pause.

You dinnae frigging get it, you dinnae SEE it, do you?

Pause.

Look, it disnae matter, see, the great thing aboot it, the great thing, disnae matter a fuck you trust me or no . . . you get on the inside, boy, you get yoursel a gaffer's job, you dae what the fuck you like, see?

Pause.

What is this dumb bastard routine, eh? Fuck is it wi' you? I'm standing here, I'm talking to you, Salter. What is this? Left your tongue up the warden's erse?

Salter *shines his cap lamp into* **Hessel**'s *eyes.*

Salter Somebody once said that if the lamp's bright enough, and close enough, it can melt the pupil in a cunt's eyeball.

Hessel Jesus, that place's melted your fucking brain.

Salter That place, Hessel? And what would you ken aboot that place?

Pause.

I mean, considering you dinnae even ken where the place is.

Pause.

Never been near the place in your fucking life, in fact.

Hessel   There was reasons for that.

Salter   Reasons.

Hessel   Reasons, man. Look, fuck . . . I couldnae be seen, they'd have sussed me oot.

Salter   First few weeks, aye, but efter that?

Hessel   Fucking stuff happens.

Salter   Stuff.

Hessel   See, like I've been saying . . . you got nicked, I had to make the best of it . . . had to move with the flow, ken what I mean . . . and when you're moving with the flow, you have to keep yoursel *clean*, see what I'm saying? One visit you in the nick, I'm doon as a bastarding criminal . . . and then it's fuck the promotion, boy, away and make the frigging tea.

Salter   Oh it widnae dae for you to be thought of as a criminal, now, would it?

Pause.

Hessel   Na, you're no catching on here . . . what I'm saying, I'm saying stuff, right, stuff happens, but . . . but now, right, now it's frigging pay day, boy, now . . . the wages are in the bank . . . for the pair of us. See?

Salter   Fucking eight year, Hessel. How much d'you reckon that's worth?

Hessel   S'what I'm saying . . .

Salter   You're due me eight fucking year. Eight year. How many years you got in the bank? Gonnae write me a fucking cheque?

Hessel   If you'll just listen . . .

Salter   Why should I listen to you, eh? You never listened to me that fucking bridge.

Pause.

I mean, I come oot, my wife, my bairns, fucked off . . . nae hoose, nae life . . . I'm a non-person, Hessel, we're talking one fucked up life here, and you're sitting there pissing shit aboot wages in the bank.

Hessel   Wait a fucking minute here . . . I never asked you . . . you frigging . . . it was your choice, boy . . . you're gieing me this shit, I never asked you for nothing . . . *you* got yoursel caught . . . fuck was I supposed to dae?

Salter   You could've owned up. I mean, even in the court, I'm sitting there, I'm thinking, any minute now, he'll step through the door, he'll tell them the truth . . . any fucking minute . . . but you had better things to dae, a career to sort oot.

Hessel   So how come you never just tellt them, eh? You could've just shopped me, how come you never shopped me?

Salter   That what you'd have done?

Hessel   It was *your choice*, boy.

Salter   In my position, you'd have shopped me?

Pause.

Hessel   Naw, fuck . . . but, but you're forgetting stuff, here, you just remember what suits ye, you come back here like some kind of holy fucking victim, but you forget, you forget what happened, you forget *your part in this*.

Salter   My part?

Hessel   Look. I ken . . . you're the yin that's suffered, I'm no saying, I'm no . . . you've every right tae cave my fucking heid in, I wouldnae blame ye, but remember, just remember . . . you were the man with the words, the big fucking speeches.

Salter   What?

Hessel   You were the yin used tae get aw the men gaun, with your clever talk, and your list of targets, I . . .

Salter   You're saying it was *my fault*?

Hessel   Naw, I'm . . . I'm just saying . . . I believed you, the men believed you, and they listened, and they *acted*, they acted on every word you said.

Pause.

When they put you away, we were fucked, cos there was naibdy could fire the men like you.

Salter   I never asked you to kill folk!

Hessel   I remember the fucking speech, Jim . . . 'They have tae be stopped,' you said . . . 'Whatever it takes, they have tae be stopped.' Whatever it takes!

Pause.

Salter   But I meant . . . I didnae mean . . .

Hessel   Okay, so I went too far, I was fired up, I was fucking *burning*, boy, but, fuck, man, if things had been the other way aboot, I'd have done the same thing, I'd have done the same thing for you.

Pause.

What I'm saying, I'm fucking here, I'm working, setting this place up for you. I worked this oot here. I planned this.

Salter That is pure shite, Hessel, only cunt you've ever been concerned aboot's yoursel, even in the union days.

Hessel Zat right, well answer me this, right, how come they gied you your job back?

Pause.

Yaise the heid, man, d'you seriously think they're gonnae employ somebody wi' your record? See, that's what I've been telling you, you get on the inside, you get stuff *done*. So I sees your application, lying in the reject tray, I says to them, I convinces them . . . I says, 'This man's the best there is'. I get them where it's tender, in the frigging wallet, I says, 'You hire yoursel a quarryman to fire the road, you get holes in the roof sixteen feet high, you're paying men to fill up holes, for fuck's sake, this is *expensive*.' So then I says, 'You hire Salter, this cunt is the BEST . . . you need an inch off the roof, that's exactly what you get, one frigging inch . . . result, nae holes, fucking speed, and it's straight fucking profit.' So, now d'you see what I'm . . . fuck, wasnae for me you wouldnae *be* here.

Salter And I'm supposed to be grateful?

Hessel Ken your problem? You just cannae bear things to be easy. Got to be the martyr, suffering away sacrificing himsel for the workers . . . well let me tell you, the workers, the workers' memories are shorter than a hoor's skirt, and maist your fan club were first oot the gate when the real money moved in . . . everything's different, Salter . . . you need to get smart . . . I've got this place set up for us, we can make a killing here.

Pause.

Okay, fine, I cannae gie you back eight year, but fuck, man, I can . . . I've got this place by the baws . . . cos the undermanager, right . . . get shot of McGee, you and me's sitting like the devil on a doss.

Salter McGee?

Hessel Aye, cos the bastard's on his final warning . . . stupid cunt fucked up a brand new shearer cutting through rock.

Salter Would've been my faither's job, that.

Pause.

Hessel I meant to say . . . I was sorry, ken . . . what happened'n that . . .

Salter You were sorry?

Hessel I'm just saying . . . nae cunt deserves . . . I mean . . .

Salter Did you go to the funeral?

Hessel Well, funerals . . . for faimly . . . close . . .

Salter Close?

Hessel You ken what I mean.

Salter   And you werenae close?

Hessel   I wasnae faimly, I . . .

Salter   Christ, Hessel, he used to treat you like a second son!

Pause.

Hessel   I just . . . I cannae handle funerals.

Salter   They widnae let me oot for the funeral.

Hessel   I mean . . . I wanted to go, I wanted tae . . . just didnae seem right.

Salter   So how come you were sorry?

Hessel   I was . . .

Salter   Couldnae make the funeral, but you were sorry?

Hessel   Look, man . . .

Salter   Every cunt's *so fucking sorry*. See, it's easy to be sorry . . . means you can forget . . . means you dinnae hae to deal wi' the thing, you you dinnae hae to think . . . cos you can just say, 'Oh, I'm sorry, I'm sorry, what a fucking shame the silly auld cunt fucked up, forgot the button . . . what a fucking shame the crazy auld bastard topped himsel' . . . and then nae cunt remembers what really happened.

Hessel   I remember what happened.

Salter   Tell me.

Hessel   You *ken* what happened.

Salter   Naw, naw, what *I* ken, what I ken's what they *said* happened . . . stupid fucking inquiry said it was my faither's fault . . . but you and me and every other bastard kens different . . . cos you and me kens whae was working that day . . . whae was efter the same job as my faither . . .

Hessel   You mean . . . fuck . . . you mean McGee? Fuck me sideways . . . you mean . . .

Salter   So dinnae stand there gieing me official versions . . . my faither would never work on a conveyor belt athoot putting on the safety switch, he was always a pain in the erse aboot things like that, used to drum it intae my heid, always check the button, check the button, check the fucking button . . .

Hessel   Wait a minute, wait a minute here . . . if what you're saying . . .

Salter   So you see, you can keep this place and your wages in the bank, only thing I want is to set the record straight . . . and there's only one man can help me dae that, and I'm no gonnae rest till I've wrung the truth oot that lying bastard's throat.

Hessel   Fucking hell, if what you're saying's true . . . see, what I'm thinking, what I'm saying . . . seems to me we're efter the same frigging . . . I mean, we want to get thegither here.

Salter   I dinnae need your help.

Hessel   So, what you gonnae dae, you gonnae wander up to McGee, 'Excuse me Mr McGee, but did you no kill my faither cos you were efter his job?' 'Why certainly, Mr Salter, d'you want that in fucking writing there?' Fuck. Off. What you need, and believe me, I ken aboot this stuff . . . what you need's a bit CLOUT, boy . . . I mean, we're talking aboot an immovable object here, this man practically lives in this place . . . it's his frigging wife for fuck's sake . . . you think he's gonnae chuck it away at your request? Naw, you get some clout, you force the issue . . . see what I'm saying . . . a wee bit orginisation . . . see, the way I see it, McGee, right, he's had this final warning . . . *in writing* . . . he cannae afford one fucking slip . . . so here's the perfect oppurtunity . . . the day, right, the general manager and the new board directors coming doon the pit . . . McGee's laying on a demonstration cut . . . so you've got yoursel a bargaining position right away . . . you get yoursel in the faceline, you threaten to blow the place to fuck, you say to McGee, what's it to be? A wee confession, or your job . . . he gies you the gen, you fuck up the cut anyway, he's oot the gate, you and me are set.

Salter   Ah, now I get it, the reason you got me back my job, it was a career move . . .

Hessel   Fuck, man, for once in your life will you let things be EASY!

Pause.

Listen . . . see, it suits us baith to see the cut fucked up . . . and it's frigging simple . . . I can get McGee oot the road, and I can get the faceline cleared, then you could sort of sort of . . .

Salter   Dae your dirty work.

Hessel   Listen . . . you could . . . arrange a few setbacks . . .

Salter   Christ, I'm no back five minutes, you want me to blaw the place up?

Hessel   Na . . . I mean . . . well . . . aye. It makes frigging sense . . . see, see, you could . . . you'd hae a wee bit clout . . . and the cut gets fucked up, McGee's oot the frigging gate, boy.

Salter   And you're the new undermanager.

Hessel   But you get what you want, I get what I want, everybody's happy.

Pause.

Salter   And what if your wee plan disnae work?

Hessel   Then you can rip McGee's heid off his shooders, either way, you get satisfaction. My way, you get some information and all.

Pause.

What do you say?

Pause.

Salter   I'm fucked if I'm gonnae trust you Hessel, I made that mistake eight years ago.

Hessel   Jim, Jim, look at me, look . . . it's *me* you're talking tae, remember? Okay, so I fucked up, I *admit* that, I *admit* it, christ . . . I was feared, I was . . . I wasnae thinking straight, but I'm still *me*! You said it yoursel, and I'm no expecting you tae . . . it's no an easy thing, but I'm fucking *trying*, here I'm trying to make up for it, you gie me the chance.

Pause.

Salter   So I'm just meant to forget, is that . . .

Hessel   Naw, I'm no saying forget, I'm saying *move on*, cos you and me's got a future, here.

Pause.

Let me dae this, let me help you *nail* the bastard.

Pause.

Salter   You'll clear the faceline?

Hessel   Nae problem.

Pause.

Salter   You fuck up, and I'll break your fucking legs.

Hessel   I fuck up, and I'll *help* you break my legs.

They exit inbye.

Scene Three

The howf. **Sandy** *is making a half-hearted attempt to clean the coupling. He coughs, and has another slug of whisky, just as* **Salter** *pops his head in the door.* **Salter** *and* **Hessel** *enter quietly.* **Salter** *carries a shotfiring box.*

Salter   Thirsty work, Sandy?

Sandy *gets a hellish fright, chokes on the drink, and coughs.* **Salter** *advances.*

Sandy   Salter!

Salter   Some water bottle you've got there . . . this new system cannae be so bad, Hessel.

Sandy   You keep away, ya bastard.

Hessel   You've nae frigging idea, boy . . . champagne piece-times.

Salter   Waitress service?

Hessel   Fucking topless.

Sandy   Just you fuck off, right. You're no wanted here.

Salter   That's nae way to talk to a fellow workmate.

Sandy   You're nae fucking mate of mine. Get to fuck . . . keep away.

Salter *stops his advance.*

Salter There's a funny smell aboot this place, d'you notice that, Hessel?

Hessel *Some*thing . . .

Salter Like decayed flesh.

Hessel Like rancid skin.

Salter Like a stinking rotten suppurating *scab*!

Sandy (*brandishing the wire-brush*) You come near me and I'll gub ye.

Salter Careful with that wire-brush, Sandy, you might clean somebody with that.

Hessel I've heard it said he's a vicious wee bastard wi' a wire-brush.

Sandy I ken your game, Salter, you're here to make bother, you're efter something.

Salter Shit. The game's up, Hessel.

Hessel Caught oot again.

Salter Okay, Sandy, you're right, I'm efter something . . . I'm efter your job.

Hessel D'you think you could manage it?

Salter How d'you mean?

Hessel I mean, aw that sitting aboot, daeing fuck all . . .

Salter Drinking whisky . . .

Hessel Wait . . . you're forgetting . . .

Salter What?

Hessel The wire-brush.

Salter Bastard.

Hessel Takes years of practice.

Sandy Youse think you're so fucking clever, just fuck off and leave us alane.

Hessel By rights, I should seck you, Sandy . . . contraband doon the pit . . . that's an oot the gate, behind the bars offence.

Sandy Salter should ken all aboot that, then.

Salter Maybe I'm wrong, but I'm picking up some bad shit, here, Hessel, I don't think we're near the top of Sandy's list of friends.

Hessel D'you think there is such a list?

Salter Well, it's no exactly a list, mair a sort of *name*, really.

Hessel What name?

Salter *and* **Hessel** (*together*) McBastard!

Salter How is our lord and master these days, still a total bastard?

Hessel Worse than ever. Spends mair time undergroond than a frigging corpse.

Sandy   He's a better man than you pair'll ever be.

Hessel   Better at being a bastard, right enough. Sandy's a big fan, ain't that right, Sandy? Gonnae tell us the one aboot the auld faither and the nursing hame?

Sandy   Get to fuck.

Salter   What's the crack, Hess?

Hessel   Well, it seems, correct me if I'm a wee bit oot, here, Sandy, but our hero, McBastard had a faither, which is a total surprise in itsel. Onyway, this faither, being an inconsiderate auld bastard, goes and gets himsel a dose of terminal cancer, so, being the faithful son, right, McBastard sticks the auld cunt in the cheapest, nastiest, nursing hame he can find . . . the sort of place where the only entertainment is the electric shock machine . . . but the auld get manages to hing on there for six month, and where is oor hero all this time? N12 faceline . . . never once went to visit . . . no even when his faither was on his last legs . . . and get this, right, when they kent the auld bastard was on his last lungful . . . the wife phones the pit to tell McBastard to come right away . . . and he was heard on the phone, he says , 'I'm too busy, there's a cut ready.' Too busy to go see his ain faither on his death bed. That no right, Sandy?

Sandy   It wasnae like that . . . it was a busy time.

Hessel   Oh, is that no what happened?

Sandy   He's still a better man than you'll ever be.

Hessel   Maybe some of us need him mair than others.

Sandy   Fuck d'you mean by that?

Salter   I think what Hessel's trying to say, Sandy, is that it's aboot time you extracted the auld tongue, there.

Sandy   You'll no be so fucking clever when McGee gets back.

Salter   My erse is streaming.

Sandy   Your faither was right.

Pause.

Salter   What?

Pause. **Salter** *takes a vacuum flask from his pocket, turns it around in his hands.*

Right aboot what, Sandy?

Sandy   Never mind.

Salter   Naw, come on, I'm interested.

Sandy   It was nothing.

Salter   What were you gonnae say?

Sandy   Fuck all, I'm telling you.

Salter   Come on, oot with it.

Sandy I dinnae want to talk about it, right?

Salter Stop fucking me aboot, Sandy.

Sandy I'm no . . . I just . . .

Salter If there's one thing I cannae stand, it's being fucked aboot.

Sandy I'm telling you . . .

Salter *smashes the flask into the wall close to* **Sandy**.

Sandy Fuck!

Salter You want to tell me now?

Hessel I'd tell him, Sandy.

Salter (*to* **Hessel**) YOU . . . keep oot of this.

Sandy (*coughing*) You're off your fucking heid, you.

Salter Just . . . tell me what you were gonnae say. My faither was right?

Sandy Aye, your faither was fucking right, he used to say, he said . . . he seen right through they union cunts . . . leeches, he cried them . . . sooking the blood oot the men like leeches . . . he said they filled your heid wi' daft ideas . . . wasnae ideas they filled your heid wi', it was bastard craziness.

Pause.

Salter He was never a union man.

Hessel Maybe he had a point.

Salter Like fuck he had a point . . . he was a stubborn auld bastard, baith feet planted firmly in the days when miners worked for fuck all and died wi' even less. He used to take pride in kenning his place. He was the maist aggrevating man you'll ever meet, I mean, he would just say hello, and you'd want to hit him.

Sandy That's no true. (*To* **Hessel**.) Geordie Salter would've done onything for you.

Salter (*also to* **Hessel**) Oh, he'd dae anything, as long as you wernae faimly . . . as long as you wernae a fucking liability, and he could twist you, and mould you, so you looked just like him.

Sandy Geordie wasnae like that . . . he was . . . we were a team, me and him, and he never once let me doon . . . he was the last of the auld-fashioned miners . . .

Salter Thank fuck.

Sandy He went back to the days when there was still some pride aboot this place . . . when the job was still worth something . . .

Salter Aye, ten bob a week, and if you were lucky, a lick at the owner's hole. C'moan Sandy, he was a crabbit, pig-heided auld . . .

Sandy (*on 'pig'*) He was the best belt man I ever seen.

Pause.

Salter Some belt man, forgets to put the button in.

Sandy He . . . (*Pause.*) I ken fuck all aboot that.

Salter D'you no think it's funny, Hessel, you work wi' a man all your life, and yet . . . on the very day he dies, you just happen to be somewhere else.

Hessel A bit peculiar that . . .

Salter And funnier still, don't you think, that the gaffer that day should end up the only name on your list of friends?

Hessel That makes it *damn* peculiar . . .

Salter Damn peculiar . . . Sandy and McBastard . . . bosom buddies.

Hessel Inseper-*ate*-able.

Salter Like a couple of fucks.

Hessel Like a couple of bum-boys.

Salter Like a pair of testicles.

Hessel Like a couple of *junkies*.

Sandy Fuck's that supposed to mean, eh?

Hessel Tell us, Sandy, where were you the day Geordie Salter died?

Sandy What's it to you, Hessel? What's your fucking game, siding with this cunt? You want to watch what your daeing, he's fucking mental, kicks fuck oot auld men . . .

Salter Only if they're crippled.

Sandy Once broke a cunt's thumbs wi' his bare hands.

Salter They never hitchhiked again.

Sandy You just wait, he'll turn on you, Hessel.

Salter Have you no forgotten something, Sandy?

Sandy If I was you . . .

Salter What aboot the hame for crippled weans I burned doon, efter locking all the doors . . . or what aboot that job I had as a serial killer . . . I used to get my victims, Hessel, right, and I'd kill them by removing their lips, and letting them bleed to death . . . you must have heard of me . . . they called me Jack the Lipper.

Sandy   Just think on, Hessel . . . what kind of man chucks a boulder off a motorway bridge? Think on . . .

Pause.

Salter   Gaun fetch my flask up here for me.

Sandy   Get it your fucking self.

Salter   Naw, cos . . . cos you're closer, Sandy.

Hessel   I'll get it.

Salter   LEAVE IT. Now, Sandy, be a nice auld man, and use one of your nice healthy thumbs fetch my flask up here.

Pause.

Sandy (*rising*)   Fuck's wrong wi' your legs, eh?

Sandy *picks up the flask and tosses it to* **Salter**.

Salter   Hey, watch what you're daeing, man, you'll break it. (*Holds the flask to his ear and shakes it.*) See what you've done, it's fucked.

Sandy   Get to fuck, that wasnae me.

Salter (*grinning*)   Zat no terrible that, breaking a cunt's flask.

Hessel   You want to be mair careful, Sandy.

Sandy   Fuck off the pair of you.

Salter   My favourite flask. My first ever flask. The flask I cairried on my very first day.

Hessel   That's tragic.

Salter   This flask has been handed doon through generations.

Hessel   Away.

Salter   Two world wars . . . the General Strike . . . christ, Arthur Scargill himself once had a cuppa from this very flask.

Hessel   So it's a sacred flask. A grail.

Salter   I never thought I'd see the day I'd hae to let it go.

Hessel   But you never reckoned on Sandy the Bastard.

Salter   Nope. Sandy the Bastard Scab has put an end to all of that.

On the word 'that', **Salter** *crashes the flask into the wall again.*

Sandy   You're completely off your heid, you ken that?

Long pause.

Salter   When will the tourists arrive?

Hessel   It'll be piece-time, the general manager likes to catch the sleepers.

Beep from the hailer.

McGee (*on hailer*)   Where's that bastard Hessel? Hessel? You lying aboot that fucking howf?

Hessel   His master's voice.

McGee   Hessel!

Hessel *goes to the hailer.*

Hessel   Aye, fucking aye . . . (*Into hailer.*) Hullo, Wullie, this is Hessel, what's up?

McGee   Fuck are you playing at oot there? Get your arse that faceline this fucking minute, or you'll be looking at your P forty-fucking-five.

Hessel   Aye, on my way, Wullie. (*Off the hailer.*) Bastard! (*To* **Salter**.) . . . You ready to go?

Salter   I'll be doon later, when I've finished here.

Sandy   I want tae go with Hessel.

Hessel   We want to get a move on, Jim.

Salter   You want some company, Hessel?

Hessel   I widnae mind a big shaggable blonde.

Salter   You and me are gonnae hae a wee chat.

Sandy   I dinnae ken nothing.

Salter   Oh but I think you dae, Sandy, you ken plenty.

Sandy *has a coughing fit.*

Hessel   Come on, Jim, Sandy's no gaun naewhere.

Salter   I said! I'll be doon later.

Hessel   You'll no forget oor wee team talk?

Salter   You just buy some insurance for your legs.

Hessel   My legs are safer than a vicar's knob.

Exit **Hessel**. *There is a long pause, during which* **Sandy** *gets himself onto the bench, while* **Salter** *sits on the high seat, and stares at* **Sandy**.

Sandy   Fuck are you gawping at?

Salter   Last time I saw my faither alive, he mentioned you, Sandy. It was in the nick . . . he came to visit me, just the once . . . it was the first and last time he was ever in such a place. He just sat there, across the table, scratching . . . clawed at his heid, at his neck, his nose . . . shoving his hand under his shirt to have a guid howk . . . the man was just one big itch. Ken why he was there? Course you dae, cos that's what he said, he said . . . 'Only person kens I'm here is Sandy, cos I tell Sandy everything.' He was sat there in his funeral suit . . . and . . . I tried to look at him . . . to catch his eyes, but he . . . he couldnae . . . widnae . . . I couldnae catch them . . . he looked at the flair, at the table at the windies, but he just couldnae bring himsel to look at *me* . . . and, ever since . . . I've been trying to remember . . . I've been trying, but . . . I cannae remember his eyes, Sandy . . . it's like I've never actually seen them . . . ever . . . like he never once in his life ever actually looked at me . . . I can remember his face . . . but just . . . empty sockets . . . and he sat there, no looking, and he spoke, and I can remember every single word he said, he said. . . 'I'll no call you son, cos nae son of mine could've done what you've done.' And I wanted to tell him . . . I wanted *so bad*, to scream it at him . . . 'It's no true, Da. I never done it! I never done it!' I was shouting it inside my heid, hoping maybe he'd hear inside his . . . but he just looked at his feet, and said, 'From now on I want you to stop thinking of me as your faither . . . I'll visit you from time to time . . .' and I stood, and my heid was . . . the room was whirling, and I thought I was gonnae vomit ower the table . . . and I think I said . . . 'dinnae bother' . . . and I fell oot the room . . . and I never . . . he never bothered . . .and that was that . . . the times I've went ower they words in my heid . . . and I keep hearing him say . . . 'I tell Sandy everything'. I mean, why tell me that? Why? It disnae make sense. Does it make sense to you?.

Sandy   If it's sympathy you're efter . . .

Salter   I dinnae want your sympathy, Sandy . . . I just need . . . did he tell you aboot any of this?

Sandy   Why should I tell you?

Salter   Cos this is *important*, Sandy.

Sandy   He tellt me was gaun to see you, that's it.

Salter   Did he say why?

Sandy   Fuck does it maitter now?

Salter   Did he, Sandy?

Sandy   He said . . . what d'you want me to say? He said what you just said.

Salter   And what else?

Sandy   Nothing.

Salter   You're fucking me aboot again.

Sandy   I'm no . . . I've tellt you what he said . . . there's nothing else.

Salter   You're lying.

Salter *makes for* **Sandy**.

Sandy   Fuck off.

Salter   Just . . . tell me.

Sandy   He said he was gonnae teach you a lesson you'd never forget.

Salter   Oh he done that awright . . . he . . . (*Pause.*) so, what else?

Sandy   Jesus . . . that's it, for fuck's sake.

Salter I mean efter the visit.

Sandy Nothing.

Salter You never discussed it?

Sandy Never.

Salter Never said nothing?

Sandy I *tellt* you.

Salter What have I tellt *you*, Sandy, I hate getting fucked aboot.

Sandy I'm no. I just . . . I saw him on the stretcher, on the way up the pit, that's all, honest, I swear.

Salter Did you speak to him?

Sandy I just seen him.

Salter Did you speak to him?

Sandy He was deid, for fuck's sake.

Salter You're lying.

Sandy I'm no . . . you werenae there . . .

Salter How did it happen?

Sandy I dinnae ken.

Salter I think you dae.

Sandy I ken fuck all, I'm telling you.

Salter Whae was carrying the stretcher?

Sandy Fuck should I ken? Fuck should I tell you, even if I did?

Salter *advances again,* **Sandy** *hides his hands behind his back.*

Sandy No my thumbs, dinnae break my thumbs.

Salter What in fuck's name you slavering aboot? Why would I want to break your thumbs?

Sandy You've done it before.

Salter Whae . . . I dinnae believe this. I wouldnae ken how to break your thumbs, Sandy. Whae's been feeding you this shit?

Sandy Hessel tellt me aboot auld Davy Thompson.

Salter Hessel tellt ye?

Sandy Said he watched you dae it with your bare hands.

Salter I dinnae fucking . . . Hessel said that? What else has Hessel been saying aboot me?

Sandy I'm no saying another word.

Salter Will you stop cowering away, I'm no gonnae hurt you.

Sandy You threw a flask at me.

Salter I lost the heid . . . christ, everybody loses the heid . . . I dinnae believe this, I mean, eight year, eight year I gave that bastard, and this is what he goes and does . . . nae wonder he never had the nerve to come and see me, nae wonder naibdy wants to talk to me, he's got everybody thinking I'm a fucking psychopath. Look at you sitting there like a battered dug . . . you actually thought I was gonnae break your thumbs, actually believed it. This is no fucking real.

Pause.

Sandy What do you mean, you gave him eight year?

Salter Nothing. I meant nothing, right?

Sandy Doesnae soond like nothing to me, soonds like you're saying . . .

Salter (*standing*) I'm saying nothing . . . I said nothing, okay? OKAY?

Salter *heads for the exit.*

Sandy I was only asking.

Salter Well dinnae. Dinnae even gie it a second thought. I mean, God forbid you should believe anything *I* say. If you want me, I'll be the faceline, breaking some cunt's thumbs.

Exit **Salter***.*

Scene Four

A roadway. On the wall, two hailers, either side of stage. Also, a lockout box. Two exits, uphill, downhill. Enter **McGee***, pursued by* **Hessel***, from uphill.*

McGee I said later, Hessel.

Hessel Look we have to . . . will you wait a frigging minute.

McGee (*stopping and turning*) I dinnae have a fucking minute. The tailgate still no advanced from the nightshift . . . bastard general manager through the lockers . . . and now the bastard belt stopped.

Hessel But that's what I'm talking aboot, s'what I'm saying . . . general manager comes doon, last thing you need's a frigging *crisis*.

McGee Crisis? Is this aboot Salter, cos . . .

Hessel No, no, no Salter . . .

McGee What then?

Hessel It's got . . . listen . . .

McGee   There's nae bastard time . . .

Hessel   I ken that . . . just . . . right . . . whae's in chairge, here?

McGee   I dinnae believe this, pit's falling to bits, you're gieing me bastard Mastermind. (*Walks away.*)

Hessel   No . . . wait . . . listen, it's just you, right, just you, so whae's gonnae take care of this bastarding place, when you're fucking aboot wi' Salter?

McGee *stops.*

McGee   What are you saying?

Hessel   See . . . Salter's doon here, wants to see you fucked. (*Pause.*) What you want . . . what you need for fuck's sake's a cunt on *your* side.

McGee   So what you're saying you want another promotion?

Hessel   You and me's got a vested interest, Wullie.

McGee   Fuck, I just gied you promotion, Hessel.

Hessel   It makes sense.

McGee   What mair d'you want, eh?

Hessel   Listen . . . Salter's a trouble-making bastard . . . last thing we want's cunts like him coming doon here fucking aboot. You put me in chairge, I get shot of the bastard for you.

McGee   And I'm supposed to trust you?

Hessel   You want to try trusting *him*? (*Pause.*)

McGee   I cannae just . . . na, no way, Hessel.

Hessel   But you're no making any sense.

McGee *turns to leave.*

Hessel   Cos the longer Salter's doon here, the mair likely he'll find stuff oot.

McGee *stops, nods head.*

McGee   I wondered when you would get roond to that.

Hessel   It's no me . . . dinnae get me wrong . . . I wouldnae . . . see, I want shot of Salter just as much as you . . . so, I wouldnae . . . but it's auld Sandy . . . see, okay, it sounds bad me bringing this up, but this is what I'm saying . . . you have to think about this stuff, Wullie, it's no . . . look, okay, I might've bent your airm a wee bit the last . . . but this is different . . . this is . . . I'm no aboot to go shooting my mouth off to frigging

Salter, but Sandy . . . Sandy's an auld man . . . and frig knows how . . . I mean, I dinnae ken how often he needs how much you how much you . . .

McGee It was only the once, for fuck's sake . . . my bastard luck to get seen.

Hessel Fine, fine, that's fine, but . . . d'you see what I'm getting at here?

McGee Aw I can see, Hessel, 's a blackmailing bastard.

Hessel Na, no, listen, you're no getting it . . . see . . . Sandy . . . the stuff . . . it's a weakness . . . and Salter sniffs oot a weakness like a dug sniffs oot a bitch . . . and then he frigging *rams it right in* . . . and auld Sandy . . . well, he wasnae looking too clever when I left him.

McGee With Salter?

Hessel I'll tell you, thon's one mental bastard.

McGee You left auld Sandy with Salter?

Hessel Christ, you were bawling ower the hailer, what was I supposed to dae? I'd have secked him on the spot, I had the frigging power . . . that's what I'm telling you.

McGee Fuck, I thought Salter would come right doon.

Hessel So, now, you see what I'm saying? You go get the tailgate advanced, I go get Salter up the frigging pit, right? But I need the power, I need some authority, here, he's gonnae listen to me.

McGee And what if I dinnae gie you it, Hessel?

Hessel Then . . . nothing. I'll no say nothing . . . but it's your funeral, Wullie.

Pause.

McGee I'll hae to think aboot it.

Hessel Fuck man, there's nae time, you said it yoursel.

McGee I *need* time . . . how do I ken . . . last time you said that was it, Hessel . . . you said you widnae bring it up again . . . so how can I trust you, eh?

Hessel It's no a question of trust, it's a question of making sense.

McGee Cos I'm telling you, I go, you go.

Hessel I ken that . . . that's what I'm saying. I get shot of Salter, you get on with the cut, you dinnae hae the hassle of having to face up to Salter.

McGee I'm no feared of Salter.

Hessel I'm no saying . . . fuck, what are we, bairns here? I'm just saying when it comes to the crunch, you're no as young as you used to be, and Salter's a vicious wee bastard, so it would be easier . . .

McGee Okay . . . this is how it is . . . *I'm* gonnae take care of Salter, you get the tailgate advanced . . . I'll *think* aboot the promotion . . . I'm promising fuck all, mind . . .

Hessel Fuck, Wullie, you're no listening . . .

McGee No, you listen, Hessel . . . I've made up my mind.

Pause.

Hessel You'll go check auld Sandy?

McGee Aye, aye, just as soon as this belt's . . . what's this sudden concern for Sandy?

Hessel You never saw Salter, he looked fucking vicious, boy.

McGee I'll take care of Salter. Now fucking move it.

Hessel I'm gaun. How long afore you let me ken?

McGee As long as it takes.

Hessel Dinnae mess me aboot, Wullie, I want to ken afore piece-time.

McGee Hessel, for fuck's sake!

Hessel Piece-time, Wullie.

Exit **Hessel***, downhill.*

McGee (*into hailer*) Conch, Conch, fuck's up wi' the belt, fuck's up wi' the belt?

Pause.

Conch (*on hailer*) Safety button in the belt, Wullie, button in the belt.

McGee A button? (*Into hailer.*) Whae's got a button in the bastard belt, whae's got a bastard button in?

Pause. Enter **Salter***, from uphill. The men don't see each other, they are at different hailers.*

McGee This is the undermanager, here, whae's got that button in?

Salter (*on hailer*) There's somebody working on the belt . . . man working on the belt.

McGee Well get the fuck off . . . get the bastard thing . . . right, whae's the stupid bastard?

Pause.

Salter (*on hailer*) Geordie Salter's on the belt, Wullie, Geordie Salter's working on the belt.

McGee *is momentarily shaken, then it dawns on him.*

McGee Salter ya bastard, get that fucking button oot.

Salter I tellt you Wullie, man working on the belt . . . you cannae start the belt when there's a man working on it.

McGee (*heading for the exit uphill*) That bastard.

Salter (*on hailer*) Man working near the fucking gable-end, near the gable-end . . . near the fucking gable-end . . .

McGee *moves towards second hailer.* **Salter** *is in the shadows.*

McGee Bastard.

He goes to the lockout box, unlocks the button.

(*Into hailer.*) Okay, Conch, start the belt, start the belt.

Pause.

Conch (*on hailer*) Still a button in, Wullie, still a button in the belt.

Salter Man working on the belt, Wullie, I tellt you.

McGee You! Ya bastard . . . how many buttons you got in?

Salter No checking, Wullie? No checking to see whae's working on the belt? Somebody could get hurt. (*Steps out of the shadows.*)

McGee Just . . . dinnae gie me your shit.

Salter Somebody could get *killed*, Wullie.

McGee Oot my road.

Salter And let you take aw the buttons oot, when there's a man working on the belt?

McGee There's nae cunt on the belt, now, oot my fucking road.

Salter I'll get oot your road, soon as you me's had a wee chat.

McGee Oot my fucking road, I said.

Salter And I'm saying we're gonnae hae a wee chat.

Pause.

McGee Look Salter, I dinnae ken how you swung this job, but you fuck me aboot, your feet'll never touch the grund, d'you hear me?

Salter What's the problem, here, I'm only trying tae talk to ye.

McGee I've nothing to say to you.

Salter A wee chat, aboot the auld days, aboot you landing yoursel the plum job.

Pause.

McGee What in fuck's name you havering aboot?

Salter   Listen, Wullie, I dinnae want this getting oot of hand, I spent my last fucking favour to get this job, last thing I want to dae is fuck it up . . . but there's questions, here . . . questions that have never been asked.

McGee   Questions?

Salter   Like where were you the day my faither died?

Pause.

McGee   I kent it would be something like this, you listen to me, Salter, you want to work, that's fine. Anything else, you're back the fucking dole queue, now oot my road, afore I really lose my temper.

McGee *attempts to brush past* **Salter***, who grabs hold of* **McGee***, securing his head in an arm lock.*

McGee   Get to fuck.

Salter   What aboot the buttons that just happen tae unlock, and the belts that start by themselves . . .

McGee   I'll hae you arrested for this.

Salter   Me and Sandy had a wee chat.

McGee   See if you've hurt him . . .

Salter   Brilliant memory for his age.

McGee   Fucking let me go.

Salter   You want to tell me what happened?

McGee   You're fucking back inside, ya bastard.

Salter   Ever heard the expression 'dead man's shoes', Wullie?

McGee   You're fucked, d'you hear me . . . fucked.

Salter   Dead man's shoes is what you're wearing . . . only yours werenae handed doon, oh no, you took yours, fucking took them off the feet, right off the feet, and the body was still fucking *warm*.

McGee   You're off your fucking heid.

McGee *breaks free, and knocks* **Salter** *to the ground*.

Salter   Where did you find them, lying in the gable-end?

McGee   You listen to me, Salter, you fuck me up the day, I'm on that phone, the cops are waiting the pit-heid . . . you walk straight back inside.

Salter (*rising*)   No, you listen to me . . . cos I dinnae gie a shit, cos I'm here to put the record straight . . . even if I have to tear this place to bits, girder by fucking girder . . .

even if I end up back inside for the rest of my days, I'm no leaving here until I've found oot the truth.

McGee (*turning away, heading for the exit uphill*) I've nae time for this crap.

Salter D'you hear me, Wullie? The truth, I'll fucking destroy this place, I'll destroy you . . .

Exit **McGee.**

Salter You cannae run for ever, McBastard.

Salter *attacks the lockout box.*

Here's your precious button, Wullie, why d'you no you check to see if it's in, why d'you no . . . (*He falls to his knees, and smashes up the box.*) why . . . check . . . the button . . . check . . . the button . . . check . . . check . . . check.

Blackout.

Act Two

Scene One

Outbye the faceline. Two exits. A first-aid box.

Enter **Salter***, from outbye. He lays down his gear – the shotfiring battery, the keps, the box of gelignite. He removes his jacket, sits down, takes out a sandwich, which he proceeds to eat. Enter* **Hessel***, from inbye.*

Hessel I wondered where you'd . . . what are you dain?

Salter Having my piece.

Hessel Christ, the general manager's already doon the pit, there's nae time.

Salter Oh, there's plenty time for me, Hessel. Plenty time.

Hessel Half an hoor, and the bastard's here.

Salter I mean, I've got months, years maybe. See, I can wait, bide my time, I'll get what I want, eventually. You're the one in a hurry.

Hessel I dinnae get it, what the fuck's gaun on? I'm in there, I'm getting rid of the men, like we agreed, we've got a fucking deal . . . you're sitting aboot here like a prize arsehole.

Salter Now, Hessel, you want to be a bit careful with your insults, especially when you're talking to a man with *my* reputation.

Hessel You finally flipped, or something?

Salter Cos you get me upset, there's nae telling what I might dae.

Hessel What is your problem here?

Salter I could end up hammering nails through your taes, or . . .

Hessel Na, you've lost me . . .

Salter . . . or crushing your teeth with a pair of pliers, or . . .

Hessel What the fuck is this?

Salter . . . or maybe breaking your thumbs with my bare hands.

Pause.

Come on, Hess, any ideas? You seem to be pretty sherp on the auld psychopathic story front.

Hessel Am I meant to ken what you're talking aboot?

Salter You ken *exactly* what I'm talking aboot.

Pause.

Hessel What is it you want, can you maybe gie me a clue?

Salter What do I want? I want tae just sit here, dreaming up new methods of geriatric torture, new techniques for breaking thumbs.

Hessel Listen to me, Salter, I've kept my side the bargain, the maingate's cleared, the job's set up, all you have to dae is finish the thing off.

Salter You finish it off.

Hessel What?

Salter Here, gelignite, battery, keps, you finish it off. Cos I'm finished with you.

Hessel Fuck, man, you cannae dae that, we had a deal . . . you're gaun back on your word.

Salter And you're the man of honour, eh? Never break your word, never go sneaking aboot ahint a cunt's back, spreading vicious lies and rumours.

Hessel Aw, for fuck's sake, show a wee bit savvy, here, Salter. So, maybe I said a few things here and there, when the situation . . . a few exaggerations . . .

Salter Hessel, I gied you eight fucking year! I come doon here, I dinnae recognise mysel.

Hessel We've been through aw that . . .

Salter Aw that shite, aboot you waiting for me tae come back was just shite. Hessel . . . you wernae waiting, you were fucking . . . destroying me doon here . . . I'm lying in that hell-hole, daeing your fucking time, and you're here inventing some kind of monster . . . Salter the Psycho . . . hide your fucking thumbs, I mean . . . *what the fuck you playing at?*

Hessel I never fucking . . . yaise the heid, man, I mean, there's times, right, when stuff's needed, when you're looking for a wee bit leverage . . . and things get said, and then they get forgotten . . . you forget . . . you canne be held responsible for every slip of the tongue.

Salter Slip of the tongue? Auld Sandy was shaking, he was terrified of me cos your slip of the fucking tongue.

Hessel Auld Sandy, I might've fucking guessed, what's he been saying?

Salter He didnae need to open his mooth, he just sat there, trembling.

Hessel C'moan, man, the auld cunt's no the full shilling, you ken that . . . christ, winding up Sandy's part of the frigging training doon here . . . you were winding him up yoursel . . .

Salter Aye, but I wasnae trying to convince him that you were the bloke fae the Texas Chainsaw Massacre.

Hessel Okay, look, I'm sorry here, right? I apologise . . . you can beat my brains oot with a big stick, I'll volunteer for a guid kicking, but *later*, okay . . . there's a job to be done, and I'm talking aboot yesterday.

Salter   You . . . d'you have any idea . . . you want me to risk my neck for the likes of . . . efter . . . you have got to be . . . look, there's the gear, faceline's that way.

Hessel   It's no me that *wants* this, christ . . . McGee's on the way oot anyway, the job's already my fucking pocket, boy, this is *your* opportunity, here, I'm only trying tae help you oot . . . you dinnae want my help, then that's *fine*, that's *fine*, I dinnae fucking *need* this . . . I'm taking chances here I dinnae need tae *take*, and I'm daeing it for you, cos I reckon I'm fucking *due you*. But you want tae miss this, then that's fucking fine.

Salter   You . . . you've never helped anybody but yoursel . . . you . . . you fucking . . . weasel away wi' your smart-arse garbage, everybody's pal, everybody's buddy . . . words dripping fae your mooth like shit . . . I dinnae buy it anymair, Hessel, d'you hear me? I dinnae. Fucking. Buy it!

Pause.

Hessel   You try tae dae a cunt a favour.

Salter   I dinnae want your favours, I've had enough your kind of favours.

Pause.

Hessel   Fair enough.

Pause.

But I'll tell you, you'll never get another chance like this.

Pause.

First chance he gets, McGee'll see your erse through the gate.

Pause.

But you just want tae let him away wi' it, that's fair enough . . . your reputation's mair important than your faither's.

Salter   Dinnae push me, Hessel, you fucking push me, I'll . . . I'll fill the shoes you made me, and I'll break your neck, never mind your thumbs.

Pause.

Hessel   So that's it then. You're just gonnae gie up?

Salter   Whae said anything aboot gieing up?

Hessel   So what you gonnae dae?

Salter   I dinnae need to dae nothing . . . you're gonnae help me oot.

Hessel   Fuck, man, what have I been . . .

Salter You see, seems you're forgetting what the facts are here. Cos I would hate to have to broadcast your wee mistake the motorway bridge.

Pause.

Hessel Now wait a fucking minute . . .

Salter And I cannae see the bastards upstairs being too keen on a murderer for undermanager.

Pause.

Hessel You think anybody's gonnae believe you?

Salter You want tae take that chance?

Hessel A criminal? You think . . . you think you're gonnae waltz in the office wi' your wee fairy tale, they're gonnae buy it? You've nae proof, Salter, nae evidence . . . it was *you* they convicted . . . far as the bastards upstairs are concerned, you're the guilty fucking party . . . you dinnae ken what . . . you'll . . . you'll come acrosss like the nutter they think you are, they'll fucking laugh at you, boy, they'll fucking . . .

Salter What's the maitter, Hess? The past breathing doon your neck?

Hessel FUCK YOU WANT FROM ME?

Pause.

Salter I want you to speak tae auld Sandy.

Hessel Auld Sandy?

Salter Tell him the hail story, starting wi' the bridge.

Pause.

Hessel I dinnae get it.

Salter You dinnae need to get it, you just need to dae it.

Hessel But fuck's sake, man . . .

Salter The hail story, Hessel.

Hessel Think aboot this . . . I tell Sandy, it'll be aw roond the pit, you and me's fucked.

Salter Naw, you'll be fucked, I'll be some kind of good guy, but what's your alternative, here? Cos you dinnae go tell Sandy the hail story, I might be tempted to stick a poster up the noticeboard, your name at the top!

Hessel I just dinnae . . . what frigging use can Sandy be?

Salter Sandy kens something, but he's too busy shaking to dae any talking.

Hessel Did you tell him anything?

Salter That's got nothing . . .

Hessel   You *tried*, didn't you, you tried to tell him, but he wouldnae listen . . . and that's what I'm telling you . . . naibdy's gonnae listen, Salter, naibdy's gonnae *hear* your story.

Salter   And that's why you're gonnae tell him.

Hessel   Am I *fuck* gonnae tell him. Jim, you're . . . you ken what you're risking here? You no hear anything I said to you? It's . . . its's madness is what this is . . . fucking . . .

Pause.

Okay, okay, I'll make a deal wi' you. (*Sits.*)

Salter   Nae deals.

Hessel   No, hear me oot, hear me . . . what you're asking . . . it's fucking *big*, boy, this is a big . . . and okay, I can see that you think . . . but let me make this thing clear to you . . .

Salter   I said nae fucking deals!

Hessel   I dinnae have to dae this. That's the situation . . . I dinnae have tae dae any of this . . . but I'm thinking, I'm thinking . . . I might be . . . willing to consider this here, if I kent there was some kind of *back up*. Think aboot it, I go tell auld Sandy, and even if he buys it, which I dinnae think . . . but even if he does, you've nae guarantee he's gonnae come up wi' an answer . . . I've stuck my neck oot for nothing, and you've missed your chance, see what I'm saying? You need to be ready for that, you need to be . . . so, I'm suggesting . . . you *go ahead*, you *go ahead* oor wee plan, just in case . . . you've got some back up.

Salter   I dinnae have tae, Hessel. I can wait see what happens.

Hessel   No you fucking . . . the bottom-line, here . . . we're running oot of time, it'll take me half an hoor to go tell Sandy, by that time it's too fucking late.

Pause.

Salter   Too late for *you*, Hessel.

Pause.

Hessel   Okay, here's the story . . . I'm no taking a risk like this for nothing, you get me? I'm no daeing it, Jim. I need that faceline fucked up, and that's the deal.

Salter   Now we're getting tae it.

Hessel   You fuck up the face, I gie Sandy the gen. You want tae sit aboot here, it's another game, Jim, a game you cannae win, cos you've got fuck all credibility this place.

Salter   No, you seen tae that, ya bastard.

Hessel   S'a fact, Jim. A fact. You want tae waste your time fighting me, then fine, but let me tell you, I'll go the fucking distance, boy, and by that time McGee'll be long fucking gone.

Pause.

But if that's what you want . . . (*Rises.*)

Salter   Hessel, you think I'm fucking stupid? I blaw the faceline, they'll put me back inside.

Hessel   But I've tellt ye, I can handle that . . . you say McGee wanted a bit off the roof, I back you up, the hail thing's *his* fault. There's nae risk.

Pause.

So, we on, or what?

Salter   Okay, you just listen up, you dinnae tell Sandy, when I'm finished wi' McGee, I'm coming efter you.

Pause. **Hessel** *nods.*

Hessel   I'll be waiting, I hear the bang, I put him straight . . . I gie you my word.

Salter   Your word?

Hessel   My mother's life.

Salter   You never had a mother.

Salter *heads for the faceline.* **Hessel** *exits outbye.*

Scene Two

A roadway. Two exits, inbye and outbye.

Enter **McGee***, in a hurry, followed by* **Sandy***.*

McGee   I mean, I thought Salter'd killed you, the way Hessel was talking. You're sitting there, no a fucking scratch.

Sandy (*struggling to keep up*)   And that's my fault, is it?

McGee   Hurry up, for fuck's sake, Salter's half-way to the face, I'm fucking aboot with you, you're no even marked.

Sandy   What d'you want me to batter my pus off a wa'.

McGee   I'll batter your pus off my fist, you dinnae hurry up.

Sandy   Ah, hell . . . hing on, Wullie. (*Sits down. His breathing is laboured.*)

McGee   Fuck is it now?

Sandy   Stane, in my bit. (*Removes boot.*)

McGee   A stane? First it's a drink, then it's your lamp, now it's a bastard stane.

Sandy   Must be in my sock. (*Removes sock.*)

McGee   If you'd stayed back in the howf like I said.

Sandy   I'll no be long.

McGee   Look, Salter'll be breaking the place up.

Sandy   I'm nearly there. That's it.

McGee What? I never saw a stane.

Sandy It rolled.

McGee Where? I never saw it.

Sandy It maybe wasnae a stane.

McGee Well, what was it, then.

Sandy I dinnae ken, a bit skin or something.

McGee A bit skin? You said it was a stane.

Sandy I thought it was a stane.

McGee A bit skin, like a stane?

Sandy Aye.

McGee You said it rolled. I've never seen skin that rolled.

Sandy Well maybe it was roond skin.

McGee It would need to be ball-shaped to roll.

Sandy WELL MAYBE ONE OF MY NUTS HAS DROPPED OFF.

Pause.

McGee Listen, Sandy, d'you no think it would be better if you stayed here, you can hardly walk.

Sandy I'm staying with you, and that's final.

McGee Naw, look, you'd be daing me a favour, see, cos there's a hailer up the road, you could keep an eye open for the general manager, and let me ken. It would gie me that wee bit time.

Sandy You ken exactly where he is, so dinnae gies your shit.

McGee Naw, but it would be a help to have it confirmed.

Sandy I'm coming with you. You get in there, I might no see you again.

McGee I could get in there and back oot twice the time it's taking with you. Will you no see sense.

Sandy Soon as you get in there, you'll forget all aboot me. (*Coughing fit.*)

McGee Christ, man, you're coughing up blood. (*Pause.*) Na, I'm no having this, I'm getting you up the pit.

Sandy No . . . wait, Wullie . . . doesnae mean nothing, it's happened before.

McGee But you're coughing up blood.

Sandy Some stuff, I'll be okay.

McGee I'll hae to go *get* you some stuff.

Enter **Hessel**, *from outbye.*

Hessel   Wullie, quick.

McGee   Fuck are you daeing here?

Hessel   Salter's on the face, he's gonnae blaw the frigging place to bits.

McGee   Away to fuck . . . you should've stopped him.

Hessel   What did I tell you, what did I say? I said, gie me the power, I'll get shot of him, but no, you needed time to think.

McGee   You could've stalled him till I got there.

Hessel   The cunt's *mental* Wullie, if you seen the look on his face . . . he says he's gonnae blast a hole the frigging surface.

McGee   I'll hae to go, Sandy.

Sandy   Dinnae leave me Wullie, no with him.

McGee   It's only Hessel, Sandy.

Sandy   I ken whae it is . . .

Hessel   You better move it Wullie.

McGee   I'll hae to go. You'll be fine here, I'll be back quick as I can.

Sandy   You'll no come back.

McGee   I will, I'm telling you.

Sandy   You never come back.

McGee   What's that supposed to mean?

Sandy   You *ken* what I'm talking aboot.

McGee   Dinnae you push your luck, here, or I'll no bother coming back.

Sandy   Well dinnae fucking bother then.

McGee   Right. I'll no.

Sandy   Fine.

Hessel   Jesus fuck, the faceline's a fucking timebomb, you're fucking aboot here like Bill and bastard Ben.

McGee   Okay, okay, I hear you Hessel. (*To* **Sandy**.) I'm coming back, right, whether you like it or no.

Sandy   Suit yoursel . . . even if you do, I'll no be here. No if you leave me with that bastard . . . you dinnae ken what he's like . . .

McGee   What are you havering aboot?

Hessel   C'moan Wullie.

Sandy   Hessel. See, Salter let something slip . . .

McGee   Aye, aye, awright . . . you'll be fine when you've had some stuff.

Sandy   Naw, naw, listen to me Wullie, listen . . .

Hessel   Salter's gonnae hae the place wired up.

McGee   There's nae time, Sandy.

Sandy   You hae to listen . . .

Hessel   He'll be turning that key any minute.

McGee   Later, Sandy.

Sandy   But Wullie . . .

McGee (*close to* **Hessel**)   Listen to me, you're responsible here, okay? Anything happens to Sandy, I will personally shove your heid so far up your erse, it'll look as if nothing's happened. D'you hear me?

Exit **McGee**.

Hessel   Bastard. (*Pause.*) So, Sandy, how's it gaun?

Sandy   Fuck do you care?

Hessel   You're looking a wee bit fucked, there, man, what's up?

Sandy   Nane of your fucking business.

Hessel   That cunt Salter been fucking you aboot?

Sandy   What's it to you?

Hessel   Hey, you heard the man, I'm your guardian angel, here.

Sandy   I dinnae want any help fae you.

Hessel   Naw, but we dinnae seem to hae much of a choice, seeing as how McGee's gied me the job looking efter you, ken what I mean?

Sandy *has a coughing fit.*

Hessel   S'a bad cough you got there, Sandy, you want to dae something aboot that, you want to see a doctor.

Sandy   I dinnae need nae fucking doctors, it's just a cough, right?

Hessel   Must be a bad cough that needs the stuff McGee's been feeding you.

Sandy   Get to fuck.

Hessel   I'm only concerned, Sandy.

Sandy   Aye, like fuck.

Hessel   How long d'you reckon you've got?

Sandy   There's nothing wrong wi' me, right?

Hessel How long afore the pain gets too big? What I'm saying, you *need* some protection here, cos if the word gets oot, your erse will be well fucked.

Sandy Dinnae gies your shit, Hessel.

Hessel Shit, is it? Well, you'll no be interested in this, then?

Hessel *reaches into an inside jacket pocket, produces a dose of morphine.*

Sandy Where d'you get that?

Hessel McGee's no the only yin wi' keys the first-aid boxes, and that's what I'm telling you, I'm the only yin can *protect* you here.

Sandy I dinnae . . . I dinnae want your protection.

Hessel Christ, you ken the risk I took get this for you?

Sandy I dinnae need that.

Hessel You dinnae *need* it?

Sandy I dinnae fucking want it.

Pause.

Hessel You dinnae want it?

Sandy No.

Pause.

Hessel Fair enough. (*Starts to put it away.*)

Sandy Wait! What is your fucking game, Hessel?

Hessel I tellt ye, I'm only concerned . . . cos, you me kens what a bad bastard Salter can be, I mean, if he finds oot . . . cos I can tell you, I was dead worried when I left you, back in the howf . . . I was worried what Salter might dae to you.

Sandy He never touched me.

Hessel Well, that surprises me, it really . . . I mean, it strikes me as strange that he didnae batter fuck oot you . . . so, the very fact you're sitting here, still in one piece, makes me wonder what went on, ken what I mean . . . makes me wonder . . . did he try something? Cos he's good at that, Salter, he was always shit hot in negotiations . . . tell the gaffers anything get what he wanted . . . he must've said something, tellt you something get you on his side. He must've made something up.

Sandy He tellt me fuck all.

Hessel Naw, you maybe *think* he tellt you fuck all, cos that's where he's clever, that's how he gets you. Just drops in a wee hint, lets you make up the rest. D'you see? Think, Sandy, think aboot what he said.

Sandy I dinnae hae to think, he didnae hae to say fuck all, I figured it oot for myself.

Hessel What? What did you figure oot?

Sandy   Aw they stories you fed me, aboot Salter breaking thumbs, how he was such an evil bastard, your best mate, you're spreading stories aboot him . . . and you never went to visit him, never once in eight year, you let him lie in that place aw they years for something he never done, na Hessel, I've got it figured oot, I've got *you* figured oot.

Hessel   What the fuck you havering aboot, man?

Sandy   Aye, I've figured it oot, awright. It was *you*, wasn' it . . . it was you dropped that boulder fae the motorway bridge . . . and my mate Geordie Salter found oot, didn't he, he found oot . . . and that's why you took the safety switch of the belt.

Hessel   Oh it was me took the button oot the belt now?

Sandy   You think you can shut me up wi' a few drops of fucking morphine? Na, nae mair, Hessel, cos I ken it was you . . . cos I was there, I seen you take that button oot, and aw these years I've kept my mooth shut, cos I thought it was a mistake . . . nae mair, Hessel . . . cos you killed Geordie Salter!

Sandy *lunges towards* **Hessel**. **Hessel** *grabs him by the thumbs.*

Hessel   You listen to me, yan auld cunt . . . whatever shite Salter's been stuffing doon your disgusting auld throat . . . forget it, d'you hear me, forget it . . . else I'll . . . I'll . . .

Sandy   Drop a boulder on my heid . . . aah, my thumbs . . .

Hessel   You ever heard a thumb break, Sandy? You can hear the crack a mile away.

Sandy   I fucking kent it . . . gaun, break them, ya murdering bastard.

Sandy *spits in* **Hessel**'s *face.* **Hessel** *throws him to the ground, and picks up the morphine syringe.*

Sandy   What you gonnae dae? You cannae dae this! You cannae . . . they'll ken it was you, they'll ken.

Hessel   An auld man in pain . . . desperate enough tae steal some morphine . . .

Hessel *grabs* **Sandy**, *injects him.*

Sandy   Yin dose, Hessel, yin fucking dose . . .

Hessel   You listen to me, yan auld cunt, I'm coming right back wi' some mair . . . and you're never gonnae fucking wake up.

Exit outbye. Blackout.

Scene Three

Faceline. Two exits – one down faceline, the other outbye.

Enter **Salter**, *crawling from down the faceline. He carries a shotfiring box.*

McGee (*from outbye*)   Salter?

Salter   Shit!

He takes a key from his pocket, which he pushes into a hole in the shotfiring box.

McGee   Salter, you in there?

Pause.

Salter?

Salter *positions the battery on his knee, and grips the key.*

Salter   In here, Wullie.

McGee *enters, cautiously.*

Salter   That's far enough, Wullie.

McGee   Fuck you think you're daeing?

Salter   What's wrong, Wullie, concerned aboot your precious faceline?

McGee   Stop fucking aboot, where have you put them?

McGee *looks around, notices the cable, reaches for it.*

Salter   Leave it, you wouldnae be quick enough.

McGee   Salter, this is stupid!

Salter   Just get away fae the cable.

McGee   This is gonnae get you naewhere.

Salter   Back, Wullie.

McGee   Fucking . . . right, right, this far enough for ye? Or would you prefer me up the pit and oot the fucking gate.

Pause.

Salter   Ken, it's kindae funny . . .

McGee   Oh, it's bastard hilarious.

Salter   Naw, d'you no think . . . you me sitting here like a couple of reps, trying tae screw each other for whatever we can get . . . takes me back.

McGee   You've lost it, you ken that?

Salter   Cairds on the table time, Wullie . . . negotiations underway . . . session in progress.

McGee   Look, will you stop this fucking aboot . . .

Salter   You'd have never made it as a negotiator, Wullie, you're meant tae observe the rituals of mutual admiration . . . I'll go first . . . I must say, Mr McGee, you've made a damn fine job of this face.

McGee   I'll make a damn fine job *your* face, you dinnae cut this oot.

Salter   Na, you've just provoked a six-month overtime ban, Wullie, you're no trying.

McGee   Salter!

Salter   See, it's aw aboot what I used tae call the dummy compromise . . . letting the other guy think you're meeting half-way, when you're really dragging him across the table, screwing him up the erse. Lubricate the ego, and the erse'll follow suit . . . see what I mean?

McGee   Aw I can see's a fucking nutter, wi' a chip his fucking shooder the size a girder.

Salter   That's an all-out strike, Wullie, you're no getting the hang of this.

Pause.

McGee   Ken your problem, Salter? You're no actually here, are ye? You're stuck back in the auld days of the pit-heid meeting, and the black ballot-box . . . well, they took away the boxes, and they threw away the lids, now they're sitting the manager's office, filled wi' fucking rubber plants!

Salter   This could be a prolonged dispute.

McGee   Still back in the trenches, eh Salter, only every other cunt's away hame, and there's nothing left tae shoot . . . so you have tae make something up, anything'll dae . . . mysterious deaths, cover-ups . . . anything that'll feed the fire, let you feel sorry for yoursel.

Pause.

Salter   Okay, so this is what's called a roond of hard talks, which is just a nice way of saying everybody chucking insults at each other . . . but I dinnae have tae go doon that road, Wullie, cos I haud the winning hand, here, nae maitter what happens . . . cos I'm in what you might call a strong bargaining position . . . here's the situation . . . I've got two rounds of explosives wired up, one doon the faceline, the other above oor heids . . . and you dinnae ken which one I've connected first . . . now, the way I see it, you can take a chance that I'm no crazy enough tae top masel, and make a grab for the cable . . . or you can take the sensible option, and offer me a few concessions.

McGee   There's nae fucking point to this, there's nothing to gain.

Salter   I think there is.

McGee   But think aboot it, man, what's gonnae happen? You go through wi' this, you'll either end up deid, or back inside the rest your days.

Pause.

Salter   I can see that this might be a long session.

McGee   Look, okay, you want a deal, you want a fucking . . . you gie me that battery, and you have my word I'll no say nothing. Naibdy'll ever hear aboot it, it'll just be between you and me. You'll still hae a job, you'll still be a free man.

Salter   Are you suggesting a cover-up, Wullie? I would never have thought you capable of such a thing, seeing as how you're always such a stickler for the rules, I'm . . . shocked you should even consider such a thing.

McGee   You've got yoursel in a fucking mess, here, I'm offering you a way oot!

Salter Well, at least we're getting somewhere, we're negotiating. But you're a fast learner, Wullie, cos it seems to me you're offering nothing but a dummy compromise . . . cos, if I agree to your proposal, we end up back where we fucking started.

Pause.

McGee This is no fucking real!

Pause.

Okay, tell me what you want.

Pause.

Salter That's mair like it.

McGee Just fucking tell me!

Salter I want the truth.

Pause.

McGee The truth. What truth?

Salter The truth aboot my faither.

McGee And what version the truth would you like?

Pause.

Salter I just want tae ken what happened.

McGee Naw, you dinnae want the truth . . . you want to be proved right.

Salter The truth, Wullie.

McGee And what if the truth isnae what you want tae hear?

Pause.

Salter If it's the truth . . .

McGee IF it's the truth . . . see . . . see what I mean, there you go with your ifs and buts . . . IF it's the truth . . . how will you ken, eh? How will you ken whae's lying and whae's no? S'no the truth you want . . . it's *your version* the truth.

Salter This is just crap, Wullie . . .

McGee Is it? Cos it doesnae fit wi' your version? The truth . . . I'll tell you what the truth is . . . you want to be proved right, you want it to be *me!*

Salter You're wrong.

McGee You want it to be ME killed your faither, cos that's your version the truth, the yin you sat there aw they years and invented . . . cos you're just sat there, a fucking prison cell, and everything's happening the ootside, and there's fuck all you can dae aboot it . . . you've nae control, and you cannae handle that, so make stuff up, a version of the truth, a fairy tale . . . and now you think it's real, and god help anybody disagrees wi' you.

Salter This is just garbage, Wullie, this is . . .

McGee Okay, you want the truth, I'll gie you the fucking . . . I had nothing to dae wi' your faither's death. Right?

Pause.

Salter You were efter the same job.

McGee See? Fuck, see what I'm . . . you get the truth, you dinnae want tae *hear* it.

Salter Why should I believe you?

McGee Cos it's the bastarding truth!

Pause.

Salter I dinnae believe you.

McGee Jesus, fuck, gie me strength!

Salter I need proof.

McGee Oh, it's proof, now. I've got tae fucking *prove* it. So, I cannae gie you proof, I'm a bastard liar . . . and even if I could gie you proof, you dinnae want tae hear it . . . I CANNAE WIN, FOR FUCK'S SAKE! This your idea justice? Eh? Guilty until proven innocent, then still fucking guilty?

Pause.

Salter You're forgetting where I've just come fae, Wullie . . . and I've seen them aw, the guilty and the innocent . . . and it's a funny thing, but . . . the innocent man, the really innocent man, is always fucking silent, cos he's too numbed by what's happened to him . . . it's the pretenders, the yins that want to be innocent, that make aw the noise. I think you're a pretender, Wullie . . . you sit there screaming your innocence, cos you think if you shout it loud enough, it's gonnae be true . . . I see through ye, Wullie, cos I've seen hunders like ye . . . you hide yoursel away doon here, three thousand feet atween you and the real world, nice and secure ahint your wall of coal . . . as long as there's coal, you've got an excuse . . . but there's a world up there, Wullie, and it doesnae ken whae you are, cos you've spent too long beneath it . . . and that's a thing you me's got in common, cos *I've* spent the last eight year shut oot fae the world, and what that taught me . . . the mair you live like an animal, the mair you start tae think like yin . . . and the way they live in the real world means *fuck all* to likes of you and me . . . but what you forget . . . what goes on doon here *affects* up there, affects people . . . like my faimly . . . like your faimly . . . like your faither!

McGee That's enough, nae fucking mair.

Salter That's why you hide yoursel away this shit-hoose . . . cos you cannae handle living up there . . . cos the Wullie McGee that lives doon here's a big man . . . nae wonder the place is so fucking attractive . . . but the Wullie McGee that lives up there in the real world, left his faither to die amongst strangers.

McGee You've went too far, too fucking far! I mean, what gies you the right, eh? What gies you the right tae judge me?

Salter Cos I ken how you feel, Wullie. *I ken how you feel.*

McGee You . . . you dinnae have a fucking clue how I feel.

Salter Oh, but I dae, Wullie. It starts like a wee swelling in the pit of your stomach, a wee ball of frustration that grows and . . . till it fills your chest, till it shoots doon your veins, and you think it's gonnae burst through the tips your fingers . . . it fills your body . . . controls you, your mind, your tongue . . . you feel like there's somebody else inside you, pushing tae get oot, and it makes you want tae scream 'Leave me alane!' But it never leaves ye.

Pause.

I ken how it feels.

Pause.

So, tell me, Wullie, tell me.

Pause.

McGee *reaches for the shotfiring box.*

Salter Leave it!

McGee It's finished, Salter.

Salter I'll turn the key.

McGee I dinnae think you will.

Salter *pushes the button, there is an explosion which knocks both men to the ground.* **McGee** *recovers first, picks up the shotfiring battery, and exits outbye.* **Salter** *starts to come round. Blackout.*

Scene Four

Outbye the faceline.

Sandy *is lying on the ground, just short of the faceline entrance, in big pain, his breathing laboured. Enter* **McGee**, *from the faceline.*

McGee   Sandy! (*He rushes to help.*) What the fuck you . . . ya stupid auld . . . I tellt you, I tellt you to wait.

Sandy   Salter . . . I need . . .

McGee   Forget Salter. We need to get you up the pit.

Sandy   Naw, naw! No up the pit . . . Salter.

McGee   Come on, auld yin.

McGee *helps him back out into the roadway, where he lays him down.*

Sandy   Aw they years, Wullie.

McGee   Aye, too many fucking years, auld yin.

Sandy   You dinnae . . . under . . .

Enter **Hessel**, *from outbye.*

Hessel   There's the bastard, I've been looking for you.

McGee   Just get tae fuck, Hessel.

Hessel   What's he been saying?

Sandy   Keep him away.

Hessel   Has he said any . . .

McGee   Hessel! The man's in pain.

Hessel   Listen Wullie . . . whatever he's said, there's naibdy gonnae believe him, cos his mind's been twisted by the stuff you've fed him . . . and you still need me here . . . I stuck a button in the bogies, so the nobs are having tae walk . . . but you've got a real mess on your hands here, you need my help.

McGee   You're too late, Hessel . . . the faceline's fucked, Salter blew a hole in it.

Hessel   Fuck . . . I tellt you this would happen, what did I tell ye?

McGee   It's finished . . . you, me, this place . . . fucked, Hessel.

Hessel   Finished?

McGee   A lifetime's work, blawn tae fuck in five seconds.

Hessel   You're maybe finished, pal, I've only just started.

Exit **Hessel**, *towards the face.*

Sandy   I had tae keep gaun, till I . . . but you'll listen . . . you'll hear me.

McGee   I'm getting you some stuff.

McGee *goes to the first-aid box, and unlocks it.*

Sandy   Bring the lot!

McGee   That's too much.

Sandy   I *want* too much.

McGee *takes out a couple of doses, comes to kneel by* **Sandy**.

McGee   Here, gie me your airm.

Sandy   Did you hear what I said?

McGee   I heard you. Roll up your sleeve.

Sandy   Listen to me, Wullie, your no hearing what I'm saying.

He pushes away **McGee***'s hand.*

McGee   I ken what you're gonnae say, I dinnae want tae hear it.

Sandy   Just . . . get me the stuff. I'll dae it masel.

McGee   You ken what you're asking here?

Sandy   Wullie, please!

Sandy *is in huge pain.*

McGee   C'moan, Sandy, at least let me take away the pain.

Sandy   I WANT THE FUCKING PAIN! Means I'm still alive, still able tae feel, means I can still be fucking heard!

The pain gets even worse.

McGee   If I hae tae, I'll force you.

Sandy   And . . . hae me . . . put away . . . some cheap nursing home?

McGee   But it might no be so bad, they might be able tae help you.

Sandy   Oh, they'll . . . help me awright . . . just like they helped . . . your faither.

Pause. **McGee** *goes back to the first-aid box, comes back with the rest of the doses.*

Sandy   You're . . . a guid laddie . . . a guid laddie . . . now listen . . . afore the stuff . . . gets haud my tongue . . . there's something I have tae tell ye . . .

Lights fade.

Scene Five

Outbye the faceline.

McGee *is kneeling, holding* **Sandy***'s head to his chest. Enter* **Salter** *and* **Hessel**.

Salter   NAW!

Salter *rushes towards* **McGee**.

Salter   What have you done, yan evil bastard?

McGee   You're too late.

Hessel *picks up a syringe, holds it up triumphantly.*

Hessel   What did I tell ye?

Salter *knocks* **McGee** *out of the way.*

Salter Leave him!

Salter *tries to wake* **Sandy** *up.*

Salter C'moan . . . c'moan . . . ya stupid auld fuck . . . wake up . . . wake fucking UP!

McGee Let him be, he's suffered enough.

Hessel You shut the fuck up.

Salter C'moan . . . wake up, fucking wake up . . . you have tae wake up.

McGee *gets to his feet,* **Hessel** *restrains him.*

Hessel No think you've done enough damage.

McGee Leave him, Salter.

Salter You have tae wake up, you have tae tell me.

McGee I said leave him!

Salter You cannae be deid, you cannae . . . I'll no let you be deid . . . you have tae talk to me . . . you have tae look at me.

Salter *holds* **Sandy**'s *face.*

Salter D'you hear me, Da? D'you hear me? I want you to look at me . . . look at me Da . . . fucking look at me!

McGee Stop him, Hessel, he's fucking lost it.

Salter I want to see your eyes, Da.

He tries to force **Sandy**'s *eyes open.*

Salter I want to see your eyes . . . show me your eyes . . . I want to see them looking at me . . . I want you to talk to me, Da, look at me, talk to me, I'm your son . . . d'you see me, Da? I'm your son.

McGee You have tae dae something, Hessel.

Hessel *walks across to* **Salter**.

Hessel Come on, Salter, put him doon, there's nothing you can dae.

Salter But he has tae look at me, Hessel. He'll no look at me. Why does he no want tae look at me? I'm his son.

Hessel That's no your faither, Salter, it's auld Sandy. Come on, now.

Salter You tell him Hessel, tell him it wasnae me, make him see. I want you tae make him understand.

Hessel I will . . . I'll . . . just . . .

Salter *hands the body to* **Hessel**.

Hessel I hope you're fucking proud yoursel, McBastard.

Salter YOU! You done this!

Salter *advances on* **McGee**, *picking up a piece of rope.*

McGee Keep away.

Hessel Aw for the sake of a fucking job.

Salter *lunges forward, wraps the rope round* **McGee**'s *neck.*

McGee Fuck off, you dinnae understand . . .

Salter *tighens the rope,* **McGee** *chokes.*

Hessel He killed your faither, Salter. He killed your faither.

Salter Ya bastard!

Hessel PULL IT FUCKING TIGHT. KILL THE BASTARD!

Salter *hears the last comment, realises what he's doing. He lets go,* **McGee** *slumps to the ground, coughing.*

Salter THIS FUCKING PLACE!

He takes out his rage on equipment, smashing things up in a fury.

Salter ANIMALS!
Fucking years.
Check the button.
Fucking murder.
Animals.
DA!
I fucking checked it, I fucking . . .
Checked it, I always fucking . . .
Nae fucking life.
This place!
This fucking button.
Nae life.
Fucking years.
Nae life.

Pause. He becomes exhausted.

Nae life.

Pause.

You.

Pause.

You think you can just.

Pause.

Like fucking animals.

Pause.

Hessel   Salter, we need tae . . .

Salter   SHUT UP! Shut it, just . . . I'm no gonnae leave it, I'm fucked if I can leave it. Cos this is gonnae end here, it has tae fucking end. (*To* **McGee**.) But I'm no gonnae kill you, I'm no gonnae let you . . . I'm no gonnae let this fucking place . . . I'm gonnae make you suffer the rest your days, and every day that you're alive will make it easier for me. I'll get a picture of you, that's what I'll dae, I'll get a fucking picture . . . and every day I'll tear off a tiny bit, the tiniest fucking piece, so's I can watch you come apart, and I can count the years it takes. (*To* **Hessel**.) You . . . keep an eye this fucking animal . . . I'm gonnae phone the pit-heid, so's the cops are waiting the cage-door when we bring the bastard up.

Exit **Salter**.

Long pause.

Hessel   You okay?

Pause.

Think you got him a wee bit wound up, there.

Pause.

I mean, I thought you were fucking *away* there, boy.

McGee   I wish to fuck he *had* put me away.

Hessel   I couldnae stop him . . . what?

McGee   That no what you dae, when an animal's in pain?

Hessel   Fuck are you on aboot?

Pause.

McGee   Dinnae think I'll ever understand what drives a man like you, Hessel. What is it? Money? Fear? Hate? What?

Hessel   I dinnae get ye.

McGee   Or is it just this fucking place?

Pause.

I put it doon tae the morphine, when Sandy tellt me aboot you, but when I heard you goading Salter tae tighten his grip, for the first time my life, I saw this place for what it's worth.

Hessel   Sandy tellt ye?

McGee Dinnae fucking worry. That bastard doesnae deserve an explanation. But he's right aboot yin thing . . . you live long enough like an animal, you start tae think like yin.

Hessel What exactly did Sandy tell ye?

McGee What does it maitter?

Hessel If he was spreading stories aboot me . . .

McGee Aw, Hessel, d'you no get it? Doesnae maitter a fuck anymair. Doesnae maitter whae believes what, or what's lies and what's true . . . doon here, there's nae such thing as the truth. Just rust, that gets intae your veins, cos doon here you breathe nothing but death.

Pause.

Hessel So, you're no gonnae say nothing?

McGee What would be the fucking point? You've won, Hessel, you'll get the undermanager's job . . . does that please ye? Cos that's the reason I'm gonnae keep quiet . . . I want you tae have this job . . . if I tellt Salter, he'd probably kill you, and that's too easy for the likes of you . . . you deserve this place, Hessel . . . it's yours . . . I hope you think it's worth the price.

McGee *gets to his feet.*

Hessel What're you daeing?

McGee I'm tired, Hessel. I've spent ower long fighting for this place, I'm . . . christ I'm fucking tired.

He heads for the faceline.

Hessel Wait . . . where you gaun?

McGee Where I belong.

Hessel Haud on . . .

Hessel *tries to stop* **McGee.**

McGee Hessel, you only want tae stop me, cos you look at me, you see yoursel in another few year, cos you want this prize tae be *worth* something . . . I'm no gaun up that pit, there's nothing for me up there . . . this is what you won, Hessel, and you're stuck wi' it.

McGee *pushes past, exits towards the faceline.* **Hessel** *stares after him for a while, then sits. Pause.* **Salter** *re-enters.*

Salter They're on their . . . where is he, where's McGee?

Hessel Just leave it, Salter.

Salter I thought I tellt you . . .

Hessel Leave it, I said.

Salter You let him go that faceline?

Hessel It's what he wanted.

Salter What he wanted? What aboot what I fucking wanted? I need that bastard stand trial, that's the only way . . . of aw the fucking stupid . . . that's the only way we'll get the truth oot the bastard . . . right . . .

Salter *heads for the faceline.*

Hessel Salter ya mad bastard, you're too late, you're fucking . . .

Exit **Salter**.

Hessel SALTER! Aw what the fuck . . . gaun, ya stupid fuck, away and . . . aw the bastard same the bastard same the lot of ye!

Hessel *removes his helmet, batters it off the faceline exit.*

Hessel Aw the bastard same! (*He gives up.*) Okay . . . okay . . . that's fine . . . that's . . .

He sits. Lighting shift. **McGee** *on the faceline, clutching the shotfiring battery. Enter* **Salter**.

Salter McGee?

McGee Get tae fuck.

Salter What you think you're daeing?

McGee I'm warning you, Salter . . .

Salter Dinnae be so fucking stupid, you me baith kens you're too much a coward to dae this.

McGee You come any closer, it's coming doon!

Pause.

Salter Like fuck it's coming doon.

McGee I dinnae want this.

Salter Naw, cos you've no got the guts to bring it doon.

McGee Keep away, I'm warning ye!

Salter Gaun then, push the button, push the fucking button. PUSH IT!

Pause.

McGee Dinnae make me dae this, Salter.

Salter You cannae dae it, can ye? Cos you arnae man enough tae dae it . . . what's the maitter, Wullie, I'm no some fucked up auld man cannae fight back? Look at ye, ya gutless bastard.

McGee Gutless?

Salter Only a gutless bastard would fill an auld man wi' morphine tae keep him fucking quiet.

McGee Just . . . get the fuck oot of here.

Salter (*driving*) Only the worst kind of spineless cunt would kill a man the way you killed my faither!

Pause.

McGee Okay, you want tae ken whae killed your faither? YOU killed him.

Pause.

You're so fucking desperate for somebody tae blame, take a look at your fucking *sel*, cos it was you let Hessel walk away fae the motorway bridge.

Salter What are you . . . what . . .

McGee You think you ken aw the answers, mister smart-arse union man, you ken nothing. I watched it happening, watched you dance that bastard's tune. You'd have put him away, your faither would still BE here!

Pause.

Salter What are you talking aboot?

McGee Your faither found oot, he found oot aboot the motorway bridge. So Hessel had tae stop him, Sandy seen him take the button oot, he seen him, Salter. That's your fucking answer. And now he's standing oot there, praying you dinnae come back oot.

Pause.

Salter How do I ken you're no just . . .

McGee Sandy spoke to your faither the fucking stretcher.

Pause.

Salter What did he say, did he tell you what he said?

McGee He said you were innocent.

Long pause.

Salter He kent. Aw fuck, he kent!

Pause.

McGee Sandy only caught on you tellt him aboot the bridge.

Long pause.

Salter The BASTARD! The BASTARD! . . . if I'd just fucking shopped him . . . I'll massacre him, I'll . . .

McGee You'll never touch him, Salter. Hessel's too fast for the likes of me you. You'll never prove it.

Pause.

Salter Wait a minute, you can help me.

McGee You've got your answer, now leave it.

Salter The pair of us can nail that bastard.

McGee You cannae, can ye?

Salter You're coming wi' me.

McGee You cannae fucking leave it.

Salter You have tae help me, Wullie.

Pause.

You have tae help me. HELP ME, WULLIE!

McGee *turns the key, massive explosion, lighting shift, a single spot, stage front. Long pause.* **Hessel** *stands, goes towards the spot, breathing fast, terror in his eyes. He looks straight toward the audience.*

Hessel Salter? McGee?

Bleep from the hailer.

Voice What the fuck was that? Hullo the maingate, hullo the maingate.

Pause.

Hullo the maingate, hullo the maingate.

Hessel You'd better get some men in here fast.

Voice What's happened, what was that bang?

Hessel Just get some fucking men in here.

Volice Who the fuck are you?

Pause.

Hessel This is the new undermanager, and you've just earned yoursel a bastard warning.

Slow fade to black.

The Cut

When I first began to write this play, I had two clear intentions in mind. Firstly, I have a strong interest in classical tragedy, especially the plays of Sophocles, and the related theories of Aristotle. I wanted to write a play with a fairly strict classical structure, in an effort to challenge the myth that classical tragedy is impossible in the modern world. Secondly, most of the depictions I've ever seen or read of mining communities paint an unrealistic, almost pastoral picture of a brotherhood, united in the struggle to further the rights of the working classes. I wanted to correct this view by writing about my own experience of this community. I worked as a colliery electrician, from 1976 to 1983, at Bilston Glen Colliery, Loanhead, and, although I encountered many decent human beings, most of the relationships I witnessed revolved around a power struggle of one kind or another. Of course, the pursuit of power in even the most trivial situations is a universal human trait, but it struck me that this trait is more sharply manifest in a world as extreme as a colliery.

As the play developed, I began to uncover an allegorical level, where the characters each represented a section of the community, and this led to a third intention – to use this inherent allegory to explore one of the most important political events of this century, the demise of socialism. I didn't simply want to record this event for posterity, I also wanted to explore the repercussions for a world where socialism is considered a disease, and where 'selfism' is the new political ideal.

So, with these intentions, *The Cut* was written over a period of about a year and a half, in 1992/93, while I was part of the Mentoring Scheme at the Tron Theatre, Glasgow. The scheme mainly consisted of meetings with established writers, such as Peter Arnott, Michael Duke, Tom McGrath, Iain Heggie. These writers would read my play, and we'd meet to discuss good and bad points about the script. This was a huge learning experience for me – Peter Arnott once said I was cramming five years of learning into one, and, on reflection, I think he was probably right. I went through periods of confusion and self-doubt, until I discovered the ultimate revelation – that my own instincts and opinions were as valid as anyone else's. Towards the end of the scheme, the Tron told me they couldn't afford to fully commission and produce the play – my first real rejection. Then over the hill came the cavalry, in the shape of Wiseguise Productions.

Wiseguise is an independent co-op of excellent Scottish actors, who are absolutely committed to new writing. They offered to produce my play, then even offered to pay me for it, despite the fact they didn't have any money. At our first meeting, I remember Kenny Glenaan, who eventually played Hessel, offering to sell his house to get the play on. Their level of commitment was breathtaking. They found the money, and took the play on a hugely successful tour of Scotland. When the play transferred to the Bush in London, they organised a sponsored walk to raise the necessary funds. In rehearsals, even though I was totally inexperienced, they completely respected my opinions and ideas. And on top of all that, they produced the kind of stunning performances I've never seen before or since.

Now that the dust has settled, I've had time to reflect on whether or not my original intentions for the play were realised. I believe the second and third intentions mentioned above (the social and political elements) were, in the main, achieved. Some audiences were moved to tears, others ended up having political debates in the bar afterwards. A few were simply confused. But does it work as a classical tragedy? I don't really know yet. All of the pieces I'm currently working on – a new stage play, TV and film scripts – are further attempts to realise this elusive goal. I now see *The Cut* as the first step on the road to perhaps discovering a new form of tragedy, a tragedy that grows from those elements of modern society that distinguish us from the ancient Greeks.

Mike Cullen
October 1994

Mike Cullen was born in 1959 and left school at sixteen to work at Bilston Glen Colliery, Loanhead, where he qualified as a tradesman in 1980. He returned to education in 1987, graduating from Edinburgh University in 1992 with an honours degree in Linguistics. He started writing at university, winning the Sloan Prize for Scottish poetry in 1990. In 1992, a short play, *The Bag*, was performed at the Byre Theatre, St Andrews, as part of a John Godber Masterclass. His first stage play, *The Cut*, and a radio play, *Canary*, were given rehearsed readings at the Arches Theatre, Glasgow, produced by the Tron Theatre, Glasgow. *The Cut* toured Scotland in 1993, produced by Wiseguise Productions, Glasgow, subsequently transferring to the Bush Theatre, London, in 1994. *The Cut* was shortlisted for the Mair/Whitworth Award in 1994. Also in 1994, Mike Cullen was shortlisted for the George Devine Award. Mike Cullen is currently working on a new stage play, *The Collection*, for the Traverse Theatre, Edinburgh; the screen adaptation of *The Cut*, for Temple films, Dublin; a television film, *Vigilante* for Island World/Channel Four, and a serial for BBC television, called *The Son Of Man*. He lives in Haddington, Scotland, with his wife Lesley, and his daughter, Lynsey.

The Life of Stuff

Simon Donald

To Nan and Shaw, my mum and dad

The Life of Stuff was first produced at the Traverse Theatre, Edinburgh, during the Edinburgh Festival in August 1992. The cast was as follows:

Arbogast	Kern Falconer
Holly	Mabel Aitken
Evelyn	Shirley Henderson
Leonard	Stuart McQuarrie
Willie Dobie	Duncan Duff
Janice	Louise Beattie
Fraser	Brian McCardie
Alec Sneddon	Bob Wisdom

Directed by John Mitchell
Designed by Nick Sargent
Lighting by Peter Scott
Music by John Irvine

It was subsequently produced at the Donmar Warehouse, London, in September 1993, with the following cast:

Arbogast	Sean Scanlan
Holly	Elizabeth Chadwick
Evelyn	Mabel Aitken
Leonard	Stuart McQuarrie
Willie Dobie	Douglas Henshall
Janice	Sandy McDade
Fraser	Forbes Masson
Alec Sneddon	Patrick O'Kane

Directed by Matthew Warchus
Designed by Neil Warmington
Lighting by Rick Fisher
Sound by Fergus O'Hare

Characters

Arbogast, *forty-odd. Dangerous*
Holly, *early twenties*
Evelyn, *early twenties*
Leonard, *early twenties*
Willie Dobie, *thirties*
Janice, *mid twenties*
Fraser, *early twenties*
Alec Sneddon, *thirties*

The action takes place in and on top of Willie Dobie's newly acquired warehouse building. The spaces vary as much as possible. The basement has a puddly floor and is dingily lit, Dobie's office is fairly plush, the roof is windy and precarious. A lift connects the main spaces. A door leads into Dobie's office.

Note

Leonard pronounces the word 'eczema' correctly. Everyone else in the play always pronounces it 'ig-*zeem*-a'.

For an explanation of the punctuation see Afterword.

Prologue. Blisters

Sneddon's *Nightclub – 'Blisters'. He comes down the stairs to the stage. He tells his friends what has just happened.*

Sneddon   Mister David Arbogast walks right into my office. He walks right in. With his 'Proposition'. I say to him – Fuck off – that is not a 'Proposition' – that is not 'A Proposal'. That's a joke. He's a joke. Davey – you're a joke.

Tellin you – those people embarrass me. They make me laugh. He has no grasp of reality. Even their jokes are a joke.

He walks into my club – amongst my friends. He has the gall. The unmitigated gall – with his demands! You know? A piece of this and a slice of that. And what? I roll over and play dead? Watch him fuck with my business. All of them. What say I remove what brains you have in your skull – Buster! Shove them up your arse keep your small intestine company. Take you out the back and rip off your arms and legs, eh David. Extract your spinal column. My old china. I hand him a toilet roll. He says what's this. I say give your gub a good wipe. All the shite you talk. With your proposition. Proposal my arse, Davey.

What I have here – how I work – his kind canny understand this stuff. The value of things. Trust. Compassion. Integrity. Nitroglycerine. Seriously. I kid you not. Those people are children. He is a child. I'm laughing in Arbogast's face. He sees me laughing. Partners? *Me* do 'A DEAL' with *him*? Keugh! In your dreams pal. I explain to him 'why'. I give him a for instance.

A guy approached me once. With a money making idea. Different kind of thing. Anyway. You know the kind of thing.

Anyway. I says to the guy –

'So who'll be driving the car?'

He says

'Francetti'

I says

'Not Fast Franky "Skid Marks" Francetti?'

He goes

'No, Douglas Francetti'

Aw. I goes

'So who's handling the punters in the foyer, you know Crowd Control?'

He says

'McIndoe and Slaven'

I am stunned. I says

'Rocky McIndoe and Chainsaw Slaven?'

He goes

'Naw. Fat-Arse McIndoe and Morag Slaven'

So I says

'Listen, who's plannin this fuckin robbery anyway.'

Goes

'Arbogast'

I says

'Davey Arbogast?!'

Says

'Yup, the very same.'

I says Ay. In yer dreams . . .

1 Mutiny

Very loud club music. Late afternoon. Main party space in the warehouse. A stack of cleaning implements, buckets, mops, some shovels and rubbish bags with bits of crap hanging out. In the room are **Janice***, who is slumped somewhere asleep,* **Evelyn***,* **Holly** *and* **Leonard***. The girls are all in various versions of their best party clothes. A professional disco sound system is set up on a raised platform –* **Leonard** *is playing with it. The volume crashes up and down, the music stops and starts. The lift arrives, the lift doors open and* **Arbogast** *bounces in, a sweeping brush in either hand.*

Arbogast Righty ho! Arses in gear! People! I've to tell you there's work to be done. Turn down that din son. No – turn that racket off, Leonard.

Evelyn He says he's got to get balanced.

Arbogast Am I speaking to you, doll?

Evelyn Evelyn.

Arbogast I said there is work to be done. We've this floor to get swept for starters, eh? Fore somebody cuts themselves (*To* **Holly** *who is dancing.*) and that includes you as well, doll.

Holly Did he say work?

Evelyn He did.

Arbogast Yup, that is what he said. (*To* **Leonard**.) Turn that . . . Hey. Leonard. LEONARD! I AM KEEPING MY TEMPER HERE!

Holly What work?

Leonard Eh? I'm just getting a balance set, Mr Arbogast.

Arbogast Turn it off!

Holly I thought it was meant to be a party.

Evelyn Holly, it's only just gone four.

Leonard But I need to set a balance for the party.

Arbogast The party's not till later. Now – we've got jobs to get done. And you do NOT want to get me DEMENTED.

Evelyn Is there going to be drugs?

Leonard I thought this was my job for the party.

Holly Bound to be millions

Arbogast Playing yourself is not a job, Leonard.

Holly   Cause I'm meant to be long term unemployed. And this is supposed to be a party. So what's with all this talk about work and no guarantee of any drugs. I mean . . . fucks sake.

Evelyn   I dont think he means that kind of work. Do you?

Arbogast   What are you pair on about?

Holly   I mean I have actually been told I'm *unemployable*. Never mind just unemployed.

Evelyn   When did you get told that.

Holly   I've actually got it officially down on my records.

Arbogast   This is not that kind of . . . Look! (*To* **Leonard**.) I am TELLING YOU FOR THE LAST TIME NOW!

Holly   Not just on the one record either. So I take what he's saying quite personally.

Evelyn (*she roars at* **Leonard**)   Hoi! Can you can that racket for ten seconds, Scabby!

Leonard *turns the music off.*

Leonard   This is beyond belief. Willie said I was in charge of . . .

Arbogast   LEONARD!

Leonard   I am supposed to be . . .

Arbogast   LEONARD!

Leonard   Look, it's up to me to . . . (**Leonard** *finally realises he's got up everybody's noses.*) All I'm trying to do is get it all set up right so that when it comes to the party everybody can have a nice time, that's all – no need to all get in such a . . . (**Arbogast** *has gone to* **Leonard** *and put his arm around him.*)

Arbogast   People having a nice time is none of your concern, Leonard. Tell you what, son. (*He dangles a set of car keys in front of* **Leonard**'s *nose.*) Willie wants you to fetch up some champers out his Merc for him. Eh?

Evelyn   And give us all some peace.

Leonard   And who's that tart calling scabby

Arbogast   Probably you, Leonard.

Leonard   Cause it's eczema (*He takes the car keys.*)

Arbogast   Probably because of your pronounced eczema.

Leonard   It is not pronounced eczema, it is pronounced eczema.

Arbogast (*ultra-patiently*)   This place has got to get cleared up

Leonard   Well what about them?

Arbogast   They'll help.

Evelyn   Long as we dont have to touch

Arbogast   Now that is a wee bit uncalled for, doll.

Holly   Nervous eczema isnt contagious. Just repulsive

Evelyn   Any sort of rash makes me nervous. Stop calling me doll you.

Holly   Anyway I'll bet you can get drugs for it

Evelyn   Bet you cant at this party.

Leonard   Do this pair think they're being amusing, cause they're about as funny as senile dementia

Arbogast (*finally losing his temper*)   This is NOT a PARTY. The PARTY is NOT till LATER. Do you all UNderSTAND.

Holly   Well what has Dobie made us get all dolled up for then.

Leonard   That's 'dolled up'?

Arbogast   Will you be QUIET! . . .

Evelyn (*to* **Leonard**)   See, now you've got him demented.

Arbogast   And behave like fucking ADULTS! I have to raise my bloody VOICE all the time.

Holly   Whoah here a minute. Now I think that that is a perfectly reasonable question. Why we were told by Willie Dobie to get as dolled up as possible because he was asking us – personally In-*vit*ing us to be his own personal guests at the party of a lifetime.

Evelyn   With drugs.

Arbogast   Because when the party starts you chicks are floozy. And before the party starts you two chicks are CLEANERS. And . . . (*Indicating* **Janice**.) Bloody wake her up as well, Leonard

Leonard *goes to wake* **Janice** *up. He shakes her gently, mumbling to her quietly, as though he's fond of her. The lift arrives with* **Willie Dobie** *in it.*

Arbogast   And, I might add, you do not get to become floozy until you have acquitted yourselves as bloody cleaners.

Evelyn   So who says we're interested in being bloody 'floozy'

Arbogast   Cleaners dont get drugs.

Dobie   And THAT! if I may say so, is where you and I part company, Davey. Personally I'd be loath to describe any one of the three young ladies present as 'floozy'.

Arbogast   I know it requires a bit of a stretch of the . . .

Dobie   And I mean that in a purely constructive sense. (*To* **Janice**.) Welcome to the land of the living, petal. I have to say you look radiant after your wee siesta.

Janice *throws up on the floor. A big, splurgy, alcoholic-poisoning stomach-emptier.*

Janice   Fuck. Missed my frock. (*Everybody stares at her. She straightens her squinty wig.*) Thank God, eh? Party still going? (*To* **Leonard**.) Get your mitts off me ya scabby pervert!

Evelyn (*to* **Holly**)   Aw, right. So *that's* floozy!

Janice   Any drink? I'm totally parched . . . (*She clocks* **Dobie**.) Have you got my rent book sorted yet?

Dobie   Davey why dont you see if you can find the young lady a drink for her upset tummy and we'll get her details reorganised in due course. I mean, you know . . . Party Time!

Arbogast   Sure thing, Willie, anything you say, sir. (*He pulls her up by the arm.*) 'Mon you.

Janice *clutches a polythene bag and her own handbag.* **Arbogast** *leads her to the lift.*

Arbogast (*over his shoulder to* **Holly** *and* **Evelyn**)   You'll need a bucket and a mop as well, you pair.

Dobie   Haha. Some man, Arbogast. (*The lift leaves.*) A phenomenon (*To* **Leonard**.) Get a bucket and get that seen to like you've been told . . . eh . . .

Leonard   Leonard.

Dobie   I know that. Leonard

Leonard   Straight away, Willie. (*He gets a bucket and mop.*)

Dobie (*to the girls*)   Phenomenal guy, Davey Arbogast. A bona fide self made man. Totally. Self made. Mind you that probably explains why he's such a mis-shapen fucker. Haha. Dragged himself up from the gutter that boy did. Got himself educated at the College of Hard Knocks. The University of Life. Mind you he never graduated because he missed all his tutorials and the neighbour's dog ate his notes. Eh? (*Puts his hand in his inside pocket.*) Either of you chicks feel like helpin me do some drugs?

2   Disguise

The basement of the warehouse. **Fraser**, *in his underpants, shaves his head over a basin. A small tranny on the floor plays music. The lift arrives and the doors open.* **Arbogast** *and* **Janice** *get out.* **Fraser** *looks up.*

Fraser   Aw come on you, this isnae fair. You said you were going to bring me some clothes, fucks sake. And a towel.

Arbogast   You've just to ignore him doll.

Fraser   Aye, join the club.

Janice (*to* **Arbogast**)   That's it with the 'doll' you. Okay. Enough. (*Looking round the basement.*) You promised me there was drink down here. (*To* **Fraser**.) I've just flung up and I'm totally dehydrated. (*To* **Arbogast**.) I've met him before . . . (*To* **Fraser**.) Havent

I. (*To* **Arbogast**.) This is him that was waiting in my room, isnt it. That you sent me up to give the van keys to isnt he.

Fraser   '*So?*' (*To* **Arbogast**.) What the fuck's she doin here anyway.

Janice   '*So?*' (*To* **Arbogast**.) What does he mean '*so?*' *So* I'm just tryin to be civil and . . . confirm . . . that we've met. (*To* **Fraser**.) That's '*so*'. (*To* **Arbogast**.) So how's he got no clothes on and what's he doin to his head?

Fraser   He's burnin my clothes as evidence (*To* **Arbogast**.) Right?

Arbogast   Sure thing, Fraser.

Janice   Eh?

Fraser   So that I dont get connected to the insurance number (*To* **Arbogast**.) Right?

Arbogast   That's right enough, son.

Janice (*at the haircut*)   And that's your disguise is it.

Fraser   Oh, very good

Janice   You better grow a beard as well when you've shaved your nut.

Fraser   Oh I had had I

Janice   Uhuh you better. Cept then you'd look the same as you did before except your head'd be on upside down (*Cackles*.) Sorry Fraser. (*More cackles as she looks at him standing there with his Bic razor and his half shaved head*.) No really, Sorry. (*Pause*.) God, are you no frozen Fraser . . .? (*Mild paroxysm*.)

Fraser   Ay, I am

Janice (*through drunken giggles*)   . . . freezin Frozer?

Fraser (*to* **Arbogast**)   What is this?

Janice   Hoi . . . (*They look at her*.) Careful you dont nick your scalp . . .

Arbogast   She's pished that's what.

Janice   . . . with your razor Fraser . . .

Fraser   I can see she's pished. I can SMELL she's fuckin pished. Look at her. That's no what I mean. I mean what's she doin here. I thought I was supposed to be '*in hiding*' till you lot gave me my plane tickets for me and Raymond. How can I be '*in hiding*' if you bring stupid pished women in? I mean what if she identifies me. That's hardly '*in hiding*' is it. Do you lot not know what *in hiding* is? Or am I supposed to do an insurance number on her as well. Eh?

Arbogast   She's brought some clothes for you. (*To* **Janice**.) Havent you? (**Janice** *still hasn't recovered*.) Eh Janice? (*She looks at him*.) Clothes?

Janice   Oh right. Clothes (*She hands the poly bag to* **Arbogast**.)

Fraser   And a towel?

Arbogast She hasn't got a towel (*He empties the clothes on the floor next to* **Fraser** *and gives him the poly bag.*) Use that.

Fraser *rubs his head with the poly bag then starts to separate the clothes.* **Arbogast** *looks at the pile of clothes and picks out a pair of lime green Y-fronts.*)

Arbogast These are redundant are they? Unless you want to swap (*He sticks the underpants in his pocket.*)

Janice Nobody told me about a towel. Just clothes. For a man. (*Pause.*) But I didnt have any. (*She lights up a cigarette.*) So I went into Leonard's room. He's the room next to me. Snores like a drain. Dirty washing all over his floor.

Fraser *is putting on a pair of luridly odd socks.*

Janice And I couldnt put the light on cause me and Leonard dont get on and he'd be all over me if he woke up and saw me in his room at night going through his dirty washin on my hands and knees cause he's a sex starved pig and no wonder . . .

Fraser *is putting on a jumper.*

Fraser For fucks sake I cant wear this on a beach – it's scratchy nylon.

Janice So I definitely didnt want to wake him up.

Arbogast It'll keep you warm the now.

Janice Cause he's a light sleeper.

Fraser *is putting on the trousers.*

Fraser And these are greasy.

Janice Cause he's got weeping sores

Fraser Cryin out loud.

Janice As a result of his horrific eczema.

Arbogast (*to* **Fraser**) Quit moanin you.

Fraser (*to* **Janice**) Whose eczema?

Janice Leonard's

Fraser Leonard who?

Janice Leonard scratchy-nylon-jumper-Leonard!

Fraser Oh, NO! (*Pulling the jumper over his head.*) I'm no wearin this!

Janice Sticky socks Leonard.

Arbogast (*to* **Janice**) Shut up you. Fraser – it's fuckin NERVOUS eczema, he canny help it.

Janice (*snorts*) Help it if he wasnt so nervous about washin.

Fraser (*pulling the socks off*) Are the trousers his as well?

Janice Yup (*To* **Arbogast**.) You never said they had to get cleaned.

Arbogast (*to* **Janice**) Shut it. (*To* **Fraser**.) Fraser . . .

Fraser Right! (*Starts to take the trousers off. To* **Janice**.) Scuse me but I canny wear these.

Janice I dont care (*To* **Arbogast**.) But he doesnae ever do a laundry.

Arbogast Keep them on Fraser son.

Janice Or lift the toilet seat either.

Fraser (*to* **Arbogast**) Bugger off you (*He sits, kicking the trousers off his legs.*)

Arbogast Fraser son (*Goes to him.*) Calm down a bit.

Fraser Will you fuck off will you.

Arbogast *pinches* **Fraser**'s *nipple and wrings it hard.* **Fraser** *yelps and convulses. Everybody freezes.*

Arbogast Fraser listen to me son. I have to tell you to calm down.

Pause. **Fraser** *recovers.* **Arbogast** *does it again. Then he puts his hand on* **Fraser**'s *shoulder.*

You've to behave yourself and no be difficult or you'll just end up in more bother.

He takes the cigarette from **Janice** *and sticks it in* **Fraser**'s *mouth.*

Calm your nerves and pull yourself together and Willie'll get round to you and the doll after he's finished gettin things set up for the big party. Okay. Okay?

Fraser *stands, the cigarette dangling from his lips, nervous.*

Arbogast Okay!?

Fraser Aye, sure. That's okay then.

Janice That's my last cigarette. And we'll have less of the doll you!

Arbogast *turns to face* **Janice**. *He reaches out and does to her nipple exactly what he did to* **Fraser**'s. **Janice** *reacts in exactly the same way* **Fraser** *did.*

Arbogast I've to tell you to behave yourself as well, doll.

A beat, then **Fraser** *laughs.*

Fraser Bet that's sobered you up, eh Janice. Nothin like a good tweak round the nipples to bring us all to our best behaviour. (*Laughs.*) Well . . . fuck me, I think I've really got the eczema in proportion now. See if you see Leonard will you tell him from me that Fraser says thanks for the clothes and we all hope your weeping sore bits get better soon.

Arbogast   I'll pass that on. Anything else?

Fraser   Yes there is. Where's Willie Dobie and my tickets he promised me for Ibiza

Janice   And my rent book?

Arbogast   Everything's all goin to get taken care of for the both of you in the fullness of time. We're busy bees just now so dont be pests.

He gets in the lift and leaves.

Fraser (*holding out the cigarette*)   Here

Janice   What?

Fraser   I dont smoke.

Janice   Oh. I've got another packet anyway. I wish I was you and I could just have battered him.

Fraser   I know I should've. Who the fuck is he anyway? hurting people.

Janice   He's Willie Dobie's people-hurter. So what stopped you then.

Fraser   Because I dont have any clothes on do I. And you cant batter somedy in your underpants. And there's no way I'm putting any of that stuff on again ever.

3   Big plans

Willie Dobie, **Evelyn** *and* **Holly** *on the roof.* **Willie** *is expansive, showing off and fantasising. He opens a bottle of champagne and has a swig.* **Eveyln** *is about to put some drugs up her nose. The exact identity of the powder in use is never fully ascertained.* **Holly** *and* **Willie** *have already had some and are both sniffling.* **Evelyn** *is staying well away from the edge of the roof.*

Dobie   Take a look at that fuckin view will you. Eh? EH? I fuckin love views. They're like being in dreams

The girls take a look at the view.

Gets me every single time. First time I saw this place and looked at this view . . . I recognised my own dream. Whoof! What do you see? Eh?

Holly   Well it's quite a long way down isnt it . . .

Dobie   Every individual a dot. And every dot a customer.

Holly   I mean you wouldnt be a dot, you'd be a splotch

Evelyn   Holly dont . . .

Dobie   A Heaving Metropolis of Desperate Dots!

Evelyn   . . . do you mind if I dont look cause I'm not personally very good at heights.

Dobie   A Swirling Galaxy of Bottomless Opportunities!

Holly (*to* **Evelyn**) Look up then! (*Big sniff.*) God. My nose is all lovely and numb.

Dobie Potential? . . . Fuckin Astronomical!

Evelyn (*hesitating before she snorts*) Is this the stuff that makes you randy or the stuff that makes you think you can fly?

Holly Randy.

Evelyn I hope so cause I'm dreadful at heights.

Holly Or fly. Cant really tell yet.

Evelyn (*she lightly sniffs the powder to identify it*) Better no be or I'm off. Either way. Smells to me a wee bit like Shake 'n' Vac. (*To* **Holly**.) Did that stuff he gave you smell like Shake 'n' Vac?

Holly Nup.

Dobie Just get it up your face and take a look at this view.

Evelyn *snorts. They wait. She lifts her head up to look at the view and then drops it immediately, spluttering.*

Evelyn Fucks sake I cant see *anything*. What is this? Clean-o-Pine.

Dobie No it is not Clean-o-Pine and it is not Shake 'n' Vac and nor is it One Thousand and One Dry Bloody Foam either. It's . . . it's . . . (*Sniffs.*) It's supposed to be top quality recreational chemicals mind you it just goes to show you never could trust that swine Alec Sneddon.

Evelyn Aw God, you never bought this off Mad Alec Sneddon did you. Fucks sake (*She tries to snuffle the stuff out of her nose.*)

Dobie No you're right there, darling, I did not *buy it* off of Mad Alec 'Psycho Nutter' Sneddon.

Evelyn Cause he's responsible for a significant amount of local brain damage. Ask her.

Holly Any local brain damage I've got you've got as well, Evelyn. All you ever do is moan, you anyway. It's a waste of drugs givin you drugs. Cause you dont know how to enjoy yourself.

Evelyn Holly people who dont like heights dont enjoy being up on roofs looking at views.

Dobie Well his brain-damaging days have only just very recently ceased. Anyway, it'll no do you any harm. Keep you nice and perky till the other stuff gets here. Have a slug of this to get rid of the taste.

He passes her the champagne. She has a swill at it.

Holly Well I think it's a gorgeous view. I could just stand here and . . . in the breeze . . . It's giving me goose bumps and . . . you know what it feels like when somebody breathes on the back of your neck and then blows in your ear and you open your eyes and you're in a steamy jungle and it's not a person it's a big throbbing leopard . . . and . . . (*She tosses her hair and shivers.*) . . . could somebody put their arm round me a minute please cause my bottom has gone to jelly

Dobie *willingly does so.*

Evelyn Oh right. So it's obviously not the stuff makes you think you can fly then. Maybe if you stayed away from the edge your arse might firm up a trifle.

Dobie (*over his shoulder to* **Evelyn**) A jelly trifle, eh? Haha.

Evelyn (*miserably, to herself*) what a tube.

Holly What is it that your dream's about?

Dobie (*starting to warm to* **Holly**) My dream?

Holly Yes. The view in your dream. I mean what's the vision in your view? Apart from . . . lots of buildings. I mean I can see it's a view of all those buildings I just felt that you . . .

Dobie That I what?

Holly Well that you . . . You know. Were describing the view more sort of . . . I dont know . . . 'symbolically'.

Dobie (*to* **Evelyn**) Hear that? My my, that's awful . . .

Evelyn Tubeish?

Dobie No not tubeish, you – perceptive. Give us that here (*He swipes the champagne back and gives it to* **Holly**.) No you're quite right. It's a metaphorical view of a vision.

Holly In your dream?

Dobie Uhuh. No. Not in my dream, I mean forget the dream for a minute, I'm talking about real life here at the moment cause I'm not just some half arsed fucker that has dreams. This is about reality that I'm saying. Tough, hard, down to earth circumstances. I've bought this building. And that's a concrete reality. I mean it's one thing having a dream and it's another thing to open a nightclub in a prime site with a captive market and eliminate your competition

Evelyn You pair have had different drugs from I have.

Dobie (*to* **Holly**) I'm standing on an investment. And I'm looking at the future.

Holly Me?

Dobie No, no you, the view. Well. Maybe you as well I dont know. I mean I'm involved in the property game *and* the people game . . . but at the moment I'm only referring to the property version . . .

Holly   Although you might want to invest a stake in the right person sometime in the future.

Evelyn   Holly he's given us different chemicals.

Dobie   . . . yeah . . .

Evelyn   Cause I can see the Social Security Benefit Office from up here . . .

Dobie   Eh?

Evelyn   Behind the Magistrates' Courts . . .

Holly   So you can.

Evelyn   Next to the Police Station.

Dobie   Is that what that is?

Evelyn   Yeah. Opposite The Scottish Communist Party Headquarters

Dobie   Aye, okay, forget the fuckin view then. What I'm referring to is about what we're standing *on*.

Both girls look at their feet.

Holly   Which is what. Exactly?

Dobie   Quite literally, a veritable Gold Mine!

Evelyn   Symbolically?

Dobie   Of course symbolically are you stupid.

Evelyn   Hoi. Just because we havent got a job and we live in one of your flats and we pay you an excessive fortune in rent which, thank fuck we get off the council, doesnt necessarily mean I'm stupid, excuse me.

Holly   (*pokes him in the chest*)   Or! . . . That we're sex slaves! Frankly.

Dobie   Eh?

Evelyn   Or. Literally!

Dobie   (*a pause. Then a big hug round each girl's shoulder, pulling them to him. He cackles*)   My my, haha. It's great to see that a lifetime's dead end disappointment and unemployability hasnt dented your senses of humour.

Holly   I know. I didn't mean to offend you with that thing about sex slaves.

Evelyn   Eh?

Holly   It's just the drugs I took talking.

Evelyn   Hoi I was offended as well you.

Dobie   No offence taken . . .

Holly   Holly.

Dobie   Holly. And like I said I have a special pharmaceutical phenomenon lined up as a treat for all my people later in the evening once we get into the full swing of things.

Evelyn   I hope it's not more of Alec Sneddon's kitchen-surface scouring-agents

Dobie   No it's bloody well not. You.

Evelyn   Well what is it and where'd you get it and it better be good. Cause she promised me you promised us major chemicals

Dobie   Where'd I get it? Where? . . . Did I get it?

Evelyn   Yes. If you didnt get it off of mad Alec Sneddon cause he's the only place I know you can get any.

Dobie   And where do you think Alec Sneddon gets his, smartypants? Do you think it's delivered from outer space wrapped in tinfoil by anonymous aliens. What – is it teams of Belgian scientists testing them on bunnies in a germ free environment?

Holly   Bet it's the aliens.

Dobie   We make it. I. I have it made.

Evelyn   You?

Dobie   Yes. No not me personally, my . . . (*He gestures.*) My people. As of today.

Evelyn (*snorting*)   Your 'people'

Holly   Aliens can be people as well, Evelyn.

Evelyn   Holly . . . aliens are NOT people as well. And neither are you either Holly so shut up (*To* **Dobie**.) You mean your henchmen

Dobie   'Henchmen' . . . Now that's a lovely idea darling but who has 'henchmen' in this day and age that we live in?

Evelyn   The Mafia.

Dobie   Well you know, I suppose, in a way . . . I mean even the Mafia must have once had to start somewhere. Locally.

Evelyn   So is that who you get your drugs from.

Dobie   Darlin . . .

Evelyn   Evelyn.

Dobie   Evelyn, darlin if only it were that sinister . . . I mean as usual the facts are so much less . . . Listen. I find some kid who doesnt know his own potential, who's been stuck in a squalid rut, worrying about his pharmacy exams, and his rent's suddenly gone through the roof and his part time job for Alec Sneddon takes up all his time and only pays him washers and suddenly he's getting terrorised by guys with eczema and stringy ties. So he comes to see me for a bit of assistance in his time of trouble and I said to him, 'Raymond, son' – or whoever – 'working for Willie Dobie full time means a guaranteed weekly income of one and a half per cent gross on all retailed substances and no more trouble with rent arrears and horrible visitors and maybe one day you'll be able to afford your very own secret laboratory on a floating desert island. Inventing pills to cure the flu.'

Holly   I could tell you were a people person as well.

Arbogast *comes up the roof access ladder.*

Arbogast   Willie, there's a boy in the basement waiting to see you about a pair of tickets to Ibiza.

Dobie   Davey! Take a look at that view will you.

Arbogast   I know Willie, it's a bloody shame but it canny be helped.

4   Ibiza

Janice *and* **Fraser** *in the basement.*

Janice   Your head's all tufty bits and baldy patches.

Fraser (*brushes his hand through his mangled hairdo*)   I know. It's bloody murder this. You got a mirror?

Janice   Should have. I was in a hurry. (*Gives him a mirror out her handbag.*)

Fraser (*examines the damage in the compact mirror*)   God. That's really bad, isnt it.

Janice   Terrible

Fraser   I know, you're right. God. I cant believe I'm doin this again.

Janice   Spoil your holidays.

Fraser   I'm no goin any holidays.

Janice   I thought you were gettin two tickets to Ibiza.

Fraser   It's not for holidays – It's for me and Raymond to start a new life again.

Janice   In Ibiza? Doin what.

Fraser   Exotic dancing.

Pause. **Janice** *falls about.*

Dont laugh. It's big bucks you. (*He stands.*) Hey! What's so funny. (*He looks down at himself.* **Janice** *is helpless.*) Fucks sake, I wouldnae be doin it in my Ys. I'd have a costume. So?

Janice   So?

Fraser   So what's so funny?

She laughs some more.

Fraser   At least I'll be making something of myself.

Janice   So you will.

Fraser   No just pullin lumbers for my landlord.

Janice (*stops laughing*)   How do you know what I do for Willie Dobie.

Fraser   Cause I know.

Janice   How?

Fraser   Just by lookin at you.

Janice   I did ONE favour for him. And it's the last time I do anything for the sleazy creep and as soon as I get my rent book back I'm off. And it was not a lumber either.

Fraser   Huh.

Janice   So what did you do. Just by lookin at you.

Fraser   I told you my clothes had all to get burnt.

Janice   Oh sure thing.

Fraser   So's the insurance company couldnt link me . . .

Janice   Course

Fraser   With the burned out vehicle that he's gonnae collect a wad of insurance for . . .

Janice   Uhuh

Fraser   . . . that I drove away and set on fire for him. Which was a lot preferable to having some of my extremities severed I can tell you . . .

Janice   Well I entertained mad Alec Sneddon for him for a number of consecutive weekends in 'Blisters' Nightclub . . .

Fraser   Oh. OOOhh! Enter-*tained*.

Janice   Yes. With wit and charm. And I never lumbered him.

Fraser   Course you didnt doll.

Janice   Yes. And I can prove it cant I and dont call me doll.

Fraser   Sure thing. And dont you talk to me about that mad swine Alec Sneddon, cause Raymond and me . . .

Janice   Ask Arbogast. Cause last night when Alec finally runs me home in his van, Arbogast whapped him on the head and dumped him in the back.

Fraser   Cause Raymond and me . . . (*Pause.*) Whapped him on the head and dumped him in the back!? . . .

Janice (*pause*)   Uhuh.

Fraser   Of the van?! . . .

Janice   . . . uhuh . . .

Fraser   The back of the van . . . that I drove away and set on fire?

Janice (*pause. She turns away*)   God I'm parched. Do you think there's a drink in here?

Fraser (*pause*)   Eh. I'll have a wee look in a minute.

Pause. They reflect.

Fraser   You're right it's quite stuffy in here isnt it. (*Pause.*) Do you think he woke up.

Janice I dont . . . It was a fair wallop he got hit.

Fraser Oh. Good. (*Pause.*) So what was he like. As a person.

5 Violence

Leonard *and* **Arbogast** *in the main party space.* **Arbogast** *is slugging whisky straight from the bottle and smoking a stubby wee cigar.* **Leonard** *is drilling a pallet with his portable drill.*

Arbogast So what's the matter with your pus.

Leonard *scratches his inner thigh.*

Leonard My ointment's run out.

Arbogast (*double takes, then genuinely pained*) No, Leonard, son I didnt mean that I meant . . . I meant why have you got such a huffy expression on your face?

Leonard I know that's what you meant. Because my ointment's run out. What do you think I thought you meant. It itches like fuck when I exert myself without my cream.

Arbogast Aye, aye, okay son, I'm sure . . . spare me the clinical details. Believe you me I fully sympathise with your dermal plight, Leonard. Tell you what, stick on some Big Frank and join me for a wee snifteroony.

Leonard (*very pained*) Do we have to listen to that moanin wop . . . Arbogast?

Arbogast *gives him a big look.*

Arbogast Am I gonnae have to tell you I've to tell you to behave?

Leonard *puts on some Sinatra, 'The Wee Small Hours of the Morning'.*

Arbogast It's important to relax your soul when you get the chance, Leonard. And you and me are going to be very busy bees in the next few hours.

Leonard How can you relax to this?

Arbogast I'll have you know that bit in *The Godfather* where they garrotte the horse's head is based on this man's vocal style.

Leonard *joins* **Arbogast**. *They each have a slug of the whisky.*

Arbogast So?

Leonard What?

Arbogast How'd it go?

Leonard How'd what go?

Arbogast You and the chemist. Give me the details.

Leonard   Well . . . I gave him the prescription but I didnt have enough cash and I'd forgot my dole card so he said . . .

Arbogast   Not THAT fuckin chemist, the wee *student chemist* you paid a visit . . .

Leonard   AWW! . . . wee *Raymond* . . . Aw fabulous, fine! Absolutely fine. Fat wee fuck.

Arbogast   (*happy grinning. Ready for the details*)   So?

Leonard   So it's all taken care of and sorted out all hunky dory.

Arbogast   Yeah? . . . Come on . . . Dont keep me dangling here on tenterhooks . . .

Leonard   I just did it like you said. To the letter, you know. As per instructions. (*Modestly sheepish.*) Plus . . .

Arbogast   Yeh, plus . . .

Leonard   Plus I added one or two little improvisational extras of my own.

Arbogast   Give me a for instance Leonard son?

Leonard *takes a screwed up polythene bag out of his pocket, uncrumples it and shows the contents to* **Arbogast**.

Arbogast   Is that . . . ?

Leonard   Only a toe. Well he was in his jim-jams and I thought he'd need all his fingers for stirring and stuff. Plus!

He takes a pair of spectacles from his pocket and puts them on. The specs have scores all over the lenses. **Leonard** *looks at* **Arbogast**.

I checked he had a spare pair first . . .

Arbogast   (*not so impressed*)   Oh very frightening.

Leonard   . . . they were in his cagoule though, this is the ones he was wearing!

Arbogast   (*still not totally impressed*)   At the time?

Leonard   Aye at the time.

Arbogast   Superb Leonard . . .

Leonard   After I'd chopped his toe off, not as easy as you'd think by the way. I got him on his back and sat on his chest and then switched on my drill and leaned on his lenses.

Arbogast   Nice one son, that's a new one on me Leonard.

Leonard   Seemed to be a new one on wee Raymond as well.

Arbogast   Bloody lucky for the laddy he'd never gone for contacts. And how about the chemicals.

Leonard   Sneddon's got the boy all fitted out in a lockup garage with the whole kit and caboodle already up and running. I picked Raymond up at the hospital after he'd got his new stump dressed and recovered consciousness and ran him round there. He's gonnae have a load ready for the night.

Arbogast Marvellous. (*He sings along with the song for a line, passing the whisky to* **Leonard**.) I'll fetch them myself later. Willie'll be chuffed as fuck.

Leonard So . . . should we maybe . . . I mean . . . is Willie expecting . . .

Arbogast What.

Leonard It's just that you seem very cool about the prospect of some sudden retaliation from Mad Alec and his team . . .

Arbogast History!

Leonard How's that then?

Arbogast (*cackles, up on his feet, enthused, singing*) 'In the wee small hours of the morning' Alec Sneddon finally fucked upwards in a shower of sparks.

Leonard How . . . you didnt . . .

Arbogast Leonard. There's minds been at work round here you know. Making sure we have a tidy and viable conclusion in our grasp. I mean at first I offered this one out to tender, two hundred bucks round Willie's flats for any unemployed yo-yo keen enough to do the usual with an iron bar up the close round the back of Blisters when Sneddon closed up on the way home – and are they interested – are they buggery. The spirit of enterprise has fled the lot. See that's a direct result of the sort of campaign of terror that swine has long term waged on the populace. And the fact that they're far too comfy on the fuckin dole. So I had a look at an alternative angle. And Alec Sneddon's history and soot.

Leonard What.

Arbogast The baldy boy in the basement. He drove Sneddon's van down to the docks and torched the lot. After Janice had lured him home with her wiles.

Leonard I know, she's got fabulous wiles that doll.

Arbogast Leonard. Pay attention to what Old Blue Eyes is telling you. Wiles never phone you back.

Leonard So anyway, the baldy boy . . .

Arbogast . . . He thought he was doing an insurance number for Willie. Stupid wee prick. And Alec Sneddon was in the back.

Leonard Aw . . . So why did the baldy boy . . .

Arbogast Because, Leonard . . . him and wee fat Raymond are . . . you know . . .

Leonard What?

Arbogast . . . You know . . .

Leonard What? . . . You mean they're . . . '!?*#'

Arbogast . . . Right. So when Fraser finds his . . . his . . . you know . . . '!?*#' . . . has been savagely tortured, with his head kicked in and his toe lopped off and his eyeballs intimidated then Fraser comes to see Willie for help and Willie says do a wee insurance number on the van for me and I'll give you and your . . . your . . . !?*# a set of tickets to go away to Ibiza with and nasty men wont pester you with drills and secateurs any more.

The lift arrives and **Evelyn** *gets out. She is quite oily and dusty and she has a nose bleed.*

Evelyn They no here?

Arbogast Who's that, doll?

Evelyn Stop calling . . . Her and Dobie. he was showin us round and chatting us up and suddenly he opens up this hatch and says, on you go, you're first doll, and when I finally find a place I can turn round and crawl back out they've gave me the slip down some dark corridor. And I've been stuck in the ventilation system, crawling round on my hands and knees like something out of *Alien*. And I was fairly sure there was something crawling around behind me cept I thought it was that pair. Or maybe it was just the drugs at last cept I think the drugs has all bled out in my nosebleed. See when I find him I'm gonnae get some proper drugs off him then I'm gonnae kill him. Cept I'll have to come up with an alternative route into my system instead of up my nose. D'you think he's got that stuff I've heard about you can rub on your gums.

Leonard Oil of cloves?

Evelyn Funny guy. I only turned up because Holly promised me he promised her there'd be sex and drugs. Cept I informed her I wasnt interested in any sex. Just the drugs. I've never had good drugs. I told her I'd come if she *promised* me he'd promised her good big proper chemicals. Anyway she says she wasnt interested in the sex either and then about the first thing she goes and says to him is by the way we're not your sex slaves, which is the sort of thing she always says to men that give us drugs. So you can see his wee eyes light up and he thinks 'sex slaves – Nice Idea'. And he just ignores the 'we're not' bit. Anyway you can tell by the way she said it that she never meant it anyway. She might as well just have said to him – 'Has the idea of us being your sex slaves ever crossed your mind?' *And* he's been telling us crap jokes. Nightmare. If I wasnt so bad at heights I'd have flung myself off the roof. And there's not so much as a sniff of good drugs just this rubbish that makes both your nostrils haemorrhage simultaneously. Does either of your pair possess such a thing as a clean hanky?

Arbogast *reaches into his poly bag and pulls out* **Leonard**'s *unrecognisably screwed up underpants.*

Arbogast You can borrow this, honey pie.

He gives the underpants to **Evelyn** *who uses them to wipe away the blood from her nosebleed. Then she inspects the stain. She freezes.*

Leonard Those're my Ys!

Arbogast It's alright, the other boy didnt need them.

Evelyn (*to* **Leonard**) Sorry. (*To* **Arbogast**.) So is it okay if I keep them then

6   Membranes

Holly *and* **Dobie** *walking around in the building. He is trying to give her a guided tour but doesnt know his way about all that well.*

Holly (*breathlessly whooping with laughter at what she obviously thinks is the best joke the world has ever heard*)   So then . . . then the baby bear turns to the daddy bear and says 'Dad . . . ?' and the daddy bear says, 'What, son?' and the baby bear says, 'Dad, what kind of bears actually are we?' And the daddy bear says, 'I'm not quite sure I get your drift, son.' And the wee baby bear says, 'I mean are we koala bears or brown bears or grizzly bears . . . ?' And the daddy bear says, 'Well, son, I think we're what's commonly known as polar bears. Why were you asking son?' and the baby bear says . . . he says . . . 'cause I'm BLOODY FREEZIN!!!'

Dobie (*stares at her while she laughs, clearly not amused*)   Very good, hen.

Holly (*nearly helpless, but aware that he's not laughing*)   What . . . cause the daddy bear . . . so the wee baby bear . . . cause he thinks . . . so it's just that you dont expect that a bear's gonnae be able to . . .

Dobie   Aye I know, I get it, it's not that I dont get it, I mean I DO get it. I just dont think it's very funny.

Holly   It's a fuck of a lot funnier than that one you told me about the highly successful businessman and the cute wee labrador puppy.

Dobie (*pause. Looks at her*)   That was not a joke that was a personal reminiscence.

Holly   Oh right (*Pause.*) That's why I didnt get it then cause I didnt see why it was meant to be funny when he wiped his arse on the puppy . . .

Dobie (*taking her arm and moving on*)   So pumpkin, here's where we're going to have the . . . the . . . (*He opens a door.*) See it's heavin with potential this place, you could store coats in that wee room. (*He shuts the door.*)

Holly   You could fit in a waterbed.

Dobie   You could . . . you could fit in a waterbed.

Holly   You could have one of those machines with straps like Alec Sneddon had.

She wanders off.

Dobie   You could . . . you could have a machine . . . (*Following her.*) Hang on a tick there sugar . . . where did you hear about . . .

Holly   Cept I think that was for . . . wrapping parcels . . . It was always quite difficult to tell in the dark and some of the substances we had with Alec sort of took up all your attention. His office was brilliant though, I mean I just love the feel of linoleum against your skin. Did you know a boa constrictor is actually dry to the touch.

Dobie (*pulling a bag of powder out his jacket pocket*)   Tell you what, rub a fingerful of this on your gums, hen.

Holly   On my gums? I've already got no feeling up my nose so I dont know that I fancy numb gums as well right now. What the fuck is it anyway cause it gave Evelyn a terrible nosebleed, where the fuck is Evelyn anyway she's always doing this to me at parties.

Dobie   Away you go, the party hasnae started. This is the very Champagne of substances from my own personal . . . and, and I really dont understand why your pal was making such a fuss, cause she was uncommonly privileged to be allowed to suck a quarter of a gramme of this up her face cause this isnt the sort of thing you fling around willy nilly amongst all and sundry.

Holly   She never discovers how to let herself go.

There is a large trunk in a corner of the room. **Holly** *has gradually homed in on it. She opens the lid and reaches inside. She pulls out a jumbled armful of abattoir aprons and wellies and hats. Old and filthy and blood-caked.*

Holly   See if you flogged this clobber round the stalls you'd make a mint.

Dobie   There's every chance that's loaded with mad cow microbes. I'd leave it in the trunk.

Holly *measures an overall against herself.*

Dobie   I would really. Botulism's torture to shake off.

Holly   There's something so attractive about a helpless animal. You know. They're so vulnerable once they've been stunned. Floppy. Do you think it'll be alright if I borrow these. Evelyn'll be green.

Dobie *takes the garment from her and turns her away from the trunk.*

Dobie   Tell you what, poppet. This is the most stunning stuff you've ever had in your proximity.

Holly   Cause she's got a real thing about body fluids.

Dobie   And Vulnerable! Hnhh. (*Proffering the packet.*) Get a dab of that round your mucous membranes.

Holly   I'll have you know I dont possess any mucous membranes for your information.

Dobie *rubs a dab round his gums. He sticks his finger in the packet and holds his finger out to* **Holly**. *She eyes it suspiciously.*

Holly   I hope you dont think I'm letting you stick that up my nostril.

Dobie   I'm not interested in your nostril I'm interested in . . . Open your mouth a minute.

He prods the finger in her mouth. A pause and then she clamps her teeth on it. **Dobie** *yelps.*

Dobie   What the fuck was that for.

Holly   That was for what you did to that poor wee labrador puppy.

7 Young lovers

In the basement. The lift doors are open and **Leonard** *is unloading cardboard boxes.* **Janice** *is slumped,* **Fraser** *is restless, pacing about.*

Leonard What about you pair, huh? Fuckin Terminator 2, eh? I could probably get about five years just for having a conversation with you. D'ye think.

Janice No chance.

Leonard How no?

Janice Cause you're not having a conversation with us that's how no.

Leonard Probably just as well, eh? D'ye no think?

Janice Shut up, Leonard.

Leonard Oh, hey, sure thing Janice, anything you say. Just dont hit me on the head and tell Arnold here to set me on fire.

Fraser I see what you mean about him.

Leonard (*to* **Fraser**) Mean about who, you?

Fraser You, ya tube, that's who.

Janice (*to* **Fraser**) Dont call him names cause he's a pig and he'll batter you.

Fraser Batter me? I'll batter him, that's who'll batter who.

Leonard Fuck me that is some haircut right enough.

Fraser You're not kidding there, Leonard.

Leonard I know, Arbogast said it was and he's no far wrong.

Janice It's his disguise.

Fraser It is some haircut. Never mind Terminator 2. It's the haircut of a desperate man. Who's either getting his tickets to Ibiza or . . .

Leonard Oh, Ibiza eh?

Janice He's going to start a new life.

Fraser Or. It is the haircut . . . of an even more desperate man who's got nothing to lose if he has to stay here cause he doesnt get his tickets to Ibiza. All of a sudden.

Janice You said you couldnt batter anyone in your underpants.

Fraser That was before. I could now. Now that they've seen my new haircut.

Leonard   Aye well buster it'll no be me anybody batters shortly I'll have you both know cause when Willie Dobie gets this place done up and running he's making me head of security and the like of you pair'll no even get in in the first place because it'll be definitely no dolies allowed. Only proper public with cash to spare, never mind haircuts and underpants.

Fraser   Tough. I'll be in Ibiza by then anyway.

Leonard   Mind you I'm no sayin I'll no let you in though, Janice. In that wee number anyway doll. Willie'll most likely get you a job here anyway, off the books. Cept there's no drinkin while you're workin, except I could probably arrange it so we could probably have a staff drink together at the end of the night. Me and you. And then I'll get you up the road. What d'ye say?

He sits on a box and gingerly scratches his armpits and his crotch and behind his knees.

Fraser   Aww! It's all over him look at that.

Leonard   Hoi! Ma ointment's run out and see when I work up a sweat.

He reaches into the box he's sitting on and pulls out a bottle of 'Taboo'.

Leonard   So what do you say then, Janice. Me and you. A wee staff drink

Janice   Leonard. My head's splittin. I've been in a nightclub all last night using my wit and charm. I've flung up, apparently I've helped get Alec Sneddon, who I quite liked by the way, murdered and I cant stand you. Give it to him, he's staff.

She finds somewhere to crash out. **Fraser** *sits next to* **Leonard**. **Leonard** *watches* **Janice**.

Leonard   I got it for Janice. She's crazy about theme drinks. Look at her.

They both look at her.

Leonard   The amount of shut eye that doll needs . . . Drives me mad thinking about what she gets up to with that Sneddon animal that makes her that knackered. Her room's the one next to mine, Willie says I can move out you know but . . . I get in the bath after she's had a bath and the enamel's still warm and sometimes there's wee hairs. But I might as well no exist. She can drink millions and it has no effect on her behaviour whatsoever except when she comes back to the flat I can hear her throw up before she goes to her kip. And I fancy her rotten but no in the way she thinks, you know, no in a caring way, more like just pure . . . complete . . . animal . . .

Fraser   So you're gonnae be the new head of security.

Leonard   Dead right I am.

Fraser   What about . . . Argoblast?

Leonard   Arbo-Gast! He moves up.

Fraser   Moves up where?

Leonard In Willie Dobie's organisation. Willie goes legitimate and leaves the world of small time crime and criminal dolies behind him and Arbogast becomes his right hand man and I take over from Arbogast.

Fraser Doin what?

Leonard Whatever's . . . required. You know! I dont know do I. Whatever Willie Dobie tells us . . . like . . . you gonnae drink that?

Fraser Nup. Anything else?

Leonard (*passes him a bottle of 'Madison'*) Like . . . and dont you be gettin any big ideas just cause you've murdered somebody . . .

Fraser . . . dont remind me about . . . I havent 'murdered' anybody

Leonard Cause there's a lot more to it than that. That's the easy bit.

Fraser (*not happy with the 'Madison'*) . . . you got anything in there you can drink? . . . I've got to get something I can drink cause I need a drink. So if murderin somebody's the easy bit what's the difficult bit?

Leonard (*finds and passes him a bottle of 'Bezique'*)   The violence and the pain. Arbogast says I've got a talent for it. He says I'm like the son he never had. He says I understand discomfort because of my affliction. And it's a job you can do without workin up a sweat which is what I'd like to avoid because that's when my discomfort's at its worst. Especially, Arbogast says, if you approach it psychologically, which is how I'm tryin to think about it when I've time. So if Willie Dobie wants somebody to do something for him he sends me and Arbogast round to see them and inflict a bit of psychology on them and then he'll offer them protection because anybody who knows Willie knows they can always turn to him for a spot of help when they're in a bit of bother. Especially if it's psychological

He grabs **Fraser***'s arm and twists it behind his back, forcing him face down on one of the pallets. He digs out his poly bag with the toe in it. He inflates the bag like a balloon and rattles the toe around in it.*

Leonard Hey, Fraser. Guess what I've got in my bag.

Fraser What? I dunno.

Leonard Do you want a clue?

Fraser Okay then Leonard, gonnae give me a clue.

Leonard (*pause*) It's psychological.

He shows **Fraser** *the contents of the bag.* **Fraser** *looks at it, not knowing what it is.*

Leonard Look. That's the first piece of anybody I've ever severed. And now the rest of him works for Willie Dobie all thanks to me.

Fraser (*suddenly realising it's* **Raymond**'s *toe*)   FU-ckin HELL! Fuckin hell, man! (*He stops himself saying any more.*)

The lift arrives and **Evelyn** *gets out.*

Evelyn   Is there any bin liners in here I've got to find some Arbogast says, it's fuckin blackmail this, I'm goin out of my nut on powerful drugs and I've done in my molars with grindin my teeth and he has the gall to tell me I'm no allowed anythin to calm me down till I've helped with the sweepin up (*During this she finds a roll of bin liners.*) And he also says to tell the guy with the uncomfortable scabs to think about how it's probably about time he tried on the new clobber he's supposed to wear to see if it's an improvement (*To* **Leonard**.) I suppose he means you. (*Loudly.*) This is HELL! These chemicals are Dangerous! I'm losing my MIND! Oh . . . And I've to tell the other guy with the devastated hairdo he's to stay cool cause he'll get his tickets for Ibiza whatever the fuck he means by that your guess is as good as mine buster

The lift doors close and **Evelyn** *disappears.* **Leonard** *releases* **Fraser**.

Leonard   Must have got the Shake 'n' Vac it's fuckin lethal. Still whenever wee fat Raymond's finished his chemistry we'll no have to bother with that garbage any more. (**Leonard** *looks challengingly at* **Fraser**.)

Fraser (*after a pause. Innocently*)   Wee who . . . ?

Leonard   Fat wee Raymond McFadyen the guy that owns the other nine toes.

He fetches a pair of shoes and a bouncer's DJ and trousers in polythene.

Leonard   Used to work for Alec Sneddon till you burned him. We are talking serious amounts of Substances here. Cause now he works for us! So who is it you're going to Ibiza with, Fraser?

Fraser   Aw . . . Raymond McFadyen the pharmacy student?

Leonard   Aye. Pal of yours? (*Ripping the polythene off the clothes.*)

Fraser   Eh? . . . Not at all, no. He . . . just, he only just moved into the flat a few weeks ago. I mean of course I 'know' him. You cant not 'know' – He's the student. The chubby student. I mean you always get at least one student dont you . . . I fuckin personally hate students, you know?

Leonard (*tittering*)   I'm tellin you, Fraser, Arbogast's right about this psychological thing it's fuckin magical. I love it. (*He cackles.*) Hey, Fraser what do you think of the state of this clobber here.

Fraser *has taken a bottle out of the booze box. Johnny Walker Black Label.*

Leonard   HI! Dont even fuckin think it! That's my own for my own personal consumption.

Fraser *stares at him, opens the bottle and takes a big swig.*

Leonard   Aye okay but that's your last.

Fraser   What I think is, that Janice'll go for you in a big way in those garments, Leonard.

Leonard   Really. You think so.

Fraser   Show us your jacket on.

Leonard *hesitates*.

Fraser   Surprise Janice when she wakes up.

Leonard *puts on the jacket*.

Fraser   Show her what a difference a complete transformation can make.

Leonard   Is it okay.

Fraser   Trousers.

Leonard *puts them on*.

Fraser   It's the same as you were saying yourself that Arbogast told you. A psychological transformation. You can never underestimate the effect that nice clothes have on a chick's perception of the real you, Leonard. How else do you imagine Willie Dobie'd be investing half his income on hand printed ties and new suits.

Leonard   That better?

Fraser   Shoes.

Leonard *steps into the slip-ons*.

Leonard   Shoes and tie. Where's the tie?

Fraser (*points*)   Hangin out of your top pocket.

Leonard (*finds it. It is an untied real bow-tie*)   Aw fuckin hell, how d'ye work these bastards?

Fraser   I've never worn one. Mind you, you're right, it needs the tie.

Leonard   Trust Arbogast.

Fraser   Otherwise you just look like a half done tube.

Leonard   Fuckin disastrous!

Fraser   Hoi Janice. Look at Leonard's half done tube outfit!

Leonard   Hold on. Wait till I've got my tie tied.

He struggles with it. **Fraser** *looks at him and laughs.* **Leonard**'s *panic increases.*

Fraser   What d'ye think, eh? Janice – cool as fuck eh?

Leonard   Leave her you. Wait till I've got my . . .

Fraser   Janice!

Leonard   This fucker fixed. Help me, you.

Fraser I'm afraid personally I'm all thumbs and toes in the psychological department, pal.

Leonard Right then well leave her. While I get Arbogast to fuckin fix this. And dont fuckin dare you wake her up, cause she needs her sleep. Or it's me you'll answer to.

He heads for the lift, he points to the bottle of whisky in **Fraser**'s *hand.*

Leonard And dont even so much as even think it okay

Fraser Okay then Leonard.

Leonard That's okay then Fraser (*As the lift door closes.*) Some haircut, right enough.

The lift ascends. **Fraser** *waits for a couple of seconds, then has another big slug of the whisky.*

8 Bags

Arbogast *is sweeping up.* **Evelyn** *is standing holding a bin liner open. Some music is playing –* 'Stand By Me'. **Willie Dobie** *and* **Holly** *are doing a dance called 'The Stroll'.* **Holly** *started the dance and* **Dobie** *has picked it up. He is chuffed with himself.* **Evelyn** *watches them, staring, clenched, miserable.*

Evelyn Look she's all floppy, how come I'm no floppy, how come I feel as if I've been sharpened.

Arbogast I've told you to hold your wheesht till we've finished then I'll give you something to make you bloody FLOPPY!

Dobie (*without breaking step*) What, have the (*He mimes the word 'substances'.*) arrived yet.

Arbogast Eh? . . . naw. I've got some . . . (*He pulls a wee pill bottle from his pocket.*)

Dobie What? Is that . . . (*He gestures with his head.*)

Arbogast (*sniggers and holds the bottle away*) No . . . Willie, this is real drugs

Dobie Eh?

Arbogast You know, medical

Dobie Pfshh . . .

Arbogast Largactil.

Dobie Larg . . . The liquid cosh . . . ?

Arbogast Aye, I mean I'm fine just now, you know if I manage to steer clear of stressful situations

Dobie Well as long as you know what you're doing I've seen a documentary about the use of that stuff in high security prisons you know. (*To* **Holly**.) Largactil.

Holly Lovely

Dobie   A great social leveller. puts you on the same social level as escaped murderers haha. Eh Davey?

Arbogast   Aye, whatever you say, Willie, you're the boss.

Dobie   Ach – away, dont be like that we're a team. Eh girls. Come over here ya scrawny old bastard. C'mere. Davey! (**Arbogast** *doesnt want to move.*) Davey – c'mere

Arbogast *joins them.*

Dobie   Swing your arms.

Arbogast   What.

Dobie   Come on ya grumpy big stiffy – a bit of rhythm. Swing your fuckin arms.

Dobie *gets back into the dance.* **Arbogast** *has no rhythm whatsoever.*

Dobie   Oh look – the Link is no longer missing! Haha. Count! one an two an three an four! Arbogast! Can you no count that high, c'mon – God's sake. Imagine you're twenty years younger. (*To* **Holly**.) Mind you he'd still be in his late forties, eh? (*To* **Arbogast**.) Christ, Davey this is not the Stone Age. You're like one of those dinosaurs with spikes out of a Million Years BC. Useless! (*Gives him a shove.*) Out the way and let the talent breathe. I realise the music's a bit fuckin contemporary for you so you just get on with your sweepin up then.

Holly (*stops dancing*)   Do you ever feel like you used to be an Egyptian. And you were allowed to stay up all night and watch people from all over the world being sacrificed on a big slab. And you had a whole team of slaves covered in oil, building pyramids for you that you can lie in in the dark for thousands of years. And that one day you'll wake up and you'll be in the future like now and it'll all have just been something you dreamt. So your whole life suddenly makes sense. Have you ever felt that?

Dobie   I have felt that, yes. I knew Arbogast when I was an Egyptian. He was a dung beetle haha. (*To* **Holly**.) C'mon lets you and me go and take a look at the Nile, Princess.

He leads **Holly** *to the lift.*

Evelyn   'Princess'. Fucks sake. How come I get rigor mortis and she gets 'Princess'. How come I get lock-jaw and flashing lights behind my eyelids and menstrual cramp up the back of my spine and . . . and . . . and she gets to go and look at the Nile. Are you gonnae put some rubbish in this or have I to just stay here impersonating a receptacle till everybody's been and gone.

Arbogast *takes the top off his pill bottle and gives a tablet to* **Evelyn**.

Evelyn   Ta. How long do these take to work.

Arbogast (*shrugs*)   Depends.

Evelyn   On what?

Arbogast   Whether you're in a state of mild tension or a murderous rage.

Evelyn I know. I think all that was just uncalled for. Does he think somebody cant have feelings just because they dance like a tube and they're dead old and they've got hair loss. I hate it when people are insensitive like that.

The lift arrives and **Leonard** *gets out.*

Leonard (*to* **Arbogast**) Can you remember how you use one of these bastards?

Evelyn It goes round your neck . . .

Leonard I KNOW it goes . . . Arbogast, can you remember how to tie one of these stupid old fashioned . . . bow thingy fucks.

Arbogast (*in a temper*) I can remember millions of things. I can remember my fuckin manners for a start as well as the Origins of the fuckin Universe. And I can remember when's the right time for getting your hole and when isnt. And I can remember exactly what I'm owed by folks, Leonard and when to keep my gob shut.

He pushes past **Leonard** *into the lift.*

Leonard What's up with him? (*Pause.*) What are you standing there holding that thing like that for.

Evelyn Holly's just been talking about sex. Again.

Leonard Eh?

Evelyn She was telling Dobie how she had a fling with this guy who had a fetish about these. See in his room he had this bag full of polythene bags and his idea of a serious sexual thrill was to take a bag out of the bagful of polythene bags and then to stick the bag full of polythene bags into the bag he's taken out of the polythene bag full of polythene bags.

Leonard Eh? . . . what did he put in them.

Evelyn Polythene bags. He was very puritanical about them. She thought he maybe wanted her to wear them or something but all he wanted to do was sit on the edge of the couch with his trousers round his shins rearranging his polythene bags. She said it was something to do with his childhood.

Leonard I loved my childhood.

Evelyn Eh?

Leonard When I have a dream, and I'm walking about then the handles on the doors are all at head height. I had the happiest childhood you can have. Every night in my dreams I'm a five year old again.

Evelyn You're a five year old at the moment never mind in your dreams

Leonard No really, cause it wasnt till I was older that I got my nervous skin complaint.

Evelyn So what was it made you nervous

Leonard It was . . . I think . . . I dunno I think . . . (*Pause.*) Lack of love.

A brief, heart-stirringly emotional pause – then **Evelyn** *falls about whooping with laughter.*

Leonard See I knew you'd just laugh. Cause by the time I was six I was the only one in the family who didnt have Tourette's Syndrome. So when everybody else was gettin treatment and loads of attention in the local papers I was gettin ignored as some sort of freaky failure of nature and it made my epidermis erupt in irritating patches . . .

Evelyn *is on her knees.*

Leonard At least it clears up when I've been puttin on my ointment! At least it doesnt say anything about me as a human being.

Evelyn *has keeled over.*

Leonard Aw fuck you too . . .

Leonard *heads for the lift in a huff. A pause.* **Evelyn** *lies there. She stops laughing. She twitches.*

Evelyn Fuck. Hello. Help me up. Could somebody help me up a bit please. Leonard. Help me up. I think I can learn to love you, Leonard.

9 Guilt

Fraser *goes to the bucket he cut his hair into and pours half of the bottle of whisky into the bucket and then fills the bottle up with piss. He holds it up to inspect the colour.*

Janice Leonard has this effect . . .

Fraser Fuck, Janice, I thought you were sleepin . . .

Janice That's what I'm sayin, he has this effect . . .

Fraser And I'm supposed to not disturb you.

Janice No I'm saying he has this effect that I feel I have to get some sleep as soon as he starts talking to me. Give me some of that my mouth tastes foul.

Fraser No way, Janice – this is Leonard's own personal supply for his own personal enjoyment and he trusts me to see nobody arses it.

Janice Anyway I wasnt really asleep, I was only kiddin so he wouldnt annoy me with his chitchat. I thought you were scared of no man with your new haircut.

Fraser Neither I am

Janice Anyway I cant sleep. I've got such a thing as a conscience you know and so should you have too.

Fraser What for?

Janice For having murdered Alec Sneddon, that's what for.

Fraser I didnt 'murder' anybody. I wish everybody would stop saying . . . I have never 'murdered' a soul in my entire life!

Janice Well now you have. Thanks to Willie Dobie. You and me are worse criminals than pigs like Leonard and just as bad as murderers like Arbogast.

Fraser Leonard *nearly* killed wee Raymond

Janice Thanks to Willie Dobie.

Fraser Stop saying 'Thanks to Willie Dobie' all the time, Janice Thanks to Willie Dobie I'm a murderer and my best pal's had his toe chopped off. That's 'Thanks to Willie Dobie'

Janice Your *best* pal?

Fraser That Leonard left bleedin unconscious all over my bedroom rug.

Janice Your *bedroom* rug?

Fraser And they said at the hospital they could have sewn it back on if I'd packed it in ice and kept it cold except I couldnt find it cause Leonard's got it in a polythene bag as a memento. Even though I searched the whole of the flat.

Janice That Willie Dobie owns.

Fraser So I went to see Willie Dobie cause like Leonard says, you can always turn to Willie Dobie for a spot of help when you're in a bit of bother.

Janice Dont I know it. Cept it turns out to be him that's the source of all everybody's trouble. GOD! I need a drink.

She chooses from amongst the bottles and has a wee drink.

Do you know what I think, Fraser

Fraser No?

Janice I wish Alec Sneddon was here. I never lumbered him but he was dead nice to talk to.

Fraser Huh. It was him got Raymond all involved in making drugs again.

Janice I know. I mean I know all that, that he was a drug . . . baron and everything. I'm not talking about that though. He was going to sort out all my rent problems with Dobie. He wasnt even scared of Dobie and that lot in the slightest. And now we've gone and murdered him. And I always had quite a nice time with Mad Alec – not special, just nice. I mean he never did anythin I wanted to kill him for. So maybe that makes it worse. Or better. I mean I hardly knew him really though. I dont know.

Fraser I know.

Janice I mean if you look at it the other way though, it wasnt really us that murdered him, even though it was.

Fraser That's what I've been saying Janice.

Janice Although *we* did the *act*!

Fraser Except I didnt know Alec Sneddon was in the back of the van.

Janice   Hopefully Alec Sneddon didnt know he was in the back of the van either. Specially after you set it on fire.

Fraser   Look! I really dont want to keep getting reminded . . . All I want is my tickets to Ibiza and me and Raymond on the plane and we're out of here. Vamoose!

Janice   Ibiza what? So housewives can stick pesetas down the front of your underpants?

Fraser   I'll have a costume!

Janice   You've got a costume. You've got the haircut of a desperate man. And you should use it. Anyway what makes you think this lot are going to let you just vamoose!

Fraser   Or you.

Janice   Or me either except dont forget I'm the object of Leonard's deepest fantasies.

Fraser   Aye except dont you forget Arbogast.

Janice   Except Leonard is the son Arbogast never had, mind you which makes him lucky he never had a son.

Fraser   So to stay in with Arbogast and Dobie you're prepared to lumber Leonard who you cant stand?

Janice   No I cant. I fancy Leonard like I fancy cancer. I'd shag Alec Sneddon's charred corpse before I'd let Leonard rub his rash against me.

Fraser (*really quite horrified*)   That is just . . . sick!

Janice   Sicker than setting somebody on fire?

Fraser   Will you stop . . . Bloody . . . That just hasnt sunk in. I've seen Leonard's skin condition.

Janice   I'm sure it's no worse than the condition Alec Sneddon's is in. Anyway I dont have to lumber either of them and there's no need for you to be so crude.

Fraser   Oh I'm SORRY – well I take that back then.

Janice   Thank you. I just feel very strongly that a new rent book and two plane tickets isnt really . . .

Fraser   Isnt really what?

Janice   . . . Adequate. For you and me getting turned into murderers without anybody even asking our permission.

Fraser   Right. So. I dont understand what it is you're suggesting that we do. I mean I quite fancy the option of running away you know.

Janice   What I'm saying is! . . . That we should fully consider our options. We should . . . we should . . . just work out if there's something that we can both . . . '*get*'

Fraser   So you think we should actually . . . '*get*' something.

Janice   I do. I definitely do think we should try to . . . to . . . '*get*' . . . something.

Fraser   Uhuh. You're going to have to give me a for instance.

Pause.

Janice   Okay. I'm going to have to have another drink. Then I'll try to give you a for instance.

10   Animal magnetism

On the roof. **Dobie** *is semi-astride the railing, popping another bottle of champagne.* **Holly** *is leaning on the railing. Both of them are a bit inflamed.*

Holly   The bit I loved was the bit where she goes (*She does an American female accent.*) 'I did it for you, Doc' and he goes 'Three years in the slammer, a man cant hide his feelings . . .'

Dobie   I know . . .

Holly   And after that, the bit . . .

Dobie   And the bit . . .

Holly   And the bit where . . . where . . . they're both . . .

Dobie   Waiting for the train . . .

Holly   Yeah – where she gets his gun out the left luggage locker . . .

Dobie   The pump action sawn-off . . .

Holly   And the bit where . . . she's running . . .

Dobie   You cant get them here you know, not even a replica.

Holly   . . . she's running in slow motion through the puddles outside the prison farm

Dobie   And he's waiting in slow motion inside the gates . . .

Holly   And then at the end it's dead good when he's . . .

Dobie   When they hitch a lift in the back of that farmer's rubbish truck

Holly   And they get to the border and she gets off the lorry to buy cigarettes and the baddies blow him to pieces and the poor Mexican farmer as well.

Dobie   . . . I know I didnt like . . .

Holly   And she really suits it when she cries.

Dobie   . . . yeah . . .

Holly   I sobbed buckets. Mind you she got the bag with all the money in it. So I suppose . . . I loved it.

Dobie (*takes a swig of his champagne and then faces her – excited*)   I really didnt enjoy the end though. But up till then I loved it. – I mean I *really* loved it! cause – Cause the guy, all the way through you know, he's got a Vision! I mean that bag of money doesnt just represent a bag of money! It's their future for both of them. Even though he gets blown up which I thought was absolutely gratuitous. and he's not afraid of . . . of . . . you know he never got scared by his responsibilities. Me! Look at me here – I mean I am *drowning* in responsibilities. And . . . it's the same, you know . . . the hard fact is. The fundamental fact of the matter is if you dont have the strength to face your responsibilities then you drown. And nothing can change that simple, since time immemorial fact, as very many poor, sad, deluded people have learned to their ultimate cost. Guys with no sense . . . of themselves . . . their Destiny . . .

Dobie *is seriously thinking about trying a kiss.* **Leonard** *arrives on the roof up the access ladder.* **Leonard** *coughs.*

Dobie   What the fuck are you after. What the fuck is he wearing. What the fuck are you wearing, Leonard.

Leonard   I was wondering if you . . . or . . . or . . . knew how you tied one of these . . . her.

Dobie   Alec Sneddon had no sense of himself and that was the downfall of the man (*To* **Holly**.) Eh?

Holly   An animal.

Dobie (*to* **Leonard**)   Why dont you just get an elasticated one. (*To* **Holly**.) The things that are put in a man's path to try him, eh?

Holly   And the things that an animal puts in a woman's path to . . . to . . .

Leonard   I dont know if I can get an elasticated one.

Dobie   Eh . . . ? God. Bring your neck over here then Leonard. And bring your bow-tie with it.

Leonard *does so.* **Dobie** *ties his tie for him.* **Holly** *watches.*

Dobie   They say that's the ultimate in human trust, did you know that.

Holly   What?

Leonard   What?

Dobie   . . . allowing another man to place his hands around your throat, it goes back to the earliest beginning of civilisation, when we were all still animals and everyone was at each other's throats the whole time. Men and women

Holly   I only ever use my throat for swallowing.

Dobie (*to* **Holly**)   And that's . . . you know that's as it should be (*To* **Leonard**.) Meanwhile . . . Leonard. You should be able to feel the magnetic animal power in my fingertips and your personal feelings will be telling you whether or not you trust me. (*To* **Holly**.) Just like the bit where the man cant hide his feelings after three years in the slammer. See what I mean . . . respect is what it all boils down to (*To* **Leonard**.) It's good for me to know that Leonard. That you trusted me to tie your tie for you. It means I know you can be trusted. On a very intimate level. It's one of the few ways you can read a man where he cant lie to you. (*He steps back. The tie is very badly knotted.*) And there's fuckin few of them my son. So we must pay heed to them when they happen.

Leonard (*to* **Holly**)   Does it look okay?

Holly   It's a bit . . .

Dobie   That is not the point! Whether it does or does not look okay. It's what the tying of the tie signifies to me about him in the most profound sense that matters. Not whether or not the bow-tie looks okay.

Holly   It looks a bit like an ordinary tie only you dont know how to tie it.

Arbogast *also arrives on the roof.*

Dobie   I know that but the point is not about whether . . .

Arbogast   Excuse me a minute Willie I've got to . . .

Dobie   WHAT!

Arbogast   Sorry, I'm saying . . .

Dobie   WHAT?! Eh? Say it! What NOW?

A very uncomfortable pause. **Dobie** *is over-reacting and everybody feels it.*

Holly   Some party this is turning into. Shouting . . .

Dobie   You are absolutely right, and I apologise, sir. You'd be well within your rights to give me a smack for that, Davey, that was right out of line. Or. (*He grins and goes into a boxing pose.*) You could try anyway, eh? Haha. (*He clips* **Arbogast** *with a couple of jokey slap punches.*) I'd like to see you give it a try, eh, Davey. Square goes, you and me, and the best man's the one with all his own teeth at the end. Though that puts you out the runnin from the off, eh, Davey.

He drops the boxing pose and turns serious. He marches to **Arbogast** *and takes his elbow.*

Dobie   What can I say, sir – I'm under a lot of pressure here, so we all have to make allowances, come on down to my office and we'll get everything sorted out

He leads **Arbogast** *down the stairs – leaving* **Leonard** *awkward with* **Holly.**

Leonard   Pair of lethal bastards eh?

Holly   Who.

Leonard   That pair. I'm telling you there's no way Arbogast would stand for that if he didnt . . . you know . . . I mean it's like . . .

Holly   Like what.

Leonard   Well I know him and I've seen him when he's got his dander up and it's just . . . phwoof!

Holly   So?

Leonard So I'm only saying, if either of them ever took exception. I mean I've seen Arbogast . . . I mean I didnt even know what a tracheotomy was.

Holly And now you do?

Leonard Yeah. Same as an appendectomy apparently only on your throat. That's how you can tell they respect each other cause I've seen Arbogast.

Holly Oh. Right.

Leonard Or else it would just be mayhem.

Holly Uhuh.

Leonard It would be just . . . just . . . Like what Willie was saying when he had his hands round my neck about how we're really all just animals. That's what it would be like. Only probably more psychological than animals. You know with real human blood.

11 Late afternoon of the Living Dead

Fraser *and* **Janice** *in the basement. Both perked up, excited and a bit pished. The little tranny is playing.* **Janice** *is singing and keeping time, bottle in her hand.* **Fraser** *is dancing and singing along. They argue about the lyrics without dropping the rhythm of the song.*

Janice Aga do do do
Push my apple pull my tree . . .
Aga do . . .

Fraser Pineapple! . . . do do

Janice Pineapple?

Both DA DA DEE-DEE-DEE-DEE-DEE!
AGA DO DO DO
PUSH PINEAPPLE

Janice } pull my tree
Fraser } Grind Coffee!

Janice *stops.*

Janice What's that one?

Fraser *stops as well.*

Fraser Grind Co-Fee.

Janice Uh?

Fraser Janice the words are 'Pull pineapple grind coffee! . . .

The lift arrives and the doors open. **Evelyn** *stands there. She is exceedingly dazed and incapable of getting out of the lift.*

Fraser   Not . . . 'Push my apple pull my tree' for fucks sake. I mean what is it you think this song's about in the first place?

Janice   Sex!

Fraser   Well you're wrong.

Janice   It's you that's moving your pelvis

Fraser   I am not moving my . . . I'm dancing. (*To* **Evelyn**, *who is standing in the lift with her mouth hanging open, drooling lightly and staring.*) It's not about sex it's about . . . working on a plantation or something. It's traditional. Isnt it?

Janice   Keugh. Traditional?

Fraser   That the natives invented.

Janice   What natives.

Fraser   The natives that invented the song in the first place that they used to sing when they were working on the . . .

Janice   Bucks Fizz?

Fraser   It's not . . .

Janice   Cause they never worked on a plantation . . .

Fraser   It isnt by . . .

Janice   Unless it was in one of their videos that I never saw . . .

Fraser   IT ISNT BY BUCKS FIZZ!!! Sorry. The song is a song about voodoo and how you can . . . you can numb yourself to the daily drudgery of digging up coconuts on a plantation by swallowing this potion that makes you into a kind of zombie that does whatever anybody tells you all the time even if it's against your will normally . . .

Evelyn   Sex slaves!

Fraser   . . . Yes. Well . . . – maybe. Not necessarily.

Janice   You dont dig coconuts . . .

Fraser   Whatever . . . bananas then

Evelyn   Is this the party?

Janice (*quietly*)   I'm fairly sure you dont dig bananas either . . .

Fraser   No this isnt . . . are you okay?

Evelin   I'm sick.

Janice   I know. I was sick earlier

Evelyn   I'm gonnae BE sick.

Fraser   Do you want me to smooth your brow?

Evelyn   Eh?

Janice   He's dead sympathetic. Really. He really is.

Fraser *gets the poly bag he wiped his hair on and snaps it open for* **Evelyn** *to use to be sick in. He goes towards her.*

Evelyn I'm not a sex slave.

Janice He's not saying . . . have you been drinking.

Evelyn I've had medicine. (*She clocks the polythene bag, then she looks at* **Fraser** *and* **Janice**.) Perverts! (*She collapses.*)

Janice I told you that song wasnt just about coconuts.

12 Respect

Dobie *and* **Arbogast** *in* **Dobie**'s *office. There is a desk and an angle-poise lamp.*

Arbogast I mean you're right and I cannot disagree, Willie, she's a lovely lookin doll.

Dobie She's a princess. And also a sense of humour.

Arbogast Not to be laughed at, Willie.

Dobie I know and . . .

Arbogast Can I ask you something?

Dobie Fire away, Davey, s'what I'm here for.

Arbogast Have you got things sorted out for this evening?

Dobie You know me better than that, son.

Arbogast I know.

Dobie Exactly

Arbogast So what I'm saying is . . . concentrate here because I'm thinking hard about all this myself.

Dobie Oh – 'CONCENTRATE!' . . . no on you go . . .

Arbogast Because somebody has to. I want to know if the folk who've got invited . . .

Dobie Of course . . .

Arbogast The important folk . . .

Dobie Uhuh

Arbogast That a lot hinges on.

Dobie (*pouring champagne into his glass*) Our vision, Davey.

Arbogast . . . and those special guests that are going to distribute our product upon whom we depend . . .

Dobie A shared dependancy. Haha

Arbogast Uhuh. That when they turn up eventually, they're going to be met with a . . .

Dobie One whale of a time

Arbogast With a semblance of. With something not just . . . With all the ground work done and the problems sorted out

Dobie (*proffering a glass*) You joinin me?

Arbogast Willie. Can we talk straight?

Dobie Well I can, Davey, but with regard to yourself I have some doubts . . .

Arbogast *steps towards* **Dobie**, *fast and angry.*

Arbogast Well you can cut that shite out for a start – it's not one of your idiot fuckin dolies you're talking to here.

Dobie (*squares up to deal with this insubordination*) Now just you steady on a wee minute here . . .

Arbogast *goes Chernobyl meltdown on him, grabbing* **Dobie***'s throat in one hand and his scrotum in the other.*

Arbogast Dont fucking steady on a wee minute here me ya little prick! I have had enough of your arsing around to last me! If you fuck me up in this I will rip out your spinal column. I will swap the brains in your skull with the shite from your bowel. And vice versa! Now is that fathomable for you?

Dobie *nods. They pause.* **Arbogast** *dusts him down a little.*

Arbogast Eh? Good God man.

Dobie No you're right. That's perfectly fathomable and I apologise. (*He offers his hand.*) It's not that I dont respect you cause I do. Mutual respect.

Arbogast (*pauses*) Willie. Keep things simple eh? (*Takes* **Dobie***'s hand but doesnt shake it, just clamps it in a superhuman vice grip.*) Now answer me a question or two. Are you or are you not the man in charge?

Dobie (*can hardly think for the pain*) Am I or am I not . . . ?

Arbogast . . . the man in charge.

Dobie I . . .

Arbogast . . . Yes?

Dobie . . . am.

Arbogast You are. Good. Excellent. We know where we stand. Have you, as the man in charge – Seen to your responsibilities?

Dobie (*cant believe the pain*) Pffew . . . eh . . .

Arbogast What I mean by that, Willie is . . .

Dobie Uhuh.

Arbogast (*giggles*) It's fuckin funny really, just look at you ya trumped up wee jerk. (*Releasing* **Dobie**'s *hand. Leaving* **Dobie** *on his knees.*) I'll tell you some news shall I, kiddo.

Dobie Uhuh.

Arbogast I mean you've worked dead hard and done well for yourself, nobody's denying you that. There's all your tenements chock full of dolies paying you DHSS money and doing you favours – I mean that's all very commendable. And you've saved up and bought this place. And you've got your own wee tame chemist to make the stuff for you. And you've got Alec Sneddon out the way. Now. Do you know what that all adds up to?

Dobie Tell me?

Arbogast A very useful foundation. And so. See I need to know if you're up to your responsibilities. That if you set something in motion you wont let it all just fall apart on your head. On everybody's head. Are we speaking our language?

Dobie We are. That is my language you're speaking. I'm just not a hundred per cent sure what you're actually talking about.

Arbogast The thing that has to be done. The two pests in the basement. Now in so far as I took care of things up to here as YOU requested, you now find yourself with the opportunity to tie the whole business up in the one go.

Dobie That is the way it seems isnt it.

Arbogast So it is.

Dobie Where is it the boy wants his tickets to again?

Arbogast (*patiently*) No no no no no no (*He goes to* **Dobie** *and puts his hands on his shoulders.*) No no no no no Willie. Listen to me. You go out to the car park . . .

Dobie Should I not be . . .

Arbogast Just! Listen to me a minute.

He holds up a bunch of car keys. **Dobie** *takes them.*

Arbogast Under the front seat of my Volvo you'll find a sawn-off shotgun and you go down to the basement and you shoot the boy first and then you shoot the doll . . .

Dobie . . . shoot . . .

Arbogast In the head, then burn the bits.

Dobie . . . shoot . . . (*He gulps.*) . . . I could never . . . then burn . . . I couldnt . . .

Arbogast You're a big boy, you'll manage.

Dobie Davey . . . Davey I could never . . . You couldnt . . . For God's sake (*He cackles.*) You're some man, Davey I mean everybody knows . . .

Arbogast Everybody knows the doll's been seeing Sneddon and now he's burned to death in the back of his van. And the boy's been doin his nut about his tickets. And the boy was in her room the night Sneddon disappeared. And everybody knows what a mad dog Alec was. So he found out and he would've murdered the boy. But the love birds murdered him first before they ran away together to . . .

Dobie (*softly*)   Ibiza.

Arbogast   Ibiza! The very same. (*He goes to the lift.*) And who can blame them for that. A very lovely place this time of the year despite what you read. I've been there myself. Under the front seat, Willie. (*He stands in the lift waiting for* **Dobie**'*s acquiescence.*) . . . Willie?

Dobie   Under the front seat. Shoot them in the head. Burn them.

Arbogast   I knew it. Same language all along. You just need it spelt out a bit.

The door closes. The lift descends.

13   Spleen

In the basement. **Fraser**, **Janice**, **Holly**, **Leonard** *and* **Evelyn**. **Janice** *and* **Fraser** *are leaning over* **Evelyn**. **Holly** *is a bit spaced.* **Fraser** *and* **Janice** *sit* **Evelyn** *up. Her face and arms are covered in red blotches.*

Leonard   Is she breathing?

Janice   She's wheezing a bit.

Holly   I knew he was contagious.

Fraser   It's an allergic reaction.

Holly   Well it's not as though we've been stuffing our faces with prawns is all I'm saying. So who knows.

Leonard   I never laid a finger on . . . anyway I'm not bloody contagious, you so will you stop making remarks your pal's dying.

Holly   Okay. I'll stop if you stop. Anyway it's her own fault she's always doin this to me at parties. So where did she get the spots.

Leonard   Fuck knows.

Holly   Who're you callin fuck nose, pizza features. (*She giggles.*) sorry that's just the drugs I took making me say things I dont mean again they were doin that before.

Janice   Anyway. She'll be okay when she gets better.

Leonard (*fetches the Johnny Walker whisky bottle*)   Give her a glug of this that'll buck her up.

Fraser   Dont give her . . . no you shouldnt give somebody alcohol when they've got food poisoning.

Leonard   No?

Holly   We've not had any food. In fact I'm bloody famished. Has anybody got any?

Leonard   Grub? Aye sure doll.

He gets the bag with **Raymond**'s *toe out of his pocket and passes it to* **Holly**, *who is nicely surprised by his generosity.*

Holly Ta. What is it. Looks foul. Looks like a bit of sausage gone rancid

Leonard (*winks at* **Fraser** *as he unscrews the whisky bottle*) They're lovely. Marks and Spencer's do them. We are talkin taste bud sensation here.

He takes a slug of the whisky as **Holly** *pops* **Raymond**'s *toe in her mouth. For a second they eye each other, then* **Holly** *starts chewing and* **Leonard** *swallows. He retches.* **Holly** *takes the toe out of her mouth and looks at it.*

Holly They're a bit chewy I dont know if I like them. (*To* **Janice**.) Try it?

Janice I'll save it for . . .

Leonard Fucks sake . . . who's been . . . has somebody been . . .

Fraser Ah God she's stopped breathing, quick, undo her . . .

Evelyn *sits up and looks round as the lift arrives and* **Arbogast** *gets out.*

Evelyn Touch me and you die I've got the whirling spinnies I'll be fine when I've . . .

A pause. She plonks back down again.

Arbogast I thought you three were supposed to be upstairs sweeping up, what's the matter with her?

Janice She'll be fine if she gets a breath of air.

Arbogast So she will as well. Why dont you take the lassie outside Leonard.

Holly (*going to the lift*) Yeah come on . . . Bring her up on the roof, it's lovely up there. You can see all the way to Ancient Egypt

Leonard Me?

Fraser Yeah, you're security you're meant to be in charge of things like this.

Leonard You're right. No problem (*He picks* **Evelyn** *up in a fireman's lift. To* **Holly**.) Gonnae get the lift, fuck nose.

Holly (*a beat*) Only cause she's my best pal, but Willie Dobie'll kill you if I get a rash off your poisonous sausage, plooky. (*As they head for the lift.*) I meant that thing you got from Marks and Spencer's not that thing you've got in your underpants.

Leonard I got my underpants from Marks and Spencer's as well . . .

The lift departs.

Fraser (*to* **Arbogast**) Right then have you got my tickets.

Janice And my rent book.

Arbogast Willie's sortin all that out he's good at that kinda thing. Paper work.

Janice I want to ask you something.

Arbogast Uhuh.

Janice As a for instance if somebody just asked you, just hypothetically speaking, how much would you say it would cost them to pay to get somebody else murdered.

Fraser Janice . . .

Janice Just off the top of your head.

Arbogast Off the top of my head? depends

Janice (*to* **Fraser**) see I told you.

Fraser (*to* **Arbogast**) I told her you wouldnt have the faintest clue what she's talking about.

Arbogast Absolutely. I think Willie Dobie's your man for that sort of question.

Fraser That's what I said.

Arbogast Just hypothetically speaking of course.

Fraser Sure. So would he know as well how much it would cost to get somebody beaten up so badly that they have to get taken straight to the hospital with bits chopped off them.

Arbogast You know, Fraser, that haircut of yours makes you look as though you've had one half of your head shot away.

Fraser Does it

Arbogast It suits you as well.

Janice My uncle Neil got shot in Northern Ireland by a soldier. Mind you my uncle Neil was a soldier as well. So I suppose it must have been an accident. Mind you, knowing my uncle Neil . . . He's no got any spleen. He says it was like, if you can imagine lying stretched out on your back and somebody stands above you with a pick-axe and then swings the point of it into your stomach as hard as they can, then that's what it felt like. Cept he was standing up when it happened. And then he got given a really nice medal.

Arbogast (*he giggles, genuinely impressed with* **Janice**) My my, you're a fly wee tinker right enough arent you. What you're askin me is what it's worth to our man Willie Dobie to buy the silence of you two hardened murderers in the light of recent events. Eh?

Fraser Hang on hang on she's saying no such thing. 'Buy the silence' – who said anything about anything like that. She's just pointing out that what we did for Willie was worth . . .

Arbogast Worth what. All going to jail for. Getting murdered for yourselves . . .

Fraser . . . two one way tickets to Ibiza and a new rent book.

Janice (*to* **Arbogast**) If Willie Dobie knew anybody he could get to murder us then he wouldnt have had to get us to murder Alec Sneddon would he? Mister Smart Arse.

Fraser Janice you go on about this nonsense more than anybody I've ever met in my life. (*To* **Arbogast**.) Dont listen to her she's daft.

Janice I didnt volunteer to get involved in Willie Dobie's orgy of death did I.

Fraser Exactly so shut up about it. Harping on all the time. What happened to make-up and babies.

Janice Oh right I'll just talk to myself about make-up and babies and you pair talk to each other about getting your hole and chopping people up.

Fraser When have I mentioned a word about getting my hole.

Janice You dont have to mention it, just take a look at the way you were dancing with me a wee while ago.

Fraser Eh?

Janice And consider what your pelvis was up to. Cause it was an obscenity.

Fraser MY pelvis?

Janice Thrusting at me

Fraser Oh not just thrusting but At You.

Janice Right in my face.

Fraser Aye in your dreams doll

Janice Huh! In my worst nightmares you mean.

Arbogast Ach I dont know. (*He goes to the lift.*) Stick him in some clothes and fix his hairdo.

Fraser Not as bad a nightmare as my worst nightmare.

Janice You've got no idea about worst nightmares Fraser cause you've got no imagination.

Fraser And you have.

Janice Yes I have. My brain is almost eighty-five per cent imaginary, so you can take that back. About not as bad a nightmare as your worst nightmare cause there's guys'd kill for the privilege pal – so dont give me 'What my pelvis' in that tone. Cause I know from years of experience that that is a totally phoney tone. Pal.

Fraser I think you . . . has it never . . .

Janice Since I was fourteen.

Fraser Listen

Janice Swine like you undoing all my buttons with their eyeballs.

Fraser I've never even glanced at your bloody buttons.

Janice Ach dont come it, Fraser. You've got the mind of a sewer. Exactly the same as all the Leonards and the Willie Dobies . . .

Fraser I am not the same as . . . Listen you! And your eighty-five per cent imaginary brain. Why do you imagine it was that it was me who took Raymond to the hospital and sat and held his hand while they dressed his stump and put bandages all round his face where he'd got drilled and then went out and got him his favourite wine gums and then sat and waited while they took him away to X-ray him for broken ribs and ruptured organs because some fat scabby bastard had been kickin him . . .

Janice (*sees him getting upset, not sure why*) . . . okay dont . . .

Fraser (*almost tearful*) 'Dont' – what are you on about '*dont*' – you cant just '*dont*' . . .

Janice Hoi Fraser . . .

Fraser Oh you mean hoi, Fraser dont get upset – eh? – Fraser dont cry.

Janice No I just meant, I meant dont . . . You . . . I'm sorry, you said he was your pal, I didnt know you meant he was . . . I'm sorry, Fraser

Fraser (*he laughs*) Do you know what's funny . . .

Janice What.

Fraser I mean Alec Sneddon was really scary and everything and Raymond and me were both terrified of him but one night at Blisters he came into his office and Raymond had been waiting for him for hours and me and Raymond were killing some time, you know and he came in and I thought . . . Fuck he's gonnae demolish us both and Sneddon goes . . . 'Boys – your bodies are your own. Just dont get any dribbles on my nice linoleum. And feed Delilah and put the lights off when you've finished'

Janice 'Delilah'?

Fraser His boa constrictor

Janice Oh. (*Pause.*) Is that like a python or something.

Fraser yup

Janice And he had one as a pet?

Fraser *nods.*

Janice In his office. (*Pause.*) I never knew that. (*Pause.*) I wish we hadnt killed him.

Fraser I know. I wish we hadnt as well.

Janice Willie Dobie said he was his pal and I'd to entertain him with my wit and charm. And see the first time, at Blisters – he didnt hardly look at me. And then the week after that I was sitting by myself and some sweaty fat guy bought me a Taboo who I told to get raffled after a minute and Alec came over and said is this guy bothering you and the guy bolted and we had a nice chat. And then the week after that he remembered my name and got me a basket of complimentary buffalo wings that I could have sworn was chicken but I didnt want to offend him. And we had a dance. And I started to like him but I was a bit pished so when he said would I like to come to his office and have a look at his big snake I got the wrong end of the stick and I though he was just as bad as all the rest.

She lights a ciggy. Her fingers are trembling. **Fraser** *has to help her with the lighter.*

Janice   Fraser I never knew he had a boa constrictor. I honestly never knew that. I thought he was just being a pig.

Fraser   He doted on Delilah.

Janice *has got quivery lip.*

Janice   I think that's so beautiful.

Fraser   What?

Janice   The name. Delilah. And everything. Being devoted to a reptile. Except we never really talked. And then last night he ran me home.

Janice *is a bit tearful.*

Fraser   Janice . . . dont. I mean . . . Have a Mirage.

Janice   Thanks, Fraser. (*She has some Mirage.*) Oh God – he was a lovely dancer.

Fraser   I know. I saw him dancing. He's a great dancer.

Janice   Do you know something, Fraser – he never even tried it on with me in the slightest. Never even so much as a feel. He never even tried to come up for a cup of coffee after he run me home in his van last night.

Fraser   He might've though, maybe if I hadnt burned him to death in the back. You know, next weekend.

Janice   Well there's no gonnae be any next weekend is there.

Fraser   . . . no there's not.

Fraser *has some Mirage too.*

14   Vertigo

Evelyn *clinging onto the metal ventilation outlet.* **Holly** *and* **Leonard** *on the roof with her.*

Holly   Evelyn if you dont open your eyes . . .

Evelyn   If I open my eyes I'll fall.

Holly   Will you open your eyes and let go of the ventilation outlet and come and get some fresh air.

Evelyn   I've got fresh air here.

Holly   That air's not fresh it's filthy everybody in there's been inhaling it for ages.

Evelyn (*very determined*)   I am not letting go of the ventilation outlet. Ever. If I open my eyes I will get sucked to the edge of the roof and fall off. I know I will!

Leonard   You'd better be careful about that cause we're six floors up . . .

Evelyn *whimpers*.

Leonard   That'll be vertigo. It's a psychological complaint. Like my eczema only in your brain. And there's jaggy cement and scaffolding at the bottom to land on as well.

Evelyn *another whimper*.

Holly   Shut it you. (*From the edge of the roof*.) Look! You wont get sucked off and fall.

Leonard   Plus rats and mice and slugs and spiders.

Holly (*yelps and steps away from the edge of the roof*)   Slugs?

Leonard   That'll be a psychological fear of slugs.

Dobie *appears at the top of the ladder*.

Dobie   Leonard stop fartin about with the fuckin floozy and get your arse into my office. Pronto!

Leonard   Straight away, Willie, sir. (**Leonard** *goes to follow* **Dobie**. *He turns back to the girls*.) Dont worry about the slugs, they're all in your mind (**Holly** *winces*.) Apart from the big slimy one on the back of your leg there. (**Holly** *jumps*.)

Evelyn (*still clinging with her eyes screwed shut*)   Leave her alone ya scratchy big bloody big bastard big fuck pig!

Leonard (*leaving the roof*)   Tourette's Syndrome. Another terrible mental affliction.

Evelyn   Holly come over here and cuddle me, there's no slugs!

Holly   'Floozy'. Did you hear that. 'F-ing floozy'! What happened to pumpkin and petal and princess?

15   Delegation

Leonard *and* **Dobie** *in* **Dobie**'s *office*.

Leonard   So honestly I wasnt chattin her up – either of them – I was only . . .

Dobie   You've no need to explain your private emotions to me, son. You and me know a thing or two about one another that means we dont have to go into particular details the whole time because there's a trust that exists that goes beyond that, you understand?

Leonard   Perfectly, I couldnt put it . . .

Dobie   And I know for instance that if I say to you, and this is a famous quote, Leonard if I say – 'God gonnae grant me the serenity to be able to . . . to . . . change those things that I can–NOT accept and the wisdom to know how to . . . to . . . do it', then you know exactly what I'm referring to. Am I right?

Leonard   you are perfectly . . . one hundred per cent.

Dobie   Right. What?

Leonard   Uhuh. Ehmmm . . .

Dobie   That we're all lumbered if people shirk their responsibilities.

Leonard   As if I'd do that.

Dobie   Which brings us neatly to the matter in hand.

Leonard   Right. Fire away.

Dobie   I want you to go to the car, Leonard.

Leonard   That's not a problem, Willie, no sooner said than . . .

Dobie   Go to the car and look under the front seat.

Leonard   (*pulls out the keys to* **Willie**'s *Mercedes, flourishes them and heads off*)   No problem whatsoever.

Dobie   Wait a minute, son.

Leonard   What.

Dobie   (*pulling out the keys to* **Arbogast**'s *Volvo, patiently explaining*)   I dont want you to go to my Mercedes I want you to go to Arbogast's Volvo.

Leonard   (*grabs the keys*)   Oh. Right (*Heads off again. Stops.*) Why?

Dobie   Why do you think, Leonard.

Leonard   Eh . . . To get something.

Dobie   Yes. What?

Leonard   I dont know. Whatever's under the seat.

Dobie   Which is what?

Leonard   Which is . . . I dont know.

Dobie   Which is a box of cartridges and a double barrelled shotgun with the ends of the barrels sawn off so that you can hide it under your jacket and not miss when you shoot somebody with it at close range, that's what.

Leonard   Right. (*Heads off again. Stops.*) What do you want one of them for. I never even knew we had one of them.

Dobie   I dont want one of them. You do.

Leonard   Me?

Dobie   You, Leonard.

Leonard   How?

Dobie Because unless you want to kill him with your bare hands you're going to need it to blow Mister Arbogast's brains out. That's how.

16   Splatter

Janice *and* **Fraser** *in the basement.* **Arbogast** *comes in with an armful of bin bags and a mop and a bucket and a shovel.*

Arbogast You pair still here.

Janice What do you expect we've still not seen Willie Dobie, have we?

Arbogast That's who I was lookin for too hen, I thought he might need this lot.

Fraser How, you havin the party in the basement?

Arbogast Very funny, doll. Best to have the whole shooting match cleaned up and no mess to upset the party goers dont you both think. Listen I'll just dump this stuff the now and when Willie comes in you can tell him it's right here for him to get a shift on with before he sorts out your problems for you once and for all. You do that for me?

He dumps the gear. He picks up **Leonard***'s bottle of whisky.* **Leonard** *arrives in the lift.*

Arbogast Leonard, son. (*Holds out his hand.*) Car Keys!

Leonard Eh?

Leonard *stands rooted, a set of car keys in either pocket. A hand jammed in with them.*

Arbogast The keys to the car.

Leonard Eh?

Arbogast Leonard give me the keys to Willie's car now would you. Please. Now. And dont get me demented, son.

Leonard Right. Willie's car keys

He gingerly extracts a trembly fist containing a set of car keys. He holds the keys out, still clenched in his mitt.

What do you want the keys to Willie's car for?

Arbogast Because (*He taps his watch.*) Time to visit the chemist and pick up the big prescription.

Leonard No I'm fine really my skin's almost completely . . .

Arbogast Leonard?

Leonard Oh right. That prescription. Sorry

He opens the fist. Massive relief – he gives them to **Arbogast**. **Arbogast** *leaves.* **Leonard** *dances about in a paroxysm of nerves.*

Leonard   Ayargh . . . !

Fraser   What's up with your pus! Is your eczema itching?

Leonard *forces* **Fraser** *onto his back on the pallets and goes to drill his eyeballs.*

Leonard   I've told you it's pronounced fuckin eczema. It's nervous. And it's not my fault. And no wonder! (*He pulls the trigger of the drill.*) Fuck!

Janice   Leonard DONT! Leave him he didnt mean that. It'll clear up when you're older.

He releases the trigger.

Leonard   Fuck! Janice. Willie Dobie's gone daft.

Janice (*to* **Fraser**)   You okay Fraser.

Fraser *signals he's okay.*

Janice   You're a big pig Leonard.

Leonard   No Janice help me. He says I'm supposed to find Arbogast and . . .

Janice   You just found him a minute ago.

Leonard   No Janice, Listen! He says I've not to just find him, I've got to get a sawn-off shotgun from out the car and *then* find him and then I've got to shoot him with it.

Fraser (*from the floor*)   Right. Okay that's it. Stuff your ticket I'm going home!

Janice   He says WHAT?

Leonard   Do you think he's kiddin me, eh? He must be.

Janice   Kidding you?

Leonard   As a test.

Janice   He told you to shoot Arbogast with a gun.

Leonard   Yes.

Janice   With a real gun? Shoot him.

Leonard   That's what I said.

Fraser *has managed to sneak over to the lift. He presses the button and waits.*

Leonard   Then I realised on the way to the car it must be a test you know? To see what I'm made of. Psychologically. So I thought – Brilliant. I'll just get the gun out the car and then I'll go back to check with Willie and then I'll have passed the test only then I thought, Fuck! What if Arbogast finds out I actually went to get the gun he'll fuckin murder me, what the fuck does Dobie think he's playin at and then when I looked in the car there wasnt any gun anyway.

The lift arrives and **Fraser** *hauls the door open.*

Leonard   Fuck!

Leonard *belts after* **Fraser**.

Janice   No Leonard wait . . . I've got it, Leonard.

Leonard (*from the lift doorway*)   What.

Janice   Show him your toe.

Leonard   I'll show him my toe alright, I'll kick his fuckin eyeballs out!

Leonard *goes into the lift. The drill whirrs again and* **Fraser** *squeals in terror. Random banging noises.*

Janice   The toe you chopped off the student!

Pause. Then **Leonard** *emerges from the lift with* **Fraser** *under his arm, all hands on the drill,* **Fraser**'s *eyes screwed shut.*

Leonard   Eh?

Janice   Well if all he wants is to test you to see if you're up to it psychologically all you have to do is show him the toe you chopped off the pharmacy student and he'll know he can rely on you.

Leonard (*he drops* **Fraser**)   Janice that's brilliant. (*Pause.*) Fuck!

Janice   What?

Leonard   I gave it to that bird that's terrified of slugs and she ate it.

Janice   No she never she spat it out and said she'd have it later. She's most probably still got it.

Leonard   Janice you are brilliant. (*Huge pause. The biggest moment of* **Leonard**'s *life.*) I . . . Love you . . . Janice.

She's utterly and absolutely blank. **Leonard** *dies inside, then heads back to the lift. A stone killer to the depths of his soul.*

Leonard   See if that bitch has eaten it I'll fuckin kill her

He dives into the lift and leaves.

Fraser   Oh that's great thanks Janice.

Janice   What

Fraser   First he chops Raymond's toe off and kicks his head and his organs in then he kicks my head in then you go and tell him how to get his bacon saved using my best pal's chopped off toe.

Janice So would you rather I just let him keep kicking your head in, I told you he was a pig.

Fraser (*absolutely fucked and past caring*) I wouldnt care. I dont give a toss any more. And I'm bloody freezing as well. I am a frozen freezer.

Janice Fraser.

Fraser What?

Janice (*she produces the bag*) I've got the toe.

Fraser Oh. Right. So

Janice So you can give it back to Raymond.

Fraser Right. So I can.

Janice And you can tell him how you got revenge for him from Willie Dobie

Fraser (*pause*) . . . Janice . . .

Janice Cause you're in love with him arent you.

Fraser In love with him?

Janice In love with him.

Fraser . . . Yes.

Janice So come on then, and I'll help you.

Fraser . . . why. How. Why are you going to help me?

Janice Cause I was in love with Alec Sneddon. That's how.

They head for the lift.

17 Wine gums

Holly *and* **Evelyn** *on the roof.* **Evelyn** *is still clinging to the ventilation outlet. She has* **Raymond**'s *tortured spectacles in one hand.* **Holly** *is looking over the edge. She is clutching a small polythene bag.*

Evelyn Do you think Leonard's going to be okay?

Holly Definitely not. There's stuff coming out of his head.

Evelyn Holly dont. I had that earlier.

Holly It's all over the jaggy cement. It looks like slugs but I think it's his brains

Evelyn I think that happened to me earlier as well.

Holly   I know Evelyn but that was psychological. The sluggy stuff's Leonard's real physical brains. It's a horrible mess down there.

Evelyn   Holly dont look down then.

A pause. They look at each other. Then **Holly** *looks down again.*

Evelyn   Who was the wee chubby guy in the cagoule with the limp.

Holly   And the can of petrol?

Evelyn   Uhuh.

Holly   I dont know. I thought him and Leonard were chums

Evelyn   If they were chums he wouldnt have pushed Leonard off the roof would he?

Holly   Depends. Maybe they'd had a row about something.

Evelyn   What's in the polythene bag the chubby boy gave you, Holly?

Holly (*holding the polythene bag at arm's length*)   I dont know. (*She has a feel.*) They're squishy. I'm scared to look. What did he give you?

Evelyn   Some specs.

Holly   Put them on.

Evelyn   I'll put them on if you look in the bag.

Holly *opens the bag and peeks in.*

Evelyn   What are they? Eyeballs?

Holly   They're not eyeballs, Evelyn. They're wine gums.

Evelyn   Thank God, eh?

Holly   Try the specs.

Evelyn *puts the specs on.*

Holly   You probably have to open your eyes, Evelyn.

Evelyn   Fuck! That's incredible.

Holly   What?

Evelyn (*she steps away from the ventilation outlet*)   The view from up here. I've never seen anything like it. I can see right through you Holly, all the way into outer space. (*She looks at her arms.*) and my blotches has gone as well and everything. Holly?

Holly   What?

Evelyn   You look like an Egyptian Princess. Holly?

Holly   What?

Evelyn   Come and we'll just sit here and hold hands and look at the stars and we can wait here till it starts to get light and then we can watch the sun come up. Eh?

Holly   Okay. I've never seen that.

She sits next to **Evelyn**. *They wait for the sun to come. Time passes.*

Evelyn   We'll give it another five minutes then we'll fuck off and get chips.

18   Stardust

Willie Dobie *in the main party area. Sweeping up the floor himself. Some music playing. The lift opens and* **Janice** *and* **Fraser** *arrive.*

Dobie   You the exotic dancer, that is one hell of a rotten costume you've got there, son. What is it you do? A get dressed tease act. Haha

Janice   It's not a costume. First. He wants his tickets.

Dobie   Tickets?

Fraser   To Ibiza.

Janice   It's the costume of a desperate man.

Dobie   Ah. Right. Point taken. See the thing is about your tickets – Davey's got them. So you should maybe wait for him in the basement.

Janice   We've been waiting.

Fraser   And he's not got them.

Dobie   Well now then. Leonard must have got them. Do you pair not think I have better things to worry about than dealing with silly wee dolies.

Fraser   Just give me my tickets and give her her rent book back.

Janice   Fraser! (*To* **Dobie**.) Tell me what other things you've got to worry about

Dobie   (*very firmly*)   They are beyond your limits! They are outwith your comprehension.

Janice   Are they matters of life and death?

Dobie   (*he laughs at her*)   I meant it, Janice when I said you looked radiant in your nice frock. It would be a shame if you got a horrible big stain on it.

The other lift arrives. They all wait to see who's in it. The doors remain shut.

Dobie   That'll be Leonard now. (*He faces the lift.*) Leonard. Some pals of yours and I've got another wee job for you. (*The doors remain shut.*) Leonard? (*He takes a step towards the lift and considers.*) Leonard is that you in there. (*Pause.*) Davey? You seen that tube Leonard anywhere. Haha. (*Pause.*) Is one of you two floozies stuck in that lift? (*Pause.*) Eh?

The lift doors open. The semi-conscious body of **Arbogast** *topples into the room. Standing in the lift holding a sawn-off shotgun is a giant of a man in a coat and suit, his clothes covered in burnt patches and smouldering bits, his voice is similarly well-done.*

Dobie   . . . Alec . . .

Sneddon   Hiya Willie. Heard you were having a party. Fuckin funny I never got an invite. Hiya Janice. Sit down, Willie. I'd've rung you, doll but some swine whapped me on the head and drove me away and set my van on fire. My best van with me in the back. You beat that. My best van's a burnt out shell and I never even had the fucker properly insured. (*To* **Dobie**.) Are you gonnae sit down when I ask you? And see when I woke up and the van was like the inside of a furnace, I think that what happened was that some of my muscles got cooked, you know the muscles in my arms and legs and stuff, so they dont work properly any more. So if you'd sit down when I wave my gun at you, your gun really, Willie, then that'll save me coming over there and havin to try and batter you.

Dobie   I'm sittin down, Alec, look I've sat down.

Sneddon   You're lookin good, Janice. I like your hair.

Janice   Oh . . . Thank's. It's my own.

Sneddon   Right. That wig was a terrible lapse in judgement

Janice   I know that now, Alec.

Sneddon   That's good that you know that.

Janice   Alec. I didnt . . . I mean I was never aware that . . . Is there anything I can do to make it up to you . . .

Fraser   Tell him

Janice (*turns to* **Fraser**)   What!?

Fraser   Tell him Janice, what you told me.

Janice   Eh?

Fraser   That you admitted to me. When I told you about Delilah.

Janice   I couldnt.

Fraser (*to* **Sneddon**)   She loves you.

Sneddon   Eh?

Fraser   She didnt understand. But she worked it out. In the meantime. Her life was an endless stream of shite . . .

Dobie   Oh, yeah, our hearts . . .

Sneddon   SHUT IT! (*He turns to* **Fraser**.) Go on.

Fraser   Until she met you. That's what she told me

Sneddon   Did you believe her?

Fraser (*he struggles for a micro-second, then nods*)   Janice is . . . Has never faced anything till she faced up to murdering you and then she saw. (*He loses it.*) . . . Janice?

Janice   I saw . . . you were a good man, Alec. Behind . . . being a bad man. And if I hadnt . . . murdered you . . . then maybe . . . we could have been happy . . . Anyway the wig was his idea (*At* **Dobie**.) He said you couldnt resist me if I was a redhead

Sneddon (*he turns to face* **Dobie**)   And you werent wrong there, Willie. A man of taste. Like this place for instance. Nice property, Willie . . . Potential.

Dobie   Aye it needs a lot of cash spent, Alec, but you know, once we all get it tidied up.

Sneddon   Funny that cause I got an approach. From Mister Arbogast here. Desiring me to liquidate some assets. You know. My night club. Blisters. And I never realised you, William, were the man in charge

Dobie   Me? (*Giggles nervously.*) I'm not the man in . . . come on, Alec . . . Me? . . . Hey . . . guys? . . .

Arbogast *moans. Everybody looks at him. He lifts his head and looks at* **Dobie**. *He is badly injured. Concussed and bleeding. He starts dragging himself interminably and painfully across the floor towards* **Dobie**.

Sneddon   Look at that. Bleedin on the floor then rubbin it in when you're tryin to keep the place tidy. Fuckin despicable. That's David Arbogast Esquire through and through. Do you no think. Willie?

Dobie   Aye.

Sneddon   That's certainly my opinion anyway. Still. Poor bastard. That was some wallop I hit him in the car park so maybe you canny really blame him. He's probably got quite serious brain damage he'll never really recover from . . . (*Pause.* **Sneddon** *looks at* **Arbogast** *and ponders this.*) . . . I reckon. (*He cackles.*) What a hoot (*To* **Janice** *and* **Fraser**.) He's sittin in the car with wee Raymond McFadyen in the front with him, and Raymond's measuring out these pills and Arbogast's sittin next to him fuckin gloatin with a bottle of Johnny Walker's in his hand and he takes a slug and then he stares at the label and I can hear him muttering away under his breath, goin, 'What the fuck's that spotty so and so fuckin spotty balloon gone and purchased . . .' And wee Raymond's goin '123, 124, 125 . . .' And Davey gets half out the car and holds the bottle up to the light. And I get right behind him and I goes 'Psst! gies a slug of your juice' and he goes tense and starts to turn his head and I goes BATTER! Hard as I can BATTER! I gives him another one and he goes 'For pity's sake, you're killin me friend' in a wee quiet pathetic wee whiney voice and so I goes BATTER – and gives him another one for bein such a hypocrite because if there's one thing I cannot suffer in a fellow human being it's hypocrisy.

Fraser   Did you hurt Raymond.

Sneddon   Fraser – I couldnt hurt Raymond – great wee guy. Arbogast's all concussed and I says to him, what's that you're counting out there Raymond. He goes Love drugs. He says, they made me make it I dont even know if I've made it properly. So I says, why dont we test it out then, on Davey here cause he looks as though he's in need of a bit of loving, so Raymond crams a handful of his pills down Davey's throat and then I says, okay that's fine Raymond you can just hop it, which he did though I never meant it that literally, the boy must have been nervous. You love him, Fraser?

Fraser (*very nervous of* **Sneddon**)   Love him . . . eh . . . well I dont know if I'd go so far as to . . .

Janice   Fraser!

Fraser   . . . yup. I really, really . . . like him.

Sneddon   Okay. Why dont you pair go and help Raymond with the paraffin, I told him to give us quarter of an hour.

Janice   Paraffin?

Sneddon   Aye on you go. And when you're done the three of you can take Willie's car cause he'll no be needin it. (*He lobs* **Dobie**'*s car keys to* **Janice**.)

Dobie   You can borrow my car alright, Janice but I'll have to send Leonard round to get it back.

Sneddon (*laughs*)   I wouldnt worry about Leonard if I were you, Janice.

Dobie *looks at* **Sneddon**.

Fraser (*to* **Sneddon**)   I was wondering if . . . Just . . . I couldnt put on Leonard's scratchy jumper and he burnt all mine as evidence so I wouldnt get linked . . . after I did the insurance number for him . . . So I just was thinking . . . Can I get his clothes?

Sneddon *gestures to* **Dobie**.

Sneddon   Dont be a shy boy, William.

Dobie *undresses and gives* **Fraser** *all his clothes*. **Dobie** *stands in his silky black posing pouch*. **Fraser** *looks at his own grunties, then points at* **Dobie**'*s*.

Fraser   I dont suppose you'd like to swap?

Janice   Fraser!

Janice *and* **Fraser** *leave*.

Dobie   You're a bad evil bastard, Alec and you'll burn in hell

Sneddon   Was, Willie, I've reformed. Anyway I've already had a taste of the fiery afterlife courtesy of Willie Dobie Enterprises. And Raymond told me this marvellous thing once that strengthened me. Do you want to hear it (**Arbogast** *emits a horrible moan*.) Aye, you as well Davey (*To* **Dobie**.) That'll be the love drug working, the guy's probably dying for his hole. (*To* **Arbogast**.) Hoi, you, pay attention and you might learn something, scum. Might emerge a better person. (*To* **Dobie**.) Do you think he's compos mentos?

Dobie (*pleading to be finished*)   Will you please just get on with it, Alec.

Sneddon   Oh. Right. (*His attention comes back to* **Dobie**. *He concentrates.*) See Raymond told me that current thinking is that this universe was created in one huge big explosion that produced loads and loads of . . . stuff. I think it was hydrogen he said. And that's all there was. And it swirled about for . . . Oh . . . hundreds of years until it made stars. And then inside of these stars, Willie, the hydrogen got turned into other stuff. You know by the heat or something. The pressure. And I can appreciate that. I'm not a hundred per cent sure but anyway. It made gold and lead and iron and uranium and all the expensive precious stuff. And that's what makes us. All these chemicals inside us that make us work came from the inside of a star. Is that not an exceptional piece of knowledge. Willie. (*Pause.*) You agree with me. That you and me and David Arbogast and everybody else, no matter what they're like as a person, is made out of stardust. I found that exceptionally moving.

Arbogast *has reached the side of* **Dobie***'s chair.*

Dobie   What is it you're saying, Sneddon?

Sneddon   (*angry*)   Nothing. I'm saying! . . . I'm just saying isnt it delightful the way we've all got something to teach one another!

Dobie   Yes but what is it that you're saying to me?

Sneddon   I'm not 'saying' anything! I'm telling you something, Willie!

Dobie   Okay, okay. All I'm saying is I dont understand what it is you're telling me. Am I supposed to find that . . .

Sneddon   You're not supposed to find it anything, it's just a personal story to . . . so that . . . (*He gestures at* **Arbogast**, *shouting at* **Dobie**.) Dont just let the poor guy crawl around on his hands and knees all night, get up off your arse and let him sit down

Arbogast *has slumped with the effort of crawling across the floor towards* **Dobie**. *He is only semi-conscious, he dribbles and mumbles very quietly.*

Sneddon   Willie, give him a help up for God's sake, can you no see he's injured.

Dobie *hauls at* **Arbogast**, *eyes fixed on* **Sneddon**.

Sneddon   That's the way, show him a bit of care and compassion and make him comfy.

Dobie *gets* **Arbogast** *onto the seat.* **Arbogast***'s head lolls.*

Arbogast   (*almost inaudibly*)   I told you Willie. I'm going to . . . (*His voice fades away altogether.*)

Sneddon   What did he say?

Dobie   I dont know I cant hear him.

Sneddon   Lean down and listen then, you ill-mannered get!

Dobie *leans down and puts his ear next to* **Arbogast***'s mouth.* **Arbogast** *tries to speak again.*

Sneddon   What did he say.

Dobie   (*shouts*)   I cant hear him!

Sneddon   Well concentrate. Try! The pair of you. Davey speak up for God's sake.

Arbogast *tries again.*

Sneddon Eh?

Dobie *bends down and listens some more.*

Dobie He says 'I told you, Willie'

Sneddon Told you what?

Dobie *leans down again.* **Arbogast** *grabs* **Dobie** *and hauls his head down. He repeats himself.* **Dobie** *breaks free. He straightens up and faces* **Sneddon**.

Dobie He says 'I told you Willie I am going to rip out your spinal column'

Sneddon *(laughs)* Good on you Davey. Well said, son.

Dobie What do you want Alec. I can only say I'm very sorry.

Sneddon What do I want. Look at me. Well. I can only say I'm happy you're sorry. I want to see what you're really made of Bill.

Dobie Uhuh.

Sneddon I want you to do a favour for me.

Dobie What

Sneddon Then I'm willing to not shoot you.

Dobie What is it.

Sneddon But if you dont do my favour for me – I shoot you.

Dobie Tell me the favour.

Sneddon *(pause)* Strangle him.

Dobie *(pause)* Why.

Sneddon Because I want you to find out if you can do it.

Dobie I dont understand, I dont want to strangle him.

Sneddon If you dont understand then I have to shoot you. I will you know. I'll shoot off your legs and leave you here to burn.

Dobie No dont shoot me Alec, but I dont see why . . .

Sneddon *pumps the gun and aims at* **Dobie**.

Dobie *stares back and places his hands on* **Arbogast**'s *throat.*

THE LIFE OF STUFF 121

Sneddon Show me you can do it, William. Use your thumbs.

Dobie *strangles* **Arbogast**. **Arbogast** *tries to laugh*. **Sneddon** *watches*. **Arbogast** *dies*.

Sneddon Is that him murdered?

Dobie *nods*.

Sneddon Off you go then, Willie.

Dobie Eh?

Dobie *unclamps his fingers from* **Arbogast**'s *throat*.

Sneddon Skedaddle. Leave me in peace.

Dobie *backs towards the lift. He opens the door. Smoke billows out.*

Sneddon Oops. Raymond's a bit fuckin punctual with the paraffin. Looks like you stay here with me and Davey and burn.

Dobie *turns.*

Dobie In your dreams, Alec.

He hits the alarm bell and gets into the lift, he slams the doors shut and starts banging and calling and coughing. Smoke pours out the gaps and cracks. The lift glows with a fiery light.

Sneddon And believe you me, it's a whole lot worse than you can begin to imagine.

We hear **Dobie**'s *voice above the roar of the gathering inferno.*

Dobie Hey! Girls. Hey! Call the lift. Hey!! Press the button and call the lift up!! Hey. Princess. Call the . . . Hey! Petal! Pumpkin! Darlin! Would you press the button and please . . . please. call the lift up and get me out of here. Holly!

Dobie *dies. Nat King Cole sings 'Stardust'. A mirror ball descends from the ceiling and sparkly starbursts fill the room.* **Sneddon** *listens to the first verse, then raises the shotgun to his face, wraps his mouth round the barrel and looks up at the mirror ball. The sound of the Insectocutor amplified and blackout.*

The Life of Stuff

The tyrannical certainties of standard English prose punctuation arent much help in this kind of dialogue. I've employed some conventions which at least I hope are consistent and unobtrusive. If a character has a line which doesnt begin with a capital letter it indicates their confidence is relatively low. Similarly, if their line doesnt end with a full stop, they're finishing on the back foot. Only serious demands are granted question marks. Apostrophes arent treated with the respect they've come to regard as their natural due. Especially in the phrase 'fucks sake'. Similarly cant didnt, dont doesnt and couldnt shouldnt. 'Dont' is not an abbreviation of 'do not' and I find it unhelpful to signal that it is.

The relative rarity of the comma also warrants explanation. The dialogue in *The Life of Stuff* is almost wholly active – the characters are hardly ever reflective and there is only one aside in the whole play. In a very literal sense, they're speaking their minds. Whatever junk forms in their frontal lobes comes out their mouths simultaneously. Very little is preconceived. This means that they launch into complex sentences with dependent subclauses lying in wait, ready to give them a syntactical kicking at the earliest opportunity. The language is a wrestling match and the actors must resist the temptation to paraphrase clauses into submission. Characters blurt out truths, gaffes and admissions because they get trapped by their own jangled articulacy. The play is fuelled by drugs, lust, fear and alcohol – none traditionally linked with steadiness of brain. Everything is said to somebody. When Holly does her 'Do you ever feel like you used to be an Egyptian . . .' speech, she's not talking to herself, soliloquising to thin air – she's telling everybody in the room what's in her head. They dont have to listen, but that's another matter. This principle applies throughout.

The governing engine of the play is fear. In both the productions I've been involved with so far, the higher the stakes and the greater the tension then the funnier and more moving the piece became. Frank Sinatra also helps.

Simon Donald
September 1994

Simon Donald was born in Lanark and brought up in Wishaw. His plays include *A Tenant for Edgar Mortez* (for Abattoir Theatre Company), *In Descent*, *Prickly Heat* and *The Life of Stuff* (all for the Traverse Theatre, Edinburgh). He has also written for film and television, including *Doctor Finlay* Series 2 and 3, *The Hideous, Hellish Crimes of Deacon Brodie and his Abominable Crew ending in their Several Executions* and the screenplay for *The Life of Stuff*.

His theatre performances include *A Tenant for Edgar Mortez*, *The Muir* (Tron Theatre, Glasgow), *The Park* (Sheffield Crucible); and at the Traverse, *Elizabeth Gordon Quinn*, *Losing Venice*, *The Death of Elias Sawney*, *Abel Barebone*, *Playing With Fire*, *Prickly Heat*, *Conquest of the South Pole*, *Hardy and Baird*, *The Hour of the Lynx*, *Struggle of the Dogs and the Black*, *Are There Tigers in the Congo*, *Columbus Blooding the Ocean*, and *The Swan*. His film and television performances include *Soldier Soldier II*, *The Hour of the Lynx*, *Taggart*, *Down Among the Big Boys*, *Stalag Luft* and *Between the Lines*.

Bondagers

Sue Glover

For Muriel Romanes, who told me about the bondagers

Bondagers was first performed in May 1991 at Tramway, Glasgow, as part of Mayfest, then subsequently at the Traverse Theatre, Edinburgh. The cast was as follows:

Liza   Hilary Maclean
Maggie   Anne Lacey
Sara   Ann Louise Ross
Tottie   Myra MacFadyen
Ellen   Rosaleen Pelan
Jenny   Eve Keepax

Directed by Ian Brown
Designed by Steward Laing
Lighting Paule Constable
Movement Sue MacLennan
Music Pete Livingstone
Dialect Coach Ros Steen

The production was revived at the new Traverse Theatre in November 1993 and later toured Canada. The cast remained the same except that Kathryn Howden played Tottie and in Canada Carole Ann Crawford played Maggie.

Characters

Liza, *a very young farm worker (or 'bondager'), facing her first 'hiring' away from home*
Maggie, *a woman with numerous children, married to one of the farm workers*
Sara, *Maggie's age or a good bit older. Works on the farm with her daftie daughter*
Tottie, *Sarah's daughter, about fifteen. A daftie*
Ellen, *the farmer's wife. Formerly a farm worker like the others, now risen to the status of a lady*
Jenny, *another young farm worker, slightly older than Liza*
Two Warders *(non speaking). These could be played by the actors who play Liza and Jenny*

Note

Bondagers were the women workers of the great Border farms in the last century. Each farm worker was hired on condition he brought a female worker to work alongside him – if not his wife or daughter, then some other girl that he himself had to hire at the Hiring Fair, and lodge and feed alongside his own family in his tiny cottage.

It is also a play about the land . . . and the misuse of land . . .

The play is set on a Border farm of 1860. Act One – with the exception of the opening scene (the 'Hiring') – takes place in the summer; and Act Two in winter

The set should be minimal. There should be one area of the acting space that represents Maggie's house – but not defined so definitely as to be intrusive during those passages of the play in which it does not figure. The cradle is in this area – it is a statement, and should be visible. Possibly there should also be an 'area' of the acting space that represents Sara's house (when required – again not intrusive). But the 'house' area(s) could simply be used as part of the field, the barn, whatever, during other scenes, they can 'come and go' as it were.

The bondagers' dress was distinctive, almost a uniform, and something approximating it is necessary: boots or clogs; full skirts with two or three petticoats; 'headhankies' – i.e. kerchiefs that covered their heads, and could, when work required, be tied over the chin, or even over the whole lower part of the face when the dust and dirt was really flying; and black straw bonnets with red ruching (trimming). Muddy and sometimes shabby, maybe, but beguiling.

Act One

Scene One

Liza, **Sara**, **Jenny**, **Tottie** *in the market place, for the Hiring Fair.* **Maggie** *at home.*

Voices (*all the cast, cutting in on each other's phrases, some of the phrases can be repeated. Low whispers at first, growing louder*)
The Hiring, the Hiring, the Hiring . . .
Hiring Fair, Hiring Fair, Hiring Fair . . .
What a folk/ What a crowd/ What a carts/ What a people/ What a noise!
Ye get a' the clash at the Hiring.
Ye get a' the fun at the Fair.
I'm blythe to see ye
Tam/Andra/Jenny/Meg/William/Neil/Geordie/Joe/Jane/Jack.
What fettle? Fine fettle. How's the cow? Doing grand. How's a' wi you? How's the bairns
. . . and the cow? How's the wife . . . and the cow?
Did you ken about Davie/Jockie/Tam/Sandy/Nathan/Ned/Mary/Betsy/Bob?
What's the crack?/ Heard the crack from Langriggs/Redriggs/ Smiddyhill/Smiddyford/
Horsecleugh/Oxencleugh/Whitehas/Blacksheils/East Mains/Westlea.

During this **Liza** *is wandering, jostled by the crowd, looking for a place to stand.*

Voices (*these phrases more distinct*)
The Hiring, the Hiring Fair.
First Monday in February.
Coldest Monday in February.
Eight o clock. Soon as it's licht.
See the farmers bargain wi the hinds.
See the hinds bargain wi the bondagers.
See the bonny bondagers stand in a row.

Liza *has chosen her place, waits to be hired.* **Sara** *and* **Tottie** *are also standing now together, waiting to be hired.*

First voice (*low whisper*) The coldest Monday. Soon as it's licht. (*Louder, taunting.*) No bondager worth a puckle's left after ten o clock.

Liza (*outwardly defiant – not in answer to the voice, and never speaking directly to the audience*) I'll be gone long afore ten. Bound over. Hired. See if I'm not. Broad shoothers, short back, strong legs.

Sara Stand here Tottie, stand still now.

Liza
– I'll not take the arle from the first that comes,
I'm only going to a well-kent hind.
I can shear come harvest. I'm good with the horses.

I'll fettle the horses – but not your bairns.
I'll redd up the steading – but not your house,
I'll work a' day – but not in your bed.

Sara   Tut, lass, dinna talk that way.

Liza
– Broad shoothers, short back, strong legs.
The good name of Tam Kerr, deceased, to live up to,
And my brother Steenie, over the seas.

Jenny   No bondager worth a puckle's left after ten o clock.

Liza   I'll be hired by ten of the clock . . . I'll take the arle by ten of the clock.

Sara   Stand straight, Tottie, dinna look sweer.

Jenny   No cottar wife's hired till the back o twelve. *Gin* she's hired.

Sara (*to* **Tottie**)   Look sonsie, can't you?

Tottie   I'm hungry.

Sara   Maybe we'll buy a tuppenny loaf after?

Tottie   After what?

Sara   After we're hired.

Jenny   *Gin* she's hired!

Tottie   There's the Maister o Langriggs – maybe we'll get to Langriggs.

Sara   Maybe. Look sonsie, now.

Voices (*each line spoken singly, in turn, by the cast*)
Ten bolls of oatmeal
Fifteen bushels barley
Six bushels pease
Twelve hundred yards potatoes, planted
A peck of lint, sown
Three pounds sheep siller
Grass for the cow
The privilege of keeping hens
Four carts of coals

First voice   It is customary to give them their meat during one month of harvest. They may keep a pig. Their wives must shear in harvest. The hinds are also bound to hire and keep a field worker, a female servant called a bondager, commonly paid ten pence a day. (. . .) The hinds complain of this; the wives even more so.

Maggie (*at home. Very busy. Washing clothes, churning butter – or knitting – she knits on the hoof, whilst she's watching a porridge pot, or rocking the cradle. Not directly to audience*)   Coldest

Monday since Hallowe'en. I should have put straw in his shoon. He's well respected, my man Andra. Any farmer would be thankful to hire him. He was up afore dawn to be there for the Hiring. Kirk claes. Kirk shoon. And a shave like he hasnae had since the kirn. Three things a hind depends on: a good wife, a good cow – and a good razor.

First voice A good hind needs a good maister.

Maggie He can take his pick o maisters.

First voice A good hind needs a good bondager.

Maggie He can take his pick o bondagers . . . gin he knows how. But some o those lassies wear two faces – one for the hiring, and another for the farm! Just so long as the lass can shear – I can't work harvest, not with the bairns. Just so long as she takes to the bairns!

Liza I'm not going to any place hoatchin wi bairns!

Sara (*to* **Liza**) Tuts, lassie – there's bound to be bairns!

Maggie See and pick right, Andra. Pick a good maister! Dinna say yes to the first farmer that slaps your hand and offers a dram. There's questions to be asked! Two rooms! I'd like a house with two rooms. The maister at Langriggs bigged a new row of houses – all with the two rooms . . .

Sara We don't hope for much, Tottie and me. Day and way.

Liza I want a place on a big farm. Plenty lassies for the crack. Plenty plooman for the dancing!

Maggie A house near the pump. A roof without holes.

Sara (*coming in on* **Maggie***'s line*) A roof without holes.

Sara *and* **Maggie** Good pasture for the cow.

Sara Kindness for Tottie – she's slow – she has days.

Tottie Bad days! Bad days!

Liza No bairns underfoot.

Maggie And if it's a good place – maybe we'll stay – not just the year . . . longer. Same house, same farm, same kirk, same neighbours . . . (*Realising it's an unlikely notion.*) Aye! Well! – so long as it's dry for the flitting.

Sara (*coming in on her last line*) So long as it's dry for the flitting.

Tottie I doubt it'll rain for the flitting, Mammy!

Liza I'll buy a new hat for the flitting.

Scene Two

Liza, **Tottie**, **Ellen**. **Liza** *walking away from the fair,* **Tottie** *comes after her.*

Tottie (*to* **Liza**)   You, you, you. What farm are you going to? What farm?

Liza *not answering, doesn't think much of* **Tottie**. **Tottie** *insistent.*

What farm?

Liza   Blacksheils.

Tottie   So are we. Which hind will ye work with?

Liza   Andra Innes.

Tottie   We're on our own. Mammy and me. (*Trying to keep* **Liza**'s *attention.*) There's ghosts at Blacksheils. Up on the moor.

Liza (*not impressed by ghosts*)   Is it still Maister Elliott farms Blacksheils?

Tottie   The one that married Ellen. Ellen Rippeth that was. She worked with us at Blacksheils. Not last year. Before. Before she set her cap at the maister.

Liza   I know.

Tottie   *You* weren't there.

Liza   I was at Billieslaw. Over the hill. I was bondager to my brother.

Tottie   Set her cap at him, and married him and a'. That's how we got hired. For the sake o lang syne.

Liza   Ellen Rippeth never gave any favours.

Tottie   Ay, she does. She's the mistress now.

Ellen (*practising using a fan, elegantly, expertly*)   Learn to use a fan? I can single turnips in the sweat; shaw them in the sleet – I can surely use a fan! Take tea with the gentry? They talk about turnips. Yield, rotation, manure. They know about turnips. Their shoes are shiny, clothes clean, shoothers dry. We were soaked to the skin by half past eight, in the mist, in the morning. Frost, snow, sun, wind, rain; single, shaw, howk, mangle, cart. Aye. We kenned about neeps!

Scene Three

Liza *and* **Maggie**. **Maggie** *is busy, very.* (*The baby and the porridge pot both at once.*) **Liza** *arrives with her bundle of worldly goods.*

Liza   I'm Liza. The bondager.

Maggie I'm Maggie, his wife. You'll have seen the bairns, they're playing round the doors.

Liza Which are yours?

Maggie All of them, nearly.

Liza The wee laddie that kicks?

Maggie (*serene*) Kicks? Oh, no, never – you must have got in the way. My bairns wouldna kick. Now. Then. (*Proudly.*) We've the two box beds. So you can share the other one with the bairns.

Liza I'll not. I'll not sleep with bairns. I'll sleep in the roof.

Maggie (*serene*) The older bairns sleep in the roof.

Liza A couple of bairns, he said, at the Hiring!

Maggie (*serene*) Andra said that? No, no – you'll have got it wrong. Andra would never deny his ain bairns! You were gabbing to some other hind, nae doubt! Here – see to the pot while I see to the babby. (*She is busy with the baby.*) Liza Kerr? Steenie Kerr's sister? There were only the two of you after Tam crossed the Jordan. And a whole house to yourselves? But lassie – naebody round here has a bed to hisself! I dinna ken anyone that sleeps alone – save the plooman up in the steading – mind you, from what I hear, there's one of the dairymaids – still, it's early days yet to pass judgement. You'll soon love the bairns. You're a lassie, after all – you're bound to love them. (*Sharp appraisal.*) Can you shear?

Liza Aye.

Maggie You'll do!

Scene Four

All of them, except **Ellen**. *They are singling turnips. In their large hats and headhankies tied over their chins, they are not individually recognisable. The five of them are part of a larger squad, the 'field' onstage is part of an enormous field – thirty or forty acres. They work fast, each moving along her own drill, keeping more or less in pace with the others. (***Tottie*** is slower, maybe much slower.) The dialogue, when it comes, is fast, fragmented, overlapping. It comes in spurts, with pauses between. And they never stop working. Obviously the gist of the dialogue is important, equally, though, every phrase does not have to be heard. The only lines that have to be spoken by particular characters are* **Jenny**'s *and* **Liza**'s.

(*Two of them sing.*)
Woo'd and married and a'
Kissed and carried awa
And is no the bride well off
That's woo'd and married and a'

I'd bind more rags round your hands, if I were you lass!

I've nane.

Straw, then, Rope. We'll have to mak mair.

The saddler's come! That's him just passed the gate!

Aw, now, there's a bonny callant!

He'll no be staying more than a week!

That's what makes him bonny!

I'll get a bit crack with him when I redd up the stables!

I'll redd up the stables.

No, you'll no!

Saddler's mine!

Laughter. Pause.

Is he married, the saddler?

No.

Can he dance?

Can he dance!

Fiddle and dance all at once – as good as yon dancing maister frae Jeddart!

We'll hae a bit dance, then!

I'll hae a bit dearie!

Laughter.

Ye're an awful lassie, Jenny!

A'body wants the saddler!

A'body want a bit dearie!

(*Singing*)   Woo'd and married and a'
Kissed and carried awa
Was she nae very well off
Was woo'd and married an a'

Was Sara married?

Dinna ken. Was Sara married?

Dinna ken.

She was going to marry Wabster, my mother said.

She was never married.

She was never neglected.

Jenny *and* **Liza** *together:*

Jenny   Can ye spin, Liza – ye get to work up at the Big House if ye can spin.

Liza   Don't want to spin.

Jenny It's good work on a rainy day. Better than being laid off. And you get your meat, sitting down in the kitchen.

Liza I can't spin.

Ye ken yon plooman with the curls?

Kello?

By, he can dance! Tappity with his clogs – and a kind of singsong he makes all the while – right there in the glaur, at the tweak o a bonnet.

Is he a Gyptian?

Dinna ken. His eyes are black!

Of course he's a Gyptian!

A mugger!

A tinkler!

Maister Elliott hiring Gyptians!

The maister's brown as a peatbog himself!

Maister's a gentleman!

Married one of us, though!

He's still a gentleman!

Maybe the other gentry don't think so!

Nellie makes a braw lady!

Aye – the besom!

Mistress Ellen.

Mistress *Elliott*!

Was she no very well off
Was woo'd and married an a'

(*Shouts coming from the far end of the field.*) Ye can stop now, stop at the end of the drill. We're stopping – Jenny! Liza!

They rest on their hoes, flex their backs, leave the field. **Jenny** *and* **Liza**, *slightly apart from the others. Stop to talk.*

Jenny You're lucky biding with Maggie. She keeps a good kitchen.

Liza I'm aye starving all the same. And I sleep with the bairns.

Jenny So do I – I'm glad of the bairns!

Liza Could you not sleep in the roof?

Jenny And have him creeping all over me?

Liza Who?

Jenny Who! Who do you think? (*As* **Liza** *gapes, astonished.*) Close your gob, Liza, the flies'll get in!

Liza But – his wife?

Jenny It's his bairns keep me safe, not his wife. I can teach ye to spin, Liza. If you're wanting work up at the Big House.

Liza (*suddenly irritable*) I'm not wanting work at the house.

Jenny Oh, well – ! (*Walking off, then stops to call back at* **Liza**.) Besom you!

Scene Five

Liza *and* **Tottie**. **Liza** *on her own. She slumps, tired, leaning against or sitting on something, starts unwinding the rags that were bound round her hands.* **Tottie** *comes on; stands and stares at her.* **Liza** *still uncertain of* **Tottie**.

Liza Go away! Shoo!

This has no effect. Tries a frightening face or gesture.

Aaaaaargh!

Tottie *for a moment impassive, then, grinning, copies her.*

Tottie Aaaaaaargh! (*Gives* **Liza** *a shove.*) Maggie says to come and mind the babby for it's girny and she has to milk the coo.

Liza If it's girny, it's wet, if it's wet it's likely mingin'. (*Sweetly.*) You mind the babby, Tottie. Go on. Go and sing to bee-baa-babbity.

Tottie Don't you like babbies? You're a motherless bairn. *And* a fatherless bairn. And you've no brother either, for he's gone to Canada.

Liza *tries to ignore her. She lies or slumps, wanting to rest, pulling her headhankie right up and forward, hiding her face.*

Tottie My daddy's gone to Canada. My daddy's been away for a hundred year. (*The word is a talisman for her.*) Sas-katch-e-wan. Sas-katch-e-wan. (*A silence.*) There's dancing tonight.

Liza Where?

Tottie In the turnip shed. The saddler's fetching his fiddle. Maybe ye'll hae a bit dearie.

Liza What's that supposed to mean?

Tottie That's what Jenny always says. 'A'body needs a bit dearie.'

Liza Away and see to the babbity!

Liza *walks away.*

Tottie Where are you going?

Liza To the pump. To wash off the glaur!

Tottie *goes over to the cradle.*

Tottie Bee-baa-babbity. Are ye wet? Ugh! Are ye mingin'? UUUUgh! (*Hastily, in case she sets it howling.*) Don't cry, don't cry. (*Very matter-of-fact, as if to someone much older.*) I'll tell you a story. I'll tell you about the ghostie. It's true. I was up on the moors. The maister sent me. With a message for the herd. And the mist came doon – and roon – and doon. I was feared. And I shouted for the herd. But the mist smoored my words. And then I heard, very close: 'Shoough . . . shoooough . . . shooough . . .' – a plough shoughin through the ground, and whiles whanging a stane or twa. And a man, calling to his beasts: 'Cooooop, coooooop'. Like a crow. I could feel the beasts on the ground, I could feel them through my feet. Oxen. I could smell them. I wanted to walk with the plooman till the mist parted. I shouted. But the mist swirled roon and smoored a'thing. After, Jock the herd said: (*She copies his patronising tone.*) 'Naebody ploughs there, Tottie – the only rigs there are the lang syne rigs. Ye can see the marks still. Hundreds of year old. But ye'll no see ony plooman, and ye'll no see ony plough.' Aye. But I heard him though . . .

Voices (*low whispery*)
Lang syne ploughman
Lang syne rigs, rigs, rigs, rigs
Lang syne barley, barley, barley, barley
Barley means bread, oats means bread, pease means bread
Bread of carefulness
Never enough bread

Children's voices (*or the cast on stage as children; loud, matter-of-fact, unkind*)
Tottie's seen a bogle, Tottie's seen a ghostie.
Tottie's a softie, Tottie's a daftie.

Tottie (*cutting into these lines*) I'm not. Stop it. I'm not.

First child Sixpence in the shilling

Tottie Stop it! No!

Second child No all there.

Tottie I am! (*Upset, blundering about, wanting to shove, shout down her tormentors.*)

Children (*jeering, laughing*)
Your mammy lay with Wabster
Gat ye in the cornrigs
Cleckit in the barley rigs
Coupled
Covered
Ploughed

Tottie Married! (*Upset, aggressive – she has blundered into or pushed the cradle, it's rocking wildly.*)

First child In the cornrigs?

Tottie Yes.

Second child In the *cornrigs*?

Tottie   Yes. Yes. She had a babby. It was me.

First child (*soft, sly*)   And where's your daddy now?

Tottie (*whisper*)   Sas-katch-e-wan . . . Sas-katch-e-wan.

She goes to the cradle, blundering, whimpering. She has to steady the cradle, and in doing so quietens herself.

Scene Six

Sara, **Tottie**, **Ellen**, **Liza**. **Tottie** *is maybe still by the cradle.* **Sara** *busy cleaning horse tack, or patching/sewing sacks, or winding the home-made straw rope into neat oval balls: any wet-weather work.* **Ellen** *– adjusting, admiring her clothes, hat? umbrella? – half pleased at her elevated status, but half laughing at herself.*

Ellen   Sweet wheaten bread, and tea, and cream and sugar and ham! All this for breakfast! Brought by a servant girl better dressed than I ever was till now. A table like snow, a floor like a looking-glass; china, lace. Great wide windows to let in the sun – to look out on the fields. Every field fifty acres square. Hedges trim. No weeds. No waste.

Tottie *stares at her, delighted to see her. Admires and is fascinated by* **Ellen**. **Ellen** *has always tolerated* **Tottie**, *with an offhand but genuine acceptance.*

Ellen   I saw you hoeing the fields this morning. I watched till you left off because of the rain.

Tottie   We don't know what to call you now.

Sara   We must call her Mistress Elliott now.

Ellen   Aye. That's what you cry me.

Seeing **Tottie**'s *grinning welcome,* **Ellen** *goes to her, hugs her.* **Tottie**'s *reciprocating hug is uninhibited, wholehearted.*

Sara (*fearful of* **Ellen**'s *gown*)   Mind now, Tottie.

Ellen   I wear this one to take tea.

Sara   There's no tea here, Nell!

Ellen   I have just taken tea – at Langriggs.

An awkwardness. She sits down very carefully. **Tottie** *gapes at her happily.* **Sara** *motions to* **Tottie** *to start work.*

Tottie (*still with her eyes on* **Ellen**)   Ellen Rippeth-that-was. Like a lady now. She sits like a lady.

Ellen   It's the stays. Can't bend forrard. Can't bend back. I'm tied up every morning – let loose at bedtime.

Tottie   Who ties you – the maister?

Ellen (*to* **Sara**) D'you mind Betty Hope? The maister's auld mither hired her for my maid.

Sara She's got the sort of face that comes in useful for a wake.

Ellen Nae crack from Betsy. It's hot in here.

Tottie It's wet out there!

Sara Too wet for work. The lassies are throwing their money at the packman. The lads are in the stables, larking.

Tottie Larking!

Ellen By, it rained for the flitting. I watched the carts from the window, coming down the loan. Bung fu': beds, bairns, clocks, dressers, grandpas, geraniums – a'thing drookit.

Sara I've a hundred rheumatisms since the flitting. Maggie's bairns have the hoast yet.

Ellen My shoothers are always dry now. If my stockings are soaked, or my shoes, someone fetches another pair.

Sara 'And was she no very well off – / That's woo'd and married an a'!'

Ellen Here, Tottie – let loose my stays! (*Shows* **Tottie** *where to loosen the laces under the bodice.*)

Sara (*shaking her head at* **Nell**'s *old ways*) Mistress Elliott!

Ellen *flops on the straw.* **Tottie** *imitates her.* **Sara** *never stops working.*

Tottie Bad Nell!

Ellen Not now! I'm a married lady now!

Tottie Are you having a baby? Is it in there yet?

Ellen No . . . Not yet.

Sara (*after a pause; softly*) There's time enough.

Ellen A hind wouldn't think so! Some of them would have you swelled before they called the banns, even!

Sara Och, now, Ellen –

Ellen Well, it's true!

Sara Not at Blacksheils. The maister wouldn't stand for it. He's stricter than the minister.

Ellen He's – he's – a fine man. Keeps his passion under hidlings, though!

Sara And his mother, the widow?

Ellen   She calls me 'the new blood'. 'No sense growing prize turnips, Gordon, without prize sons to mind them!'

Sara   Well, you know what they say: the bull is half the herd.

Ellen *lolls in the hay. More like the bondager she used to be.*

Ellen   Is that true for folk, as well as beasts?

Sara   Must be. Surely.

Ellen   He had a son. It died before it got born. It killed its mother before it was even born.

Tottie   How could a baby kill you?

Sara   The Elliotts have farmed here since I don't know when. His grandfather drained those cold fields of clay. He died before they were ever first cropped. Look at them now. Tatties, clover, the finest neeps in Europe. People come from all over – Germany, England – just to look at Blacksheils, and talk with the maister.

Ellen   A son for Blacksheils. Of course he wants a son.

Tottie (*tormenting* **Ellen***, pulling at her*)   How could a bull be half the herd? How could a baby kill you?

Ellen   Babies are mischief. Like you, Tottie! No telling what they'll do.

Liza *appears.*

Sara   It's Liza, Mistress Elliott. Liza Kerr. Andra's bondager.

Tottie (*to* **Liza**)   You must cry her Mistress Elliott, now.

Liza *gives a bob.*

Ellen (*getting up, brushing off the straw – but not put out at being caught lolling there by a servant*) I would hardly have known you. You've grown.

Ellen *is going.*

Liza   Steenie's in Canada.

Ellen   Yes, I heard. I hope he's well?

Liza *doesn't answer.* **Ellen** *goes.*

Liza (*muttering after her*)   No thanks to you if he's well. No thanks to you!

Tottie (*softly*)   Sas-katch-e-wan.

Liza   Steik yer gab, you!

Gives **Tottie** *a shove, as she goes.*

Tottie   Sas-katch-e-wan.

Scene Seven

Ellen, **Maggie**, **Sara**. *They are not 'together', but in their separate areas.*

Ellen Steenie Kerr. He was only a bairn. Lovesick loon! Heart on his sleeve. Scratching my name on the steading walls.

Sara Poor Steenie. I felt heart-sorry for him.

Ellen He played on pity. Punished me with other folk's pity. Used me.

Maggie She led him a dance.

Sara Well, he wouldn't take no.

Maggie She drove them a' wild, the plooman.

Sara Such a beautiful summer.

Maggie Not for Steenie.

Sara They were a' mad for dancing – danced every night. Till the first field was cut. And the night of the kirn – the moon was so bonny, a real harvest moon.

Ellen I was angry. I'll show you, I thought. Steenie, all of you. I felt angry. Wild. The maister was there in the fields every day, keeping an eye on things. In the fields. At the kirn . . . Ye'll hae a dance, maister? . . . Anither dance, maister? . . . And ye'll hae a bit mair dance, maister . . . He looked that – modest! He made me laugh. He made me want. Stricter than the minister, a'body said. I'll have him in the hay, efter, I thought. Why not? A'body needs a bit dearie. And then I thought – never mind the hay, Nell – ye can mak it tae the bed. Ye can mak the Big Hoose. Ye'll can cry the banns. I could see it in his eyes. Feel it in his bones. (. . .) He cried out when he loved me. Not blubbing like Steenie, not like I wasn't there at the end, but like he was wanting to take me with him . . . Just a bit dearie. And what do I get? A'thing. I got a'thing.

Scene Eight

Maggie, **Sara**, **Liza**, **Jenny**.

Maggie Did you hear about Marjie Brockie? Buckled up wi Jamie Moodie! Buckled up at Coldstream Brig. Ca' that a wedding?

Sara It's legal.

Maggie The minister wouldn't say so. Folk should marry in kirk with the full connivance of the Almighty. A lad and lass walk into the inn, and someone says 'Who's the lass, then?' and the lad says 'O, she's my wife!'! Ca' that a wedding?

Sara Well, it's legal!

Maggie It's a scandal!

Sara It's cheaper that way. Kirk weddings cost. No wonder they run off to Coldstream under hidlings. After the fair. Or after the kirn.

Liza Did you run away to Coldstream?

Sara No, Liza. We were handfasted, Patie and me. We lived together, man and wife, for nearly a year, to see how we would do.

Maggie Handfasting! And who's left holding the bairn?

Sara But that's what they're waiting for, often as not, to see if there's a bairn. It's the baby leads them to the kirk, eventually.

Maggie Or sends the man fleeing. To Canada, for instance.

Sara Patie loved the baby. She was a queer bit babby, wheezy and choky. He knew she wasn't quite natural. But he loved her, you mustn't think he didn't, she was ours. He was restless, though. He wanted – something, adventure, Canada. It was me said no, I wouldn't go. This parish was my calf-ground: Langriggs, Blackshiels, Billieslaw; the fields, the river, the moor up yonder with the lang syne rigs. Patie loved the land. 'Her'. But maybe I loved her more. When it came to the bit. When it came to Greenock – and even there the land seemed foreign. And the sea; and the ships. A sad, sad place. A great crush of folk, all quiet, and a highland lass singing. Then a voice cried out, loud: 'Hands up for Canada! Hands up for Canada!' A rushing, like wings, all the hands held high. And the baby screamed like she'd never grat before. Such a stab in my heart it made the milk spurt from me. I couldn't step forward. I couldn't go on. And Patie couldn't stay. I knew he couldn't stay. He crossed the ocean; I looked for the carter to take us back home. Patie Wabster. I think of him every day, many times every day.

Maggie Fourteen years! He'll have bairns of his own now.

Sara I hope so surely. He was made for happiness, Patie.

Liza and **Jenny** *are all ears, gripped by all this.*

Maggie Well! (*She hasn't heard so much of this story before, is shocked, disapproving, of* **Sara**.) Well, you've made your bed, you must lie on it.

Sara (*laughs easily*) I've no leisure for my bed!

Maggie As ye sow, shall ye reap! A cottar wife's bound to be hard-wrought!

Sara (*serenely*) Day and way!

Maggie (*annoyed, and shows it in the way she is working, with thumps and bangs – feels* **Sara** *should be regretful and guilty about this*) Well, it takes all sorts! . . . There's naught so queer as folk! . . . (*Exasperation.*) A kirk wedding would have bound you both! . . . (*More to* **Liza** *now.*) You have to bring them to account. Andra wouldn't ask me. He *wouldn't*. He was never going to ask. So when he was standing with a crowd of the lads, I flew to his neck and measured him for the sark. His wedding sark.

Liza and **Jenny** *start to giggle at this.*

Maggie Once word got round I was sewing him the sark, well, he had no choice, he had to call the banns. And not before time.

Maggie *either goes offstage, busy on some errand, or busies herself with some work; has left* **Sara** *and* **Liza** *on their own.*

Sara (*to* **Liza** *and* **Jenny**) She doesn't understand. And neither do you, I daresay. And neither did I, at the time. Patie was lovely, like no one else. Happy, clever. But he needed to wander, he wanted the world. I have to bide still, I have to stay where I am.

Jenny But you don't bide still – you flit every year!

Sara (*laughs*) Aye, so I do! But I never flit far. I've never been further than the three, four farms; never been further than – oh – twenty miles, maybe.

Liza But you went as far as Greenock once.

An assent from **Sara**.

Liza I could go to Canada.

Sara Well, you could. And join your brother.

Liza Saskatchewan. I could go there. Is it a big place?

Sara It's a place I think about every day. But I don't know what it's like. I wonder: do they have peewees. Patie loved the peewees, he'd never plough a peewee's nest, he'd steer the horses round it. We understood each other. Tottie's part of that, part of Patie and me. That makes her special.

Scene Nine

Jenny, **Liza**, **Tottie**. *Night. Candlelight. They have a candle, a looking-glass, an apple. With lots of shushing, they arrange themselves, so that* **Tottie** *has the candle,* **Jenny** *the glass,* **Liza** *the apple.* **Liza** *places herself in front of, and not too near, the glass. A clock begins to strike twelve. This is what they've been waiting for. Immediately, solemnly,* **Liza** *bites into the apple, throws the bitten-out chunk over her left shoulder.* **Tottie** *wants to retrieve the bite of apple –* **Jenny** *restrains her. They take the apple from* **Liza**, *hand her a comb. Ceremoniously she combs her hair, staring all the while into the mirror, peering into the space over her shoulder in the mirror. The others are waiting expectantly,* **Tottie** *tries to look in the glass, obscuring* **Liza**'s *own view of it, they signal* **Tottie** *to move away. Suddenly* **Liza** *bursts into excited laughter, doubles up, dances around, gives a 'hooch' of delight.*

Tottie *and* **Jenny** *crowding, cutting each other's lines, in a rush:*

Jenny Did you see him, Liza?

Tottie Which one, Liza?

Jenny Was it the Gyptian?

Tottie Was it Kello?

Jenny Black-eyed Kello?

Liza *still dancing about, laughing, nodding 'yes', clutching at* **Jenny**.

Tottie Do me! My turn!

Jenny (*sternly*) No!

Tottie   I want to see my man! Give me an apple! (*She looks for the apple piece that* **Liza** *threw over her shoulder.*)

Jenny   Sumph! It's past twelve o the clock! You can't tell fortunes now!

She or **Liza** *blows out the candle.*

You can't see anyone now!

Scene Ten

Liza, **Maggie**, **Sara**, **Tottie**, **Jenny** . . . *and later,* **Ellen**. *They are stopping for a piece-break, milk or water, and bannocks of some kind.* **Maggie** *has brought the food along to the field for them.*

Tottie   He was shouting – in the turnip shed. Shouting at the neeps. Nobody there, just neeps.

Maggie   It's a speech. For the meeting! He'll be practising his speech.

Jenny   For the Soiree!

Liza   (*the title – an official one – sounds glamorous to her*)   The Plooman's Soiree!

Sara   Go on, then, Tottie, tell us – what did he say?

Tottie   He said – we are not penny pies.

Liza
'Gentlemen! We are not penny pies
We must continue to press for the six-pound rise!'

Tottie   Yes, that's what he said.

Sara   Six pound!

Maggie   Rowat of Currivale gives farm servants a grand wage, and lost time.

Sara   Lost time?

Liza   What's that?

Maggie   I dinna rightly ken. But he gives them it.

Sara   Dunlop of Smiddyhill's promised to mend up his houses. Planks on the floor. *And* in the loft.

Maggie   Every year the maisters promise to mend up the houses! But syne it's time for the Speaking, and syne the Hiring, and syne the Flitting – and where are the promises?

Maggie *and* **Sara**   Snowed off the dyke!

Sara   If we didn't flit every year, they'd have to mend up the houses.

Maggie   If the houses were mended up, we wouldn't want to flit ae year.

Sara   (*quite cheerful*)   Tinklers, that's all we are!

Tottie   Penny pies. We are not penny pies.

Maggie A six-pound rise would do me fine, and a new house even finer – but what we really need is an end to the bondage.

Surprise from the others.

Maggie (*slightly abashed*) Lots of folk are beginning to speak out against the bondage.

Others not convinced.

Maggie I've barely a shilling a week to spare for her.

Liza I earn my keep!

Jenny A shilling! Is that all we're worth?

Maggie Barely a shilling for all that food –

Liza – I'm aye starving –

Jenny Even a horse can't work without food!

Maggie She takes the bed from my bairns, and the warmth from my fire –

Liza (*furious*) Where d'you expect me to –

Sara (*restrains her*) She doesn't mean you – (*To* **Maggie**.) Maggie! – (*To* **Liza**.) It's the bondage she's angry at!

Maggie Flighty, giddy bits o lassies! Pay no heed to the hind, or his wife!

Liza I'm not *your* servant!

Maggie I'm not *your* washerwoman!

Sara This'll never do now, fraying like – tinklers!

Tottie Penny pies!

Maggie Remember Rob Maxwell two year ago at the Hiring? Pleading with a bondager – a woman he didnae ken from Eve – begging her to take the arle as if his very life depended on it!

Sara Well, but it did. For his ain wife had bairns, and without a female worker who would have hired him? No maister round here.

Maggie And remember how that young bondager turned out? Remember a' that?

Liza What?

Maggie Never you mind. But a poor unsuspecting hind shouldn't have to hire by looks. A sweet face won't shift the sharn.

Liza And what about us? It works both ways.

Jenny Ay, both ways. How can we choose a decent hind by his looks?

Maggie That's just it – the farmer should hire you lassies, not the hind.

Liza We'd still get picked by our looks.

Maggie Andra's picked by his looks too, come to that.

Liza They'd still pinch our arms and gawp at our legs!

Jenny We'd still have to sleep with the bairns – or worse!

Maggie The maister should hire all the bondagers himself – ay, and lodge them too.

Sara Now, where could he lodge them, Maggie?

Liza In the Big Hoose!

Jenny In the big bed! Oooh-ooh!

Liza We should have a meeting!

Sara Who?

Liza Us! The lassies! There's as many of us as them! More lassies than men, come harvest!

Maggie and **Sara** *shrug off her anger, won't see the point.*

Liza We should make the speeches!

Maggie What do you want? A six-pound rise? And what would you spend it on? Ribbons, ruching? (*To* **Sara**.) Do you know how much this besom owes the draper?

Liza We don't get much!

Maggie I wish I had it. I hunger my bairns, whiles, to feed you! And you spend your money at the draper's!

Jenny We don't get much compared to the men.

Maggie A man's got a family.

Liza Sara's got a family.

Sara Oh, but we're not doing men's work. We canna work like men.

Ellen 'Don't be ridiculous, Ellen,' says the maister. 'We can't do away with the bondage. I can't employ a man who hasn't a woman to work with him. One pair of horse to every fifty acre, one hind for every pair of horse, one bondager for every hind. That's the way it's done,' he says. 'I'm all for progress,' he says, 'but I won't do away with the bondage,' he says. 'We need the women. Who else would do the work? . . . Women's work, for women's pay.'

Liza (*or all, taking phrase by phrase, in turn. She is kirtling up her skirts, putting on the sacking apron*) Redd up the stables, muck out the byre, plant the tatties, howk the tatties, clamp the tatties. Single the neeps, shaw the neeps, mangle the neeps, cart the neeps. Shear, stook, striddle, stack. Women's work.

Ellen Muck. A heap of it – higher than your head. Wider than a house. Every bit of it to be turned over. Aired. Rotted. Women's work.

Liza (*forking the dung*)
Shift the sharn, fulzie, muck

Sharn, sharn, fulzie, muck
Shift the sharn, fulzie, muck . . . *etc.*

Ellen (*on top of* **Liza***'s words*)   Muck is gold, says the maister.

Liza (*forking, digging*)
Sharn, sharn, fulzie, muck
Sharn, sharn, fulzie, muck

Ellen   Muck's like kindness, says the maister, it can be overdone.

Liza (*to* **Ellen**)   You mind what it was like, cleaning your claes after this? My new
bonnet – it stinks. My claes, my skin.

Sara   It's Maggie who washes your claes.

Liza (*to* **Ellen**)   What was the job you hated most?

Ellen   Howking tatties. I'm long – here – in the back. At the end of the day I used to
scraffle on all fours. I couldn't get to my feet till I was halfway down the loan. Can you
shear?

Liza   Aye.

Ellen   Striddle?

Liza   Aye!

Ellen   Are you good?

Liza   Aye. It's the corn I love best. It's the whisper it gives when it's ripe for the sickle.

Ellen   I love the speed of it all, the fury. Faster, faster, keep up with the bandster; faster,
faster, and better your neighbour. I felt like yon Amazon in the Bible. No one could stop
me, if Mabon himself had stood before me, I'd have cut him in two with a swipe o my
sickle. I gloried in the shearing. I'll miss the hairst.

Liza *and* **Ellen** *smile at each other.*

Sara   I remember my mother and her neighbour each had a rig of corn on the village
allotment. My mother was gey thrang, all her life. Too much to do, no time to do it. One
night, when the corn was ripe, she couldn't sleep. The moon was full. So she went out to
shear her corn. And as she sheared, every now and then, she'd take just a bitty from her
neighbour's rig, just as much as would make bands to tie her sheaves. Syne she went
home and slept the last hour or two till day, glad the work was done. But in the morning,
passing the field, she saw she'd reaped the wrong rig, her neighbour's rig. The corn she'd
stolen to bind her sheaves was her own corn – and she still had her own rig to shear. O,
but she grat! It was a punishment, she said.

Scene Eleven

Maggie, **Liza**, **Sara**. *Evening.* **Sara** *is working quietly – in her garden or her house* (*sewing?
hoeing?*), *near enough to hear/overhear* **Liza** *and* **Maggie**. **Maggie** *is busy* (*so is her tongue, she*

scarcely draws breath during the first part of this scene.) She could be churning butter – it calls for steady rhythmic movement, she wouldn't be able to leave her work till the milk was turned. **Liza** *is not so busy: adding ribbon to her petticoats, or ruching to her bonnet.*

Maggie   You must draw *all* the milk off each milking. Well, I've told you before, it's no use milking if you don't milk her right – she'll draw all the milk that's left back into herself, and come next milking she'll give a bit less –

Liza   Coo, coo, I'm sick o the coo.

Maggie   – you'll only get the same next time, as you took from her the time before. We need all the milk she can give. I can't bake flourocks without good cream –

Liza   I could eat a coo, I'm starving!

Maggie   – Andra's fond of flourocks. *You* eat them fast enough – And what about the teats, Liza? I said wash the teats with alum and water –

Liza   Horses – aye. Coos – no.

Maggie   – I said to wash the warts on her teats. Poor coo. A' you bondagers are the same. You know nothing of coos, or kitchens or bairns –

Liza   Bairns – never!

Maggie   The milking's important, Liza, can't you see. I can't feed the family without it!

Liza   You've plenty of your own if your coo runs dry.

Maggie (*stops short, at last, for a moment anyway*)   Aye, I have. And don't think I'm not proud of it. Oh, you wait. Wait till you're wed. Wait till you've a man to feed –

Liza   Oh, wait. You wait. You'll ken! You'll see!

Maggie   – Wait till you've bairns. You'll ken. You'll see! Canna bake, canna milk, canna sew, canna spin. Wait till you're wed!

Liza   I'm not getting wed. I'll be a cottar wife like Sara.

Sara (*more to herself than to them*)   You want to be like Sara? It's day and way for Sara. Every year gets harder for Sara.

Liza (*coming in over* **Sara***'s words*)   I'm not getting wed. Not yet. Not for years. The sooner you wed, the more bairns you get.

Maggie   That's what you wed for – bairns!

Liza   Why?

Maggie   Why? Why! (*Can't think what to say, can't see why she can't think what to say.*) Why, they keep the roof over you when they're older, that's why. They keep things going. Wull and Tam will soon be half-yins, getting halfpay, and when they're grown there'll be Jim and Drew, and the girls will make bondagers in time. Meg can work with her daddy. Netta can work with Wull or Tam. It'll be grand. We'll can take our pick at the Hiring. Ay, we'll be easy then. Soon enough.

Liza All in the one house – all in the one room? And what about him (*Indicating the cradle.*), he'll not be grown, and Rosie's still wee – and how many more? Easy! You'd be easier without.

Maggie Without what?

Liza Bairns.

Maggie Fields aye need folk.

Liza Bairns for the maister?

Maggie What's a hoose without bairns?

Liza If you think they're so bonny, what are you greeting for?

Maggie Me?

Liza What do you greet for nights?

Maggie No, not me – it must have been one of the wee ones – Rosie cries –

Liza 'Bake, cook, sew, spin, get wed, have bairns.' Natter, natter. Nothing about fighting him off in the night!

Maggie (*a gesture: meaning 'you're havering'*) Now . . . where was I . . . what was I going to do next . . .

Liza I hear you! I hear you nights! Do you think I don't hear you?

Maggie Now, what was I doing . . .

Liza You sit on by the fire, hoping he'll sleep. You fetch moss from the peat moor to stuff up your legs. I've seen.

Sara (*calling out from her own house, or garden*) Liza, fetch me some water, would you?

Liza It's bad enough listening when folk are – happy. But when they're pleading, crying – giving in –

Sara Liza! Go to the pump for me, there's my lass!

Maggie (*very upset, loathe to admit it to herself*) What's day is day . . . and night is night.

Sara Liza!

Liza, *insouciant, unrepentant, fetches some receptacle for water, and goes off to the pump.*

Maggie . . . and the bairns are my days! (*She starts – or resumes – some piece of work, then stops, goes to the cradle.*) Aye . . . wee lamb . . . my wee burdie . . . (*Picks him up.*) She doesna ken ought. Just a muckle great tawpie, that's all she is. (*Begins to nurse the baby.*) Dinna go to sleep my burdie. Tak your fill.

It is she who is being comforted by the nursing, rather than the baby.

Now . . . Now . . . I ken where I am now. I canna feel dowie when you tug like that. A'
the bairns at the breast. A' the folk in the fields. A' the bonny folk. A good harvest is a
blessing to all. Aye. That's right. Tak yer fill, burdie, I ken who I am when you're there.

Scene Twelve

Liza, **Tottie**, *all*. **Liza** *is waltzing – humming, or lala-ing the tune* ('*Logie o Buchan*'). *Then starts
to make up words for the tune, dancing hesitantly, searching hesitantly for words. Sings some or all of
this.*

Liza
O, the plooman's so bonny wi black curly hair
He dances so trig and his smile is just rare
His arms are so strong as he birls me awa
His black eyes are bonny and laughing and bra
His name it is Kello, the best o them a'
His name it is Kello, the best o them a'

Waltzing with an imaginary partner now, more confident, repeating the song more confidently . . .

A laugh heard from **Tottie***, who has been hiding, watching. She appears, kissing her own arm with
grotesque kissing noises, sighing, petting noises.* **Liza***, annoyed, gives her a shove or tries to –* **Tottie**
shoves back, hard.

Tottie Tinkler, tailor, beggar – *Kello!* (*More kissing noises.*) Tinkler, tailor, beggar – *lover!*

Liza Tak yer hook, you – go on.

Tottie I looked in the glass. I looked in the glass too. It was twelve o clock, so I saw. I
saw my man. You know who I saw?

Liza You haven't a glass. Jenny's the only one with a glass. Away wag yer mou
somewhere else. Go on!

Tottie Jenny went with the saddler. I saw them in the rigs. Not our rigs. The lang syne
rigs up by the moor. You can hide up there, the furrows are deep. The ghosts'll get them
if they don't watch out. Her claes were way up. Woosh! She's getting wed to the saddler.
That's what you do! Woosh! (. . .) I've seen you too. You went with the Gyptian. In the
turnip house.

Liza I never did. I was dancing, that's all. He was showing me the steps. And he's not a
Gyptian.

Tottie Woosh!

Liza Daftie! Come on, I'll show you the steps. Come on, come here.

Tottie I know the steps!

Liza I want to go over the steps. If you don't know them right, no one will ask you. You
want to dance at the kirn, don't you?

Liza holds out her arms, but **Tottie** *declines to dance with her.* **Liza** *starts waltzing again, singing.* **Tottie** *watches for a while, then suddenly breaks into a raucous clog (or boot) dance, in fast reel or jig time: rough, spirited, noisy. And, like* **Liza**, *sings her own accompaniment:*

Tottie
Liza loves the plooman
Bonnie black-eyed plooman
Kello is the plooman
O, he's no a tinkler
O, he's no a mugger
O, he's no a Gyptian
He's a black-eyed plooman
Bonnie black-eyed plooman, *etc.*

Which kills **Liza**'s *waltz. She stares amazed –* **Tottie**'s *dancing may lack finesse, but it's wholehearted, makes you want to dance with her.*

The others appear, join in. Someone bangs the ground with a graip (or hoe) handle, beating time, they are all singing **Tottie**'s *rhythm now, same tune, same lines, but each singing different lines to each line of the music. The dance is becoming the kirn, has led into the kirn. It stops abruptly:*

Voices (*toasts, asides, conversation*)
The kirn, the kirn, the kirn, the kirn
What a folk/ a'body's here/ mind the bairns
A good harvest/ best for years/ best in my time

Tottie (*listing the repertoire of dances*)   Reel o Tulloch, ribbon dance, pin reel, polka

Voices
All the corn standing and none to lift
I can't stay late because of the bairns
Will you look at Marjie's petticoats!
The saddler's shed his hair doon the middle!

Tottie   Tullogorum, petronella, strathespey, scotch reel

Voices
A good harvest's the envy of none
And a blessing to all
(*Toast.*) Welcome to the maister
(*Toast.*) Thanks to the maister for the harvest home
And the use of the barn
And the beer and the baps
We've a good maister
(*Toast.*) To the maister
And a better mistress
(*Toast.*) To the mistress
Health and Prosperity

A good harvest is a blessing to all
And the envy of none

They shush each other to silence as someone starts to sing (maybe Burns, the song entitled 'Somebody':)

My heart is sair – I darena tell –
My heart is sair for somebody;
I could wake a winter night
For the sake o somebody.
Ohon! for somebody!
O-hey! for somebody!
I could range the world around,
For the sake o somebody!

Ye Powers that smile on virtuous love,
O, sweetly smile on somebody!
Frae ilka danger keep him free,
And send me safe my somebody.
Ohon! for somebody!
O-hey! for somebody!
I wad do – what wad I not?
For the sake o somebody!

Scene Thirteen

Jenny, **Liza**, **Maggie**, **Tottie**, **Sara**. *Dawn, or just after, the morning after the kirn.* **Jenny** *and* **Liza** *arriving home, fits of giggles. High from lack of sleep and the night's events.* **Maggie** *has heard them coming, she's already up – splashing her face with water? fetching water? something – and 'nursing her wrath'.*

Maggie I'll thraw your neck when I come to you, lass. I'll dadd your lugs. I'll skelp you blue.

Liza We were only dancing!

Maggie Dancing! He was dragging you down the loan!

Jenny He'd had a drop! They'd all had a drop.

Maggie Gyptians! Steal the clothes off your back – and a whole lot more!

Liza Kello's not a Gyptian.

Jenny It was the kirn, Maggie.

Liza We were dancing!

Maggie Where to? Coldstream?

Renewed giggles.

And for the love of the Lord, stop that laughing. You cackled and screeched all through the kirn!

Jenny She wasn't going to Coldstream *really*! She wasn't getting wed or anything!

Liza (*mockingly*) Oooh-ooh! Buckled up at Coldstream!

Maggie You weren't? Were you? By, you'd see – !

Liza You'd lose your bondager if I got wed. That's all that bothers you.

Maggie Get ready for work, go on, the pair of you. The steward won't brook lateness after the kirn. Especially not after the kirn. He'll have a thumping head on him this morning. And not the only one. Gin you were mine – I'd shake you, lass!

Sara has appeared, been milking her cow or fetching water or firewood.

Sara Is Tottie not up yet?

They stare at her blankly.

Sara Still sleeping with the bairns, is she?

Maggie *shakes her head, is about to say 'no'.*

Sara I left her last night dancing with the bairns.

Maggie Well, she wasn't with me, Sara.

Sara (*worried, but not unduly*) I thought she was sleeping at your place. Now where can she be?

Maggie The hayloft, probably.

Jenny *and* **Liza** *exchange looks.*

Sara She didn't want to leave with me. She wanted to dance.

Jenny She followed us a way.

Sara You've seen her then – ?

Jenny Last night.

Sara Well, but now, where is she now?

Maggie (*angry, to* **Liza** *and/or* **Jenny**) You should have kept an eye on her.

Jenny ⎤ Why?
Liza ⎬ She's a pest.
Jenny ⎦ Traipsing after us.

Maggie She's been girny lately. Thrawn.

Sara She's been having bad days.

Liza What's the fuss? She never goes far. She's too daft to get far.

They catch sight of **Tottie.**

Sara Tottie, burdie, where have you been? Come here. You're a bad girl, going off like that, where have you been?

Tottie (*triumphant, but wary too – keeps her distance*) I've been married.

'Ooh-ing' or giggles again from **Liza** *and* **Jenny**.

Sara Oh, it's a notion she takes. Like the dancing.

Maggie (*to* **Jenny**, **Liza**) She was with you, then?

Sara Where have you been, Tottie?

Tottie I've been with my man. Getting wed. Liza wouldn't go. He didn't want her anyway.

Each time they approach her she withdraws.

Jenny You've never been to Coldstream and back, not without wings.

Liza You can't wed, you're not sixteen.

Tottie I'm not the bairnie now! I know things. I'm wed.

Maggie It's their fault, putting ideas in her head.

Liza } Us!
Jenny } She wasn't with us!

Tottie I was! I was. They were going to Coldstream brig, they were laughing and dancing, they were having a wedding. I wanted to go too. But they shouted at me, Liza and Jenny and Kello and Dave, and Dave threw a stone. So I hid. Then I heard them running across the field, Liza and Jenny, running and stopping to have a bit laugh, and running and stopping and laughing and running. But the ploomen didn't run cos they'd had too much ale, they couldn't loup the dyke, they stayed in the loan. So I went and asked them could I go to Coldstream instead, and Kello said yes.

Liza Kello.

Jenny You've never been to Coldstream!

Liza She's making it up, she talks like that all the time.

Tottie I'm going to have a clock and a dresser and a bed. And a baby.

The silence gratifies her.

Liza Who said?

Tottie *starts laughing, almost dancing (or lolling about in the hay, as* **Ellen** *did earlier), hugging herself with satisfaction – at last night's, as well as this morning's, attention.*

Maggie What did he do? Tottie? Which one was it, and what did he do?

Sara There's blood on her skirt.

Maggie (*slapping at, or shoving at* **Jenny** *or* **Liza**, *whichever is nearest*) Your fault, bitches!

As she speaks the farmyard bell – maybe just two iron bars banged together – is heard in the distance.

Maggie That's the steward in the yard. You're late. Go on, the pair of you, hurry up, go on. No sense everyone being late.

Sara Tell the steward we're both sick, Tottie and me. Tell him we're sick.

Maggie And Jenny – both of you – keep your gob shut!

Liza (*to* **Tottie**) Was it Kello?

Maggie Tak your hook, Liza!

Tottie (*calling after her in triumph*) You're the bairnie now, Liza!

Liza *and* **Jenny** *go slowly towards the field, collect their hoes, tie on their headhankies, aprons, etc.*

Tottie It was Kello I saw in the glass. Yon night I took a loan of Jenny's glass.

Maggie *and* **Sara** *say nothing, don't know what to say – to* **Tottie***, to each other.*

Tottie He said we hadn't got all night, we'd never get to Coldstream, we should go in the rigs. We were wed in the rigs. Lift your claes! Woosh! I wanted a look at his prick, but I couldn't see right, it was still half dark. And he never lay me doon at all, he pushed me agin the stack. 'We'll smoor the fleas together,' he says. 'It canna hurt if we smoor a wheen fleas.' But it hurt. I'm hurt.

But just when she seems distressed and ready to be comforted, she starts laughing again, excited, gleeful.

Liza They'll tell the steward and the maister.

Jenny (*to* **Liza**) What'll they do to that Kello, eh? What'll they *not* do!

Maggie There's always trouble after the kirn!

Jenny (*looking to the fields*) They're ploughing already. I can see the horses. *He's* turning up the stubble, your Kello –

Liza Not mine!

Maggie Go to work, Sara. I'll see to her now. Leave her here with me. If you don't work, you don't get paid. And the steward'll be angry if you're not in the field, it'll make him angrier at Tottie.

Sara (*more angry than sad, for once*) At *Tottie*?

But **Sara** *can't go.*

Jenny (*to* **Liza**) What'll you say when you see him, Kello?

Liza I won't see him – I won't look!

Jenny If he speaks to –

Liza I'll spit!

Maggie (*looking to fields*) They're ploughing already. Ploughing for winter.

Sara Come home now, bairnie!

Tottie Not the bairnie now!

Maggie Trouble – it comes like the first nip of frost. Sure as frost after harvest.

Liza   I wish it was last night again. I wish it was the kirn still.

Maggie   Sure as winter.

Jenny   I wish the summer would last for ever.

Liza   I wish we were still dancing!

Act Two

Scene One

It is dark, at first we barely see the characters on stage. The different sections of chorus here come fast on top of each other, sections actually overlapping – until **Maggie** *and* **Sara** *speak individually, in character.*

A single voice (*tune: traditional*)
Up in the morning's no for me
Up in the morning early
When a' the hills are covered in snow
Then it is winter fairly . . . (*Last line more spoken than sung.*)

Voices (*in a spoken round*)
When a' the hills are covered in snow
Then it is winter fairly . . .

As the round finishes, voices still saying 'Winter . . . winter . . . winter . . .'

A burst of noise: a rattle of tin cans, or sticks clattering together, or a stick drumming on tin – or something like. (It was Hogmanay, not Hallowe'en, when kids went guising in the Borders.)

A child (*calling out in a mock scary way*)   OOooooh!

A child (*calling out, merry*)
We're only some bits o bairns come oot to play
Get up – and gie's oor Hogmanay!

Some laughter, children's laughter. The rattle/drumming noise. If possible an impression of the laughter fading to distance – as if the children have retreated, and the adults, and adult worries, are coming to the centre of the stage.

Voices (*singly, in turn*)
Cold wind: snow wind
Small thaw: mair snaw
The snow wreaths
The feeding storm
The hungry flood

Sara's *and* **Maggie**'s *speeches here more definite, more individual.*

Sara   The dread of winter. All summer long, the dread of it. Like a nail in the door that keeps catching your hand. Like a nip in the air in the midst of the harvest.

A voice (*whispery, echoey*)   Cold wind: snow wind.

Maggie (*brisk, busy*)   There's beasts to be fed, snaw or blaw!

Voice   Cold. Ice. Iron.

Maggie (*with a certain satisfaction*)   A green yule makes a fat kirkyard!

As **Tottie** *starts speaking, light comes on her. Her voice gets louder. She is brandishing a graip – maybe there are tin cans or something else tied to it that make a noise when she brandishes. She is swathed for winter (as are the rest of the cast here, but not quite so wildly) – straw-rope leggings, her arms covered in extra knitted oversleeves; fingerless mitts, shawl, the headhankie pulled protectively well around the face. A right tumshie-bogle.*

Tottie (*voice becomes less childish, harsher, more violent as she recites*)
Get up auld wife and shake your feathers
Ye needna think that we're a' wheen beggars
We're only some bits o bairns come oot to play
Get up – and gie's oor Hogmanay!

Aggressive now, hitting out maybe – whanging the straw bales/stack/hedgerow with the graip or just beating about with it, or beating the ground.

Hogmanay – Hogmanick
Hang the baker ower the stick
When the stick begins to break
Take another and break his back

Tottie, **Liza**, **Sara** – *and* **Maggie**, *who talks with them, but has work to do in her own 'home area'.*

Sara   Tottie!

Tottie   No!

Sara   We'll be late for the field, Tottie.

Tottie   I want to play.

Maggie   Don't be daft, now.

Tottie (*with menace*)   Not!

Maggie   The maister'll be after you.

Tottie   A' the men are after Tottie!

Sara   Tie up yer claes, we're going to the field.

Tottie   I'm playing!

Sara   We've to work, Tottie. No work, no shillings.

Maggie   You're too big to play!

Tottie   I'm married now!

Maggie   Leave her be. What's the use when she's this way?

Sara   If I leave her be she'll go deaving the men.

Tottie   I'm going guising. Going to guise the ploomen in the chamber.

Sara   No, you're not. You're not to go there, Tottie. Leave the men alone.

Tottie (*violent. She's still apart from them, by herself*)
'Hogmanay, Hogmanick
Take another and break his back' . . .
A'body wants Tottie. A' the men are after Tottie.

Liza *watching all this, watching* **Sara** *and* **Tottie**, *miserable for herself and them.*

Maggie   Best leave her for now. Best get moving. You'll make the steward angry if you're late – aye, and the maister. No work, no pay.

Sara *goes towards the field.* **Tottie** *sulking.*

Maggie (*with venom, she's meaning* **Liza**)   Dirt! . . . Dirt!

Liza, *utterly miserable, follows* **Sara** *towards the field.*

Scene Two

Tottie *by the stacks/bales.*

Tottie (*a slow, sour version of her former jig/song*)
Tottie loves the plooman
Tottie's black-eyed plooman
Kello is the plooman

Throws herself against the stack, beats at it a bit with her body, her arms, her fists . . .

Not fair. Wasn't there. Not fair. Didn't come . . .
'Away up the moor, Tottie,' he says. 'I'll meet you up on the moor.'
But he didnae. Kello.
There was a man there, but it wasnae him.
Twixt me and the sun. Just the one man.
He was stood in the rigs, the lang syne rigs.
'A week's work done in a day,' he cries.
'We don't need you now!
We don't need folk. We don't need horses.
Machines without horses.
We've plenty bread now,' he cries.
'Too much bread.'
He was pleased. He was laughing.
But I wasnae feared. (*She's laughing a bit, it pleases her.*)
For he wasnae the ghost.
I was! I was the ghost!

Voices (*whilst speaking these lines, they are moving into position, still muffled in headhankies, mitts, etc., still 'hauden-doon' by winter. Spoken quite matter-of-factly, either singly, turn by turn, or in unison*)
Barley means bread
Pease means bread

Oats means bread
Wheat means bread
Corn means bread

Tottie (*in the middle of the above, on top of their words – the voices do not pause*)
'We've plenty bread now,' he cries.
'Too much bread.'

Voices
Never enough bread
Give us this day our daily bread
The bread of carefulness

Tottie 'Too much bread now! Mountains!' he cries.

Voice(s) The bread of progress!

Scene Three

Ellen (*polite teatime voice – a teapot or cakestand? – she's talking to the foreigners visiting the show farm of Blacksheils*)   Progress? Progress! The key to progress is rotation: Maister Elliott's six-course rotation. Famed throughout the land; throughout Europe. Corn, potatoes, turnips, and swedes, clover, and rye grass, with a good stock of sheep and cattle. Sixty tons of farm manure. Twelve hundredweight of artificials. Wheat yields – up! Potato yields – up! The rent? – up! – naturally. Raised by the Marquis according to our yields. Rotation! Rotation of course applies also to the workforce. On farms of this size we have to be exact. Twenty men and eight women in winter, eighteen extra women and boys in summer. The steward can't do with less, the master can't pay for more.

(*Not talking to the visitors here.*) If Jimmy Eagan's too frail now to work,
Then he and his family must move elsewhere,
For his house is needed for a younger hind,
And his wife and three daughters are surplus to requirements.
If Tam Neil's lad is ready for the fields,
The family will have to seek a new place at the Hiring,
We've too many young boys at Blacksheils already,
We don't need more half-yins,
We need more hinds,
We need more bondagers and unmarried ploughmen.

(*To the visitors again.*) Of course, they never move far . . . ten, fifteen miles . . . They're used to it. Some welcome it . . . 'So long as it's dry for the flitting!'

(*No longer addressing the visitors.*) 'Please God: Keep them dry for the flitting.' . . . He's a fair man, the maister. He'd have built a new row of houses by now – if it wasn't for the Marquis raising the rent. 'I overlook small faults in a good workman,' says the maister. 'I've lived here all my life,' he says. 'I know this place like I know my own hand. I know the Border peasant: honest, industrious, godfearing . . .'

He never knew me, never knew my name even, till I set my cap at him. The first year of marriage, I still had the face of a bondager: white below, where the kerchief had been tied, the top of my cheeks and my nose dirt brown. The ladies stared, and smiled behind their fans. But I'm all pale now, I'm a proper lady now.

Not once has he asked me what it was like: to live in the row, to work in the fields. Not once . . . They've made a lady of me now.

Scene Four

Maggie, **Tottie**, **Sara**, **Liza** . . . *and* **Ellen** *later. All working, or about to.* **Maggie** *working in, or for, her own house.* **Liza** *filling buckets or a burrow with neeps to feed the beasts (or crushing the neeps in the crusher).* **Sara** *helping* **Tottie** *to 'breech her claes', i.e. kirtle up her skirts, so that they're almost like trousers, ready for work.*

Sara Has he spoken to Andra, the maister?

Maggie No. Not yet. Has he spoken to you?

Sara (*shakes her head*) No. Not yet. Not to anyone yet. Not that I've heard. (*Without conviction.*) Well, there's time . . .

Liza There's hardly any time. It's past Hogmanay.

A pause. Uneasy.

Sara Maister Elliott always speaks well before the Hiring. He's good that way.

Maggie Not long till the Hiring now.

Liza First Monday in February.

Uneasy pause.

Maggie He's bound to keep some on. The steward; the herd. And he's well pleased with Andra, he'll be speaking to Andra. (*To* **Sara**.) Ellen'll see that you're kept on, don't fret.

Sara Tottie's had bad days. Too many bad days.

Maggie And who's to blame? Kello. Well, they won't keep him on, that's for sure. It's a wonder he wasn't sent packing before – straight after the kirn! Mind, the same could be said for some other – dirt!

Sara That's not right, Maggie, that's not fair!

Maggie You don't know the half of it. Don't know the half of her! Flaunty piece of – dirtery!

Sara *wants to smooth this, but can't.*

Maggie, **Sara**, **Liza**, *all speaking and shouting at once here:*

Maggie (*to* **Liza**) Her father must be turning in his grave. Dirt. If the maister only knew, he'd send her packing. Dirt – that's all she is.

Liza (*incoherent, upset*) My father – aye, he must – at you – at you and your man. What do you expect me to do – what? If my father knew – if Steenie was here – he'd – if he – it's not right – it's not.

Maggie Just like her mother. Maisie Kerr – no better than she should be. Tinkler trash!

Sara That's not true, Maggie, that's not true at all!

Liza Liar! That's a lie!

Ellen What's all this? All this noise? Haven't you work enough to keep busy? The maister's sick of all this clamjamfray. Where's Tottie – Tottie? – Tottie, come here –

Tottie *comes, without enthusiasm.* **Ellen** *hugs her, but she doesn't reciprocate.*

Ellen Why haven't you been working? Bad girl. Wild girl! (*Says this nicely, cajolingly, but* **Tottie**, *sulky, is trying to break away.*) You used to be a good worker, Tottie. You've got to be good. Hey, now, promise me, now – you'll be a good girl now.

Tottie *retreats to stack, bale, somewhere.*

Ellen (*to* **Sara**) The steward's been grumbling to the maister. She deaves all the men, she throws herself at Kello.

Maggie Kello shouldn't be here. They should have sent him away.

Ellen Yes. I know.

Maggie Then why did they not?

Ellen Because she wouldn't say. Tottie wouldn't say. (*To* **Tottie**.) You should have told them, Tottie, you should have told them what happened to you.

Maggie She said it all to us. Don't they believe it? There was blood on her claes.

Ellen I know.

Maggie He should have been punished.

Ellen (*knowing how feeble this is*) They did punish him, the men.

Maggie Oh – they douked him in the trough, and kicked him round the yard. But they feel sorry for him now. Some of the lads admire him, almost, some of the lassies even. It's Tottie they're angry at now.

Liza *very silent, very subdued – and very resentful.*

Sara He changed Tottie. He stole her.

Maggie They laugh and swear at her now.

Ellen 'I keep a steward to manage my workers.' That's all the maister says, that's all he'll say. 'I won't keep a dog and bark for myself.'

Maggie He barks when it's lassies causing the trouble. He sent Minnie packing . . . almost before we'd time to find out why!

Ellen And the steward won't budge. 'It takes two,' he says. 'Takes two to smoor the fleas.' You know how they are – maisters, stewards – they leave things be, till the turn of the year. They leave it till the Speaking, and let the bad ones go. Leave it till the Hiring, and let them go.

Maggie (*with some satisfaction*) No one'll hire Kello. That's for sure!

Ellen I wouldn't be so certain. He's good with the horses, he's a hero with horses.

Maggie (*with a venemous look at* **Liza**) Folk like that are left till last at the Hiring! Lads or lassies!

Sara It's us who'll get left, Tottie and me.

Ellen You won't need to go to the Hiring, Sara. You can stay on here, you know that surely. But see she behaves. If she won't do any work, at least keep her quiet – and away from the men. For the maister won't stand for all this – nonsense.

Sara *obviously feels this is easier said than done.*

Ellen She throws up her skirts, she rushes at Kello, the other men have to pull her away.

Sara (*very quietly*) He changed Tottie, he stole her.

Maggie If she hated him now – if she feared him, even – well, that would make sense.

Sara She's angry at him – but not that way.

Ellen You know what they say? 'Well, no wonder,' they say. 'No wonder what happened, just look at the way she behaves, poor Kello, poor man, it wasn't his fault, he'd had a few, mind, why not, at the kirn, and what was she doing there out in the field – asking for it.' That's what they say.

Sara I know.

Maggie (*going off, brisk, busy*) Not the only one asking for it. And not just in the fields, either! Sleekit piece of dirtery!

Sara (*to* **Tottie***; as she talks, she fetches* **Tottie***, and ushers her reluctantly off*) We'll spoil a few moudies in the far field, Tottie, eh? You like doing that. Fetch your hoe, we'll give the moudieworps a gliff!

Ellen (*she has been aware of* **Liza***'s reactions, and the vibes from* **Maggie** *throughout this scene*) Liza!

Liza I've the beasts to feed.

Ellen (*signals* **Liza** *to come nearer*)   There's Mary and Jenny to see to the beasts. Tell them I needed you up at the House. It's no more than the truth – there's flax to be spun!

Liza (*miserable, awkward, won't meet* **Ellen**'s *eye*)   Can't spin. I don't want to spin.

Ellen (*though never sentimental, touched now by* **Liza**'s *misery*)   Don't listen to Maggie, what she said about your mother, it isn't true. She's jealous, that's all. Your father was fierce – but a'body liked your mother.

Liza   How would you know?

Ellen   Steenie told me. Over and over.

Liza *wants very much to go.*

Ellen   Liza. It wasn't your fault. About Kello and Tottie. You're not to blame. Don't let them blame you. Jenny's not blamed. She holds up her head. Don't let them blame you.

Liza (*frustrated, near to tears*)   It's not just that . . . It's *her*!

Ellen   Maggie?

Liza   *Him*!

Ellen   Kello?

Liza *shakes her head.*

Ellen   Andra?

Liza *nods.*

Ellen (*incredulous*)   Andra!

Liza (*blurting this, chopping it up*)   It's not my fault. It's not. Just because I – because – because of Kello – since the kirn – Maggie – they all think – they all think I'm – word gets round – it's not my fault – I haven't done anything . . .

Ellen (*disbelief – not tragically shocked, because she can't take Andra all that seriously – maybe a hint of mirth already in her voice*)   Andra.

Liza (*upset*)   She won't – I can't help hearing them at night – and then he – I hate it, hearing them – she won't let him, she won't touch him – and then he – he comes and stands by the other bed. I keep the curtains drawn, I hug the bairns close, the two on the outside, and the wee one between me and the wall – but they sleep like the dead – he stands there, I can hear him – *she* can hear him, that's the worst, she can hear him, I hear her listening – but it's not my fault – it's not my fault – it's not . . .

Ellen   But he doesn't – does he? – *Andra*? What does he do?

Liza   Nothing. He stands there. Breathing.

Ellen *can no longer hold in her laughter, fairly snorts with mirth.*

Liza (*outraged at this response*)   It isn't funny. It isn't my fault.

Ellen   Andra! It would be like going to bed with a tumshie! (*Beginning to laugh again.*)

Liza (*in self-defence*) He isn't in my bed. (*Almost in defence of him.*) I don't think he's a tumshie! He's got awful bonny legs.

Ellen Oh?

Liza I've spied them through the curtains.

Ellen Ah.

Liza I like working with Andra. That wall-eyed mare, the one that kicks, she was ramming me tight against the stable wall, I was losing my breath, but Andra came along and roared and whacked her, he showed me how to roar and whack, she's been quiet with me since.

Ellen (*laughter threatening again*) Ummm.

Liza I don't want him in my bed, whatever Maggie says. I don't want him at all. I'm not a bad girl.

Ellen I know that, Liza. I know you're not bad. (*Without remorse, quite fondly.*) Ellen Rippeth was bad, Ellen Rippeth-that-was . . . I was douce with Steenie, though, I wasn't bad to Steenie . . . Have you heard from Steenie?

Liza shakes her head.

Ellen Saskatchewan. Are they douce there, I wonder?

Liza You sent him away.

Ellen (*brisk*) Thistles!

Liza Steenie left because of you.

Ellen Bonnets! He set off for Canada like you set off for Coldstream brig – he never made up his mind – he'd no mind to make up. You're two of a kind – you and your brother – fresh pats of butter still waiting on the stamp. He was ower young, Steenie. I didn't love him, Liza.

Liza (*muttering*) You don't love the maister, either.

Ellen What?

Liza But you love the maister, do you?

Ellen (*very quietly*) Almost. Almost.

A pause. Each lost in her own thoughts – of the maister; of Kello.

Liza Kello can ride the maister's black mare – make it dance, and turn in a ring. He stands on its rump, whilst it circles around, he keeps his balance, he takes off his jacket, his waistcoat, his kerchief. (*She is moving, dancing really, as she recalls watching Kello, in the summer, in the paddock.*) . . . A red-spotted kerchief. He aye keeps his balance, the mare canters round, and around, and around, and when Kello jumps off, he turns in the air, right round in the air, and lands on his feet . . . A red-spotted kerchief . . . His eyes are aye laughing, he dances so trig. He showed me the steps. He stroked my hair.

Ellen   Tinkler, sorner, seducer – thief!

Liza (*taken aback; then braving it out*)   I know.

Ellen   That's all right then, so long as you know. The maister locks the doors at night to keep him away from the dairymaids. So now he meets with the hedger's wife instead – when he's not walking over to Langriggs at night. The parlourmaid there – they meet in the woods. Bella Menteith. Huh! Who would have thought! Well, she's no chicken – and so perjink!

It's a kick in the teeth for **Liza**. **Ellen** *didn't mean to say so much.*

Liza (*face-saving; lying*)   I knew all that! A'body kens that!

Liza *goes.*

Scene Five

Ellen, **Maggie**, **Tottie**. **Tottie** *appears – maybe been hiding nearby for a while.*

Ellen (*softly; taking account of* **Tottie**'s *presence, but not directly to her*)   A'body kens that. Don't they, Tottie?

Tottie (*ditto: not directly to* **Ellen** *at this point*)   'I'll meet you,' he says. He keeps on saying – 'Away up the moor – down by the mill – along by Craig Water – I'll meet you there, soon – I'll meet you there later.' But he doesnae.

Ellen   You don't want to see Kello, Tottie. He's a bad man.

Tottie   Yes, he is.

Ellen   Then you must leave him alone.

Tottie *still has her hoe, she's been hoeing down molehills. She attacks the ground, or something, hay-bale, something, with her hoe.*

Tottie   Foxton field's plagued with moudies – moudie hillocks all over the field. Ten, two, a hundred moudies!
Hogmanay, Hogmanick
Find the moudie and break its neck
Find its hillock and ding it doon
Ding! Dang! – BANG! – Seven hillocks, seven moudies!
(*Well aware of* **Ellen**, *half an eye on* **Ellen**.)
Moudiewort, moudiewort, run to the Tweed
For your hillock's danged doon, and we all want you dead
Ding, dang – damn! (*Repeats this with quieter pleasurable concentration.*) Damnation! Damn! Damn!

But **Ellen** *is walking away (maybe not right offstage).*

Hell! Damn! A hundred moudies! Yes, he's bad. I know where he bides. He bides in the chamber up above the new stables. He's to fetch me a clock, still. And a bed. (*She's by the cradle now.*) Hasn't he, babby? Eh? Wee babby. Bee-baw-babbity.

Maggie *bustling in:*

Maggie   Now then, Tottie, keep away from wee Joe. You shouldn't be here – you've work to do. Mind what Mistress Ellen told you.

Tottie   I'm minding the babby.

Maggie   No, no. Not now. Take that hoe out of here. You're not to mind the babby any more, he's – he's too big for you to mind now.

Tottie   He's not. I'm bigger.

Maggie (*losing patience; has the baby in her arms now, waiting for* **Tottie** *to go*)   Away you go now, Tottie, get that hoe out of here!

Tottie *gives the cradle a push, maybe with her hoe, and goes, leaving the cradle rocking.*

Maggie, *still holding the baby, follows* **Tottie** *a little way, but not offstage, to make sure she's really going.*

Scene Six

Ellen, Maggie, Sara.

Ellen (*not talking directly to* **Sara** *yet – nor to* **Maggie**)   I like the idea of a winter baby. Swaddled in shawls. I'd feed him in bed by the light of the fire. I'd keep him safe from the feeding storms. When spring burst on us, he'd be fat as a lamb, he'd laugh at the leaves.

Maggie (*muttering*)   Lie in bed? All right for some! (*Busy, busy . . . self-righteousness increasing.*) Lying in bed! With a baby to look after? (*Seems to calm down . . . and then it gets to her again. With scorn and envy.*) Lying in bed! Huh!

She goes.

Meanwhile **Sara** *appears, with some quiet kind of work, maybe knitting (she would be knitting as she walked).*

Ellen (*to* **Sara**)   What do I have to take, Sara? What do I have to do? Don't say: 'Time enough!' Don't say: 'Be patient!' I need a child now! Not for me – well, not for me only – for the maister! (. . .) Sara?

But **Sara** *can't think what to say.*

Ellen   It was your mother brought me into the world. She knew all the cures. My mother always said she did. You know them, too, don't you?

Sara   Be happy, Nell. You were happy as a lark, once. And so was the maister.

Ellen He has things on his mind. Yields per acre, tiles for drainage . . . mortgage for mortgage . . . I don't know what. I'm useless in that great house! Dressing up; pouring tea. His mother minds the house, Betty Hope minds me. I'd shift the sharn if it'd help; mangle the neeps, feed the beasts. I watch him at his desk, writing, counting. He doesn't even know I've come into the room. He breaks my heart. I only want it for him. I'm plump, I'm greedy, I'm healthy! Damn it, why can't I swell? It happens soon enough for those who don't want it, who don't even think about it!

Sara Then don't think about it, Nell.

Exasperation from **Ellen**.

There's time.

More exasperation.

Be patient!

Ellen Sara!

Sara And don't let him sit at his desk all night. You can't fall for a baby while he sits at his desk!

They laugh.

Ellen (. . .) There's a herb. It cures a'thing, my mother used to say. It grows round these parts. I don't know its name. But it looked like a docken, I remember she said that.

Sara *shakes her head very slightly, as she continues knitting or whatever.*

Ellen You know about it, don't you? You know where it grows?

Sara It cured cuts and wounds. We put the leaves on the wound, and bandaged them round. I never knew it to fail for things like that. For sickness too, and fevers, and wasting.

Ellen Barrenness?

Sara (*gently*) Nell –

Ellen Tell me where it grows. I'll fetch some. I'll dig it up. Tell me what to do with it. Eat it? Wear it? I'll wrap myself in it from head to heel.

Sara It used to grow at Craig's Pool. It never had a name. 'The leaves by Craig Water', that's what we cried it. But – I'm not sure it would have cured barrenness, Nell –

Ellen I could try.

Sara You aren't barren, Nell – you're spun dizzy with nerves. You just need to –

Ellen Craig's Pool – on the crook of the river?

Sara The leaves don't grow there now.

Ellen Where else do they grow?

Sara That's the only place we ever knew of. But they don't grow there now. The maister had a wall built, some years ago – to keep the river from flooding the fields. He had the bank raised. They moved tons of earth. And build a braw dyke, and a paving on the bank so we could wash the linen. (. . .) Nobody thought. We used the leaves all the time – your mother was right, we used them for a'thing . . . well . . . (*Partly her sensible opinion, and partly trying to comfort* **Ellen** *in her dismay.*) not so much for babies, Nell, some women tried, but I don't –

Ellen I could have tried. I could have tried.

Sara Nobody thought to save any of the roots. Nobody gave it any thought . . .

Scene Seven

All (except **Ellen**). **Tottie** *brandishing a letter,* **Liza**, *desperate, furious, trying to get it back. A silent, quite vicious struggle, shoving, wrestling, pinching, kicking. And* **Tottie** *wins.*

Liza Give it me.

Tottie No.

Liza It's mine

Tottie No.

Liza It's not yours.

Tottie Sas-katch-e-wan.

Liza It's not yours.

Tottie My daddy's been away for a hundred year.

Liza You can't read anyway.

Tottie I can so, I can.
Collop Monday,
Pancake Tuesday,
Ash Wednesday,
Bloody Thursday,
Lang Friday,
Hey for Saturday afternoon;
Hey for Sunday at twelve o clock,
Whan a' the plum puddings jump out o the pot.

Throughout this recitation **Liza** *is trying to shut her up, shout her down:*

Liza That's not reading. You can't read. Daftie! You can't read, Tottie!

Tottie *is upset.* **Liza** *beginning – slightly – to take pity on her, but still irritated and fearful for her letter. A moment's pause.* **Tottie** *gets out the letter – keeping it well away from* **Liza**'s *snatching hands, begins to 'read' it:*

Tottie (*'reading' the letter*)
'Here's tae ye a' yer days
Plenty meat and plenty claes
Plenty porridge and a horn spoon
And another tattie when a's done.' (. . .) I can so, I can read.

Liza   Here. I'll read it to you. (. . .) It's a story. There's a story in the letter – from Steenie, my brother. I'll read you the story.

Very slowly **Tottie** *gives in, gives* **Liza** *the letter. As* **Liza** *opens the letter* **Tottie** *suddenly changes mood, all excitement, all smiles, jumps, dances about, laughing, yelling, yelling at the top of her voice.*

Tottie   Hey-ey! Oooo-oh! Hey-ey! Liza's got a letter. Liza's reading a letter. A letter. A story. A story. A letter. Sas-katch-e-wan!

They all come forward, as for a story (it is, for them).

Liza (*reads*)   'Dear Sister: I am writing letting you know I am in good health. The country is good if a man keeps his health. The land costs eleven shillings and thruppence an acre, but we must take up our axes and cut down the trees. Should he not take land, a man gets four shillings a day and his meat which is no bad wage. Donald McPhail is here, I am staying with him still, he has sixty acres, and Walter Brotherston from Coldstream, one hundred acres.

'The winter here is long. The ice floats in the lake like so many peats, and some the size of a house. The Indians say that Hell is made of snow and ice, and they say that heaven is alive with buffalo. There is buffalo everywhere for eating, they belong to no master. There are no masters here, and no stewards, and no pride. If a man be civil he is respected. I have dined with gentlemen and been asked to say the grace. My – (*She stops dead, astonished.*) my wife – '

They wait for enlightenment, amused, curious.

Liza (*reads*)   'My wife Emily joins with me in her best respects to you. This letter is brought by her father, Mr Monroe, who is going home to Edinburgh owing to his health.'

They wait – surely there's more?

Liza (*reads*)   'Your loving brother, Steenie.'

But surely there's more?

Liza (*reads*)   'PS. Tell John Mackintosh if he comes he need bring no axes, just the clothes for the voyage.'

Liza *stares at the letter, nonplussed, lonely.*

Tottie (*softly*)   Buffalo . . . Buffalo . . .

Maggie   Men!

Sara   But it's a grand letter, Liza, and grand news of Steenie. You must write to the wife, you'll get more crack from his wife.

Jenny (*suddenly, merrily, jigging about*)
Woo'd and married and a'
Kissed and carried awa!

She and **Tottie** *jigging about, trying to get* **Liza** *to jig/dance also – but* **Liza** *is still taking in the news of the letter, half-thrilled at the news, at any news, half let-down . . . bewildered . . . at the gaps in the news, at the fact that Steenie, now married, belongs to her less.* **Tottie** *and* **Jenny** *dance around her, jostle, even push her, but she doesn't join in.*

Tottie, **Jenny**
And is no the bride well off
That's woo'd and married and a'!

They're all thinking over the news. **Liza** *is silent, holding her letter, tracing the seal, the writing, with her finger. She pays only intermittent attention to the ensuing conversation, goes off to some quiet corner to sit with her letter, or goes offstage.*

Sara   Walter Brotherston! A hundred acres! (*She starts to laugh.*) Well, he was a young limmer and no mistake! Remember the night of that kirn at Westlea?

Maggie (*frosty*)   I certainly do.

Sara (*enjoying herself*)   There were half a dozen bairns – the wee ones, just babies – sleeping in the hay at the farthest end of the barn. Oh, they were good as gold, not a cheep out of them, and of course around dawn everyone started for home, and the mothers were tired out, and the babies sleeping like the dead. So it wasn't till later, till they were all home, that they found out what Walter had done!

Maggie   He should have been whipped!

Sara   It wasn't just him, it was Jamie as well. They'd changed the babies round. They'd changed all the clothes, the bonnets and shawls. Six babies! – and all of them home with the wrong mother!

Jenny   But they'd notice, the mothers!

Sara (*laughing*)   Eventually! What a squawking and screeching across the fields – it sounded like a fox had got amongst the hens.

Maggie (*muttering under* **Sara***'s words*)   A swearing scandal, that's what it was!

Sara   The blacksmith's bairn was away up the hill with the shepherd and his wife! And Maggie's wee Tam ended up in the village, who was he with again, Maggie, was it Phoebe?

Maggie (*grim*)   I went to feed and change my bairn – and he'd turned into a lassie! Oh, you can laugh. But there's many a baby been changed by the Gyptians – so what was I to think? He was never a Christian that Walter Brotherston – and neither's that scoundrel

Jamie Dodds. They aye watch him at the kirk! He'll more likely take money out the plate than put anything in.

Jenny   And when he does put something in, it's only a halfpenny.

Sara   There's plenty he gives that no one knows of. He gives to the needy. Many a time.

Maggie (*grudgingly*)   He's a grand worker, I'll grant you that.

Sara   Ay. (. . .) The maister will be keeping *him* on, likely.

A pause. These days they are all nagged by the same thought.

Sara   Has he spoken to Andra yet, the maister?

Maggie   No. Not yet. Has he spoken to you?

Sara   No.

Jenny   You don't need to fret, Sara. Ellen said you were biding on.

Sara   Well, he hasn't spoken yet.

Maggie   Maybe he's waiting till he's paid his rents. He'll be paying the rents on Friday – down at the inn. They say the Marquis'll be there to collect in person this year. And the usual grand dinner for the tenants.

Jenny   Hare soup. And goose. And plum pudding. And whisky 'as required'.

They dwell on this in silence. The conversation is becoming desultory, the scene ends (and light fades) quietly, conversationally.

Jenny   The chimneypiece at the inn takes up most of one wall. I've seen it from the yard, I've keeked through the window. They don't need candles with a blaze like yon.

They dwell on this too.

Tottie   Plum pudding. Buffalo.

Jenny   I wish I was a hedgehog . . . or a frog . . .

Tottie   You're a cuckoo!

Jenny   I wish I was. A frog. A cuckoo. I don't know what they do in the winter, those beasts. But you never see them working the fields.

Everyone has left by now, except **Tottie**.

Tottie
Buffalo, buffalo, run up to heaven
For they want you all dead
And you'll soon be all gone.

(*Suddenly boisterous.*) Hey for Sunday at twelve o clock
When all the buffalo jump out the pot!

I can read, I can. I can write, too. I can write a grand letter. 'Dear Kello, What fettle? I am in good fettle, hope this finds you in the same. Did you see me in the glass? I saw you in the glass when the clock struck twelve. I want a clock that strikes twelve. I want to lie down right, not leaning up agin the stack. I want a plaidie on the bed, it canna hurt that way. "Come under my plaidie, the night's going to fa'." ' (*She is maybe almost half-singing the next lines, very softly, very low.*)

Come in frae the cold blast, the drift, and the snaw
Come under my plaidie, and lie down beside me
There's room here, dear lassie, believe me, for twa

Scene Eight

Voices/Chorus. **Liza**, **Maggie**, **Sara**, **Jenny**, **Tottie**. *Couple of days since previous scene. Winter afternoon/evening. Already dark. Lamps or candles.*

From the beginning of the scene **Tottie** *hears and is aware of the commotion, but keeps separate from it . . . as if, by ignoring it, the commotion might simply disappear.*

As the lights go up, there is a great howl from **Liza**. *Then:*

Liza Sara! Andra! Jenny! Maggie! Davie! Sara! Andra!

All this goes fast:

Voices
What now?/ In the name of heaven?/ It's only Liza!
Is that Liza?/ What a racket!/ Where's the fire?
What's happened?/ These lassies!/ What's wrong?

Liza Get the maister – Oh – God! – someone – doctor – he's hurt. He's lying all – He's lying all crooked. Bleeding. Dying.

Voices (*coming in halfway through* **Liza***'s last speech*)
Who's hurt?/ Where?/ Who's hurt?
What's happened?/ Shush now!/ Calm down
Who's hurt?/ Lying?/ Dying?/ Bleeding?
Where is he? Where?
There, lass, shush now
Let her speak

Liza It's Kello. It's Kello. He's lying all crooked on the stable floor. At the foot of the ladder that leads to his chamber. Bella found him. Bella –

Voices
Bella Menteith!
Bella Menteith?

Huh, well – !
Shush, let her speak!

Liza   She shouted on me. She's there with him now. He's – It's Kello.

Voice(s)   Why didn't you run to the house?

Liza   There's no one there.

Voice(s)   Jenny, run to the house.

Liza   There's no one there.

Voices
It's the day for the rents
They're down at the inn
They're all at the inn
The steward
The maister
But where's the mistress?

Liza   There's no one there.

Voice(s)
Fetch water
Whisky
Lineament
Prayer . . .

A pause. Fearful.

Liza (*quietly*)   There's blood coming out of him. Out of his head.

Sara (*to* **Jenny**, *in fact, but as if to several*)   Fetch the trap. For the doctor. Go on now.

Maggie   Yes. Fetch the trap. Go and harness the mare.

Maggie, **Liza**, **Sara** *are now watching 'the others' (i.e.* **Jenny**) *go.* **Liza** *obviously not keen to go back to the stables.* **Tottie** *still ignoring it all.* **Sara** *can't move – neither towards the stables to help, nor towards* **Tottie**, *whom she is acutely aware of.*

Maggie (*going now too*)   I'll follow them on. If you'll mind the bairns. Keep the bairn safe from – (*She means from* **Tottie**.)

Sara   Yes, Maggie.

Maggie (*on her way*)   Lying all crooked! That's rich – for a Gyptian! (*A dart at* **Liza**.) Nothing but trouble!

All this time **Tottie** *has been determinedly trying to ignore the rumpus, trying not to care (and not to be noticed), birling the handles of her hoe or graip to and from one hand to the other, or fiddling, doodling, in some other way.*

Liza (*in shock, really*)   Bella Menteith. I was going to the dairy. She called from the yard, from the stable door.

Sara   Who else was there?

Liza   No one.

Sara   *She* found him?

Liza   He fell. There's blood coming out of him where he fell.

Sara   She saw him fall?

Liza   She found him. I don't know. Kello. He's dying.

Sara   Oh, now, you don't know that. I've seen several given up for dead. Why, my own – (*Breaks off, looks at* **Tottie***; very softly.*) my own . . .

Liza   Bella Menteith. She's no chicken!

Sara   Are you sure there was no one else there?

Liza   There was no one about. I went to the Big House. There was no one about.

Sara (*she's comforting* **Liza***, calming her*)   It's the day for the rents. They'll still be at the inn. They'll sit long at the dinner. The Marquis is there . . .

Liza   But Andra, and Tam, and –

Sara   They'll be playing pitch-and-toss at the back of the inn. With the stable boys. There'll be whisky going spare from the tenants' dinner. If the farmers drink, why shouldn't the men?

Liza   But not Kello . . . Kello was here . . . Bella Menteith . . . Maggie thinks . . . I wasn't going to the stables, I was going to the dairy . . .

Sara (*ushering* **Liza** *over to the cradle*)   Go and sit with the bairns, my burdie. Go on now, till Maggie gets back. Look after wee Joe. (*Takes her arm, pats her, soothes her – but it's* **Tottie** *who's on her mind.*) Tottie?

Tottie   No.

Sara   Where have you been?

Tottie   No.

Sara   Where have you been?

Tottie   Nowhere.

Sara   You went to the stable?

Tottie   No.

Sara   Then where have you –

Tottie   NO.

Big and strong, or small and wiry – she's more than a match for **Sara** *when roused, as now – she pushes, or threatens* **Sara***, and moves away. But she's scared . . . and she doesn't move all that far, stays onstage somewhere.* **Sara** *turns away, but stays onstage somewhere.*

Scene Nine

Maggie *is summoned before the maister. He's trying to piece together what really happened. She is answering his questions. The others are present, also summoned to the maister's 'Inquiry'. There are whisperings before/just as **Maggie** speaks – Bella Menteith's name being whispered.*

Maggie   Bella Menteith! Well, she's wrong, Maister Elliott. It wasn't like she said. Tottie wasn't – Tottie wouldn't –

Listens to the maister's questions.

Yes, sir. Well: Liza came screaming, and I ran to the stables, and Kello was lying at the foot of the ladder, and Bella Menteith –

Listens to the maister's questions.

Yes, sir. It was dusk. It was getting on for dark. But there was a light in the stables and another in the chamber. But they were all down at the inn, the men, so why would Kello – ?

Listens to the maister's questions.

No, sir. I never saw Tottie. I saw Bella Menteith. Kneeling over Kello. There was straw in her hair.

Listens to the maister's questions.

Yes, sir, I know that, sir. I know what she says. She said it all to me too, right there in the stables: she said she happened to be passing and she heard an argy-bargy and saw Tottie on the ladder, and that Tottie must have pushed him and that all Tottie said was 'it serves yourself right!'. She said Tottie laughed and laughed up there on the ladder and yelled 'it serves yourself right'. I don't believe her, Maister Elliott. It wasn't like she said.

Listens to the maister.

Yes, sir – I know Tottie deaves all the men – Yes, sir, I know she's always after Kello, but she never wished him harm, sir, she's only a bairn. That night of the kirn – there was blood on her claes. He got off scot-free. She thought she was married –

But the maister cuts her short.

Yes, sir. (. . .) Thank *you*, sir.

She is dismissed, turns away, and her next words are not for the maister, but to herself, or maybe for **Sara***, and the others.*

Bella Menteith! It wasn't like she said. There was straw in her hair.

*As **Maggie** goes, **Sara** is putting on a black shawl, picking up a bible.*

Children (*or children's voices*)
Doctor, doctor, quick, quick, quick!
The black-eyed ploughman's sick, sick, sick!

Look at the blood coming out of his head!
Doctor, doctor, surely he's – ?

Sara   So he died, and was waked. With pennies on his eyes and salt on his breast . . .
Poor Kello. He was daft himself, if the truth be known. But he had that knack – horses,
women – they softened at the very sound of his voice. And yet . . . no heart . . . no
thought . . . no soul. That's what was wrong. If the truth be known. He wasn't all there.
Poor young Kello. He was the one who wasn't all there.

Children (*or their voices. They are running around, playing at ghosties, laughing, enjoying scaring
each other*)
Oooooooh! Here's Kello!
Here's a ghostie/ Here's a bogle!
Oooooooh! Here's Kello!
Kello's coming to get you!
Tottie's seen a ghostie, Kello's ghostie!
Tottie's a daftie!
No all there!
Here's Tottie – Ooooh!

*Shrieks of delighted fear. If they are present, and not just voices, they are flapping cloths   aprons,
headhankies? – as they dart for* **Tottic,** *then dart away again in fear.* **Tottie** *trying to catch them, or
hit at them.*

Hideaway, hideaway!
Hogmanay, Hogmanick!
Hang the baker!
Hang Tottie!
Tottie's going to jaaaail!
Stone walls, iron bars.
They're going to put you awaaay!
Hang the baker ower the stick.
Hang the rope round Tottie's neck.

Tottie *lunges at them. They shriek – and run away. They are hiding somewhere, giggling, whispering,
shushing.*

Maggie(**'s voice**) (*insouciant, without serious censure*)   Now then, my burdies, what are you
up to? Eh?

Child's voice   Tottie's in a swither!

Scene Ten

Tottie, *two* **Warders, Maggie, Sara. Maggie** *and* **Sara** *are working somewhere, preferably in
the field, away from the rest of the action.* **Sara** *knows what is about to happen, but can't bear to be
there.*

Tottie, *still upset, relieved the taunting bairns have gone. Approaches the cradle, but warily since nowadays she's not allowed near. She picks up the baby's cane rattle – the old type with a bell inside the cane ball. Plays with it a bit . . . goes on playing with it while she's talking – her story seemingly less important than her concentration on the toy, as children seem, when they're trying to impart something that deeply troubles. She doesn't look at the baby, wrapped in her own world.*

Tottie (*not so maternal to the baby as she used to be*)   I'll tell you a story if you like – it's true . . . He was up there in the chamber. He heard me coming up the ladder. Creepy, crawlie up the ladder. 'We don't need you!' he shouted. 'We don't need you now! Tak your hook, you!' He tried to kick me off the ladder. He hadn't any boots on, but I fell off, he made me fall. Ding! And the ladder fell. Clatter! – Bang! And he fell, Kello, from the top, from the trapdoor . . . dunt!

Two figures in grey cloaks – **Warders** *– are creeping up on her. One of them is holding a blanket, or sheet – or maybe they are holding it between them.*

He wasn't hurt bad – he didn't make a noise. Then she started to scream up there in the chamber. Her! Huh! She couldn't get down – and it served herself right – he was giving her the clock and the dresser and the bed – he was giving her the baby – Whoosh! – I heard. Creepy, crawlie up the ladder –

She breaks off somewhere in the last line as she senses the two behind her, turns round sharply. They have the sheet ready for the capture.

(*Faltering, placating, retreating.*) What fettle? Do you want a story? I'll tell you a story. I'll tell you a story of Jackanory.

They have taken hold of her, one on each side. She is paralysed with fear, so doesn't struggle, at first. They wind the sheet around her.

Tottie No!

Sara (*she stops work, she's in pain,* **Tottie**'s *anguish is piercing her*)   Oh, no!

The **Warders** *make a straitjacket of the sheet; in two or three well-practised movements, that take* **Tottie** *by surprise, they have made her their prisoner.*

Tottie No! No!

The two **Warders** *are hustling* **Tottie** *away.*

Sara *and* **Tottie** *both cry out 'NO' two or three times – not in unison – but we can hardly tell which cries come from whom.*

Maggie (*has been watching* **Sara** *anxiously*)   Sara?

Sara (*flatly, not speaking to* **Maggie**)   No.

Maggie Sara?

Sara No.

Maggie (*not directly to* **Sara**. *Even* **Maggie** *realises* **Sara** *is beyond conventional comfort at a time like this*)   You can't keep your eyes in the back of your head. She'll be looked after where she's going. Poor maimed creature. The sheriff was right – she'll be better off there. Lucky it's not the jail. (*Lower.*) Lucky it's not the noose! And you won't have to pay for her keep. The well-off pay, but not the poor. There's a ward for the paupers –

Sara No!

Maggie I didn't mean ought. Be sensible, Sara – look at it this –

Sara I'll pay for my daughter, Patie's daughter. I'll pay.

Ellen *has appeared by now.* **Liza** *also – but not with* **Ellen**.

Sara (*turning to* **Ellen**, *a plea:*) I'll work.

But **Ellen** *doesn't speak.*

Maggie (*to* **Ellen**, *a reminder:*) It's only ten days till the Hiring. The maister hasn't spoken yet.

Ellen The maister's out. The Elliotts are out. The lease is up – out – terminated. The great Lord Marquis has had enough: the foreign visitors, the mortgages, the politics. Maister Elliott got above himself, it seems: he supports the six-pound rise, he's standing for parliament. The Marquis is angry, very angry. The lease is up and not to be renewed. There'll be no Speaking at Blacksheils. Not this year. We'll be moving on too. Like the rest of you. (. . .) Will you come with us, Sara? I won't keep Betty Hope on. I'd rather have you.

Sara (*she is still in shock at* **Tottie***'s incarceration*) But where will you go?

Ellen (*a gesture – where indeed?*) We'll not get a lease round these parts. The Marquis owns all the farms round here.

Sara (*refusing the offer*) These fields are my calf-ground.

Ellen (*softly*) Mine too.

Sara I've nothing else now.

Ellen *turns away, goes.*

Maggie (*getting back to work again, picking up a bucket to feed or milk the cow*) It'll be cold for the Hiring. Bound to be. It's been a long winter – and more snow to come! (*Wistfully.*) I'd like a house with the two rooms. Maybe we'll get to Langriggs . . .

Maggie *goes off.*

Sara
She would tell me these stories, she said they were true.
She 'saw' them, she said, on the moor, in the mist.
In a hundred years – more –
We'll be ghosts in the fields,
But we'll cry out in vain,
For there'll be no one there.
Fields without folk.
Machines without horses.

A whole week's harvest
All done in one night,
By the light of great lamps . . .
Not the light of the moon,
They won't wait for the moon . . . no need for the moon . . .

Liza   Sara? . . . We'll maybe both get to the same farm, Sara   If we do – will you teach me to spin?

Bondagers

'What's it about?' they ask before you even start to write (because of commissioning, funding, programming). Loathsome question. Of course you know – but just maybe you don't. For me, a play starts as shadows in the mind. A fused vision where a fifty-acre field (or factory floor, or housing estate) and the limiting but magical parameters of the theatre space, are one and the same thing: a real world. In this world the characters move, interact, grow – that's when you discover what they, and you, are 'about'.

Tottie, at first, was to say very little. A strong presence, not much dialogue. (I looked forward to this, something different.) But Tottie saw the 'lang syne' ploughman. She needed to tell us things. Soon she stood for the land, and not long after Kello came to stand for our (sometimes criminal) carelessness.

Shadows in my mind. And in this particular play, shadows in the fields. That's also, partly, what *Bondagers* is 'about'. More agricultural advances have been made in the last two hundred years than in the previous eight thousand. (The bondagers used a sickle that the ancient Egyptians would have recognised.) I'm not talking of nostalgia, I'm talking of cycles: periods of plenty, optimism, progress – relentlessly interrupted by leaner, less happy, less confident times: bad weather, bad harvests, bad government, disease . . . and sometimes the unfortunate, sometimes the devastating, consequences of our own innovations and discoveries. And so the ghosts in the field come and go.

But plays are not historical/sociological documentaries. The dialogue here is not authentic 1860-speak. How could it be? No reliable record of the speech of the fields (or the streets, or even of the drawing-rooms) survives. (Letters and diaries can only give clues; people do not talk as they write.) The function of the language in *Bondagers* is dramatic: to help the audience believe in the time, the place, and above all, the characters. It is honest: I do not use any Scots that the bondagers might not have used. It is not very broad Scots because I am not writing solely for a Scottish (far less a Border) audience. And if it is inconsistent – well, the Scots I hear around me every day, and the Scots that I use myself, is inconsistent: we say 'hoose' or 'noo' or 'sleekit' in one sentence, and 'house' or 'now' or 'sly' in another; and this for many, and definite, reasons: the mood, and rhythm of the sentence; the passion or humour of the speaker.

It was the actress Muriel Romanes who first told me about the bondagers, suggested I should write about them; encouraged, calmed, enthused in the appropriate measures that writers need, and playwrights, since their work must eventually be interpreted by others, need most of all. Anne M. Scott, the artist, told me more still, during the most beautiful November surely to be seen in Kelso or anywhere else. At Hawick Public Library Hugh Mackay directed me to sources that I had despaired of finding. Liz Taylor, the Border journalist, lent me valuable notes of her own (no writer does this lightly).

An award made on the strength of the script before rehearsals even start is a canny bonus for a dramatist. It gives her – and others, too? – a prop, an extra limb – of confidence – to lean on. Confidence breeds confidence. And financial help breeds confidence: without the LWT Plays on Stage Award we might have had one actor less: Ellen doubling as Jenny. (I couldn't contemplate it now.) Certainly we would have had less rehearsal, less music, less publicity. However the production would always have been Ian's – and the cast's. They believed the fifty-acre fields were there, within the cramped parameters of the old Traverse space. Two years later they revealed them again, with an even finer magic, in the new theatre building.

Sue Glover
October 1994

Sue Glover was born in Edinburgh, and now lives in North-East Fife. She writes for radio, television and theatre. Theatre work includes *The Seal Wife*, *The Bubble Boy*, *The Straw Chair*, *Sacred Hearts*. *The Bubble Boy* was one of the Glasgow Tron Theatre's opening season, and was later televised, winning prizes at both the New York Film and Television Festival, and the Chicago International Festival. *The Straw Chair* opened the Traverse Theatre's 25th Anniversary season, and was the first Traverse production to be toured by that theatre in its home country, Scotland. *Bondagers* won first prize in London Weekend Television's Plays on Stage Awards in 1990. At present Sue Glover is working on a commission for the Royal National Theatre Studio (working title, *Kinder*), and on a television project about the 'Glasgow Girls', the talented group of female artists who attended the Glasgow School of Art at the turn of the century.

Julie Allardyce

Duncan McLean

Julie Allardyce was first performed at The Lemon Tree, West North Street, Aberdeen, on 23 November 1993, in a co-production between Boilerhouse and The Lemon Tree. The cast was as follows:

Julie Allardyce	Katrina Caldwell
David Mitchell	Peter Burnett
Finn Finlay	Micky MacPherson
Gary Grant	Andrew Wardlaw
Angela Bruce	Vicki Masson
Drew Allardyce	Steve Webb

Other characters were doubled by the cast and further non-speaking parts were played by: Denise Chapman, Duncan Craig, Linda Davidson, Victoria McLennan, Kim Smith.

Directed by Paul Pinson
Designed by Bryan Angus
Lighting Designer Tariq Hussain
Music Ken Slaven
Boilerhouse administrator Rachael Bailey
The Lemon Tree administrator Shona Powell

Characters

Julie Allardyce, *twenty-two, ROV operator, originally from near Fyvie*
David Mitchell, *going out with Julie, roustabout, Aberdonian*
Finn Finlay, *from a southern Scottish city, another ROV operator*
Gary Grant, *operations – 'ops' – controller on the rig*
Angela Bruce, *Julie's best friend since school, unemployed, with a young kid*
Drew Allardyce, *Julie's brother, a couple of years older than her, works the family farm*

There are various minor parts with a few lines, e.g. David's mother and father, ship's chandler; and opportunities for as many non-speaking actors as possible, e.g. drummers, other rig workers, wedding guests.

Note   The accents of the characters have not been represented phonetically in the script; standard spelling has been used throughout. But strong north-east voices are written into the rhythms and syntax of the north-east characters, and it is intended that the actors should also use the vowel and consonant sounds appropriate to their character's age and background.

The play is set in the present day, in and around Aberdeen, including some scenes on an offshore drilling rig.

1 Getting there

The audience is sitting in a helicopter, about to fly offshore. The lights go down to black, the engines start up, whining, and gradually build to a deafening roar; there is music in this as well as real industrial noise. Take off. The seats shake and rattle violently. From time to time a distorted radio-voice can be heard saying something indecipherable.

Ahead is a narrow field of vision, sharply lit against the black. Across it bright colours begin to flash: green and yellow, green and yellow, blue and green, blue and green, blue and blue, blue and white, and blue and blue. Then a black appears, a blue and a black and more blues, then another black, then more blacks gradually taking over from the blue till there is only black. The space is filled with dense black – it's impenetrable, but not static: flowing, billowing, rippling – and the movement builds to a climax along with the noise of the helicopter engine.

Then both stop us, for a second, a large white H inside a circle is visible. Touchdown on the platform. Without any let-up, the H is replaced by an enormous roaring red and orange flame overhead. After a few seconds, dozens of small bright lights become visible against the overall darkness: stars and ships and rigs scattered across the sea and sky.

2 A proposal

Two figures appear and lean against a railing, standing close together, looking out to sea. The flare burns above them, lighting their faces with flickering red and orange. After a few seconds' silence, they speak.

David Will you marry me?

Julie Aye, okay then.

Immediately music bursts out, loud and tuneful and joyous: bits of the Wedding March and Scottish dance music especially, but also snatches of a hundred different tunes and moods: all the music from the rest of the play speeded up and sampled and mixed together. Again bright colours swirl about, dominated by white and green around **Julie***, blue circling both of them. The cast performs the whole play in thirty seconds, in abstract, concentrating on the aspects – and mostly the happy aspects – of* **Julie** *and* **David** *as a couple. A few seconds from the end, there is a glimpse of red and black, red and black, before it's back to the white and green and blue again and the movement and the music stop.* **Julie** *and* **David** *stand alone at the railing, the flare burning overhead.*

Julie But we'll have to keep it quiet.

David What!

Julie You ken the rules: no happy couples allowed offshore.

David It's not like we're doing it on the drill floor!

Julie As soon as they spot signs of happiness, we're back on the beach like a shot.

David Aye, Grant'd love that: any excuse to cause a bittie more misery!

Julie And then what? We'd get alternate shifts, we'd only meet at Dyce – you coming in just as I was going out – 'Hi Julie', 'Aye aye Davy' – no way to start a married life!

David (*looking out over the water*)   Delta looks hell of a close thenight.

Julie We'll just have to make on like we're your average bears with a sore head . . .

David It looks like you could swim it.

Julie I'd like to see you try.

He climbs up on the railing, as if about to jump. She laughs.

David Are you not going to stop me then?

Julie You'd never do it! You haven't the guts!

David And you have, like?

Julie The way I feel just now I could *jump* it, never mind swim it!

She climbs up onto a railing and makes on she's about to leap. He pulls her back, laughing.

David You're mad, Julie Allardyce!

Julie No, just in love.

David (*the start of a game they play:*)   In love? With who?

Julie With you!

David With me?

Julie With you and me and the whole North Sea! (*She climbs up on the railing again, facing out to the sea, and shouts:*) Julie Allardyce loves you!

She lets herself fall backwards off the railing, and **David** *catches her – it's like a scene from a silent film, them playing the role of the lovers – and they embrace and go to kiss. But somebody walks out towards them:* **Grant**, *going about his business.* **David** *and* **Julie** *split apart and disappear into the shadows before he gets to them. He looks after them – fairly casually, without any melodramatic emphasis – then goes on with his work, which is to shout the line that opens the next scene:*

Grant Mitchell, get those boxes shifted!

3 Lowering

Bright daylight. The noise of an oil rig at work. Drills, generators, motors; clanging and hammering; the wind, the sea; shouts, tannoy. A steady green light shines, indicating all is normal.

David *is working loading stores from one place to another. This is repetitive and hard: he lifts a heavy box from one pile, carries it ten metres, then dumps it in another pile. There are a hundred boxes to shift.* **Grant**, *the deck foreman, is watching him, every so often directing* **David** *as to exactly which box should be picked up next and precisely where it should be dumped; he checks his watch and clipboard often, and keeps* **David** *moving fast.* **Grant** *keeps an eye on everything going on around the deck of the* *rig, wandering about from time to time to have a closer look at something. In the foreground, at the edge of the moonpool,* **Julie** *and* **Finn** *are doing work that appears more absorbing: pre-dive checks on the ROV.*

The noise of the rig at work carries on throughout the scene, almost like a musical score: sometimes the dialogue is echoed, sometimes almost drowned out.

Julie   How's the docking dogs?

Finn   All three dogs secured.

Julie   On the lip?

Finn   On the fucking lip.

Julie   Docking bullet in place?

Finn   Docking bullet fucking home. I'll go and check the cable.

Julie   I already checked the cable.

Finn   I'll double fucking check.

Julie   Checked?

Finn   Check. The cable's fucking coiled.

Julie   The drum's wound – I checked.

Finn   I fucking know you fucking did, or it wouldn't been a fucking double fucking check, would it?

Julie   A fucking double fucking check?

Finn   Fucking right.

Julie   Glad I got something right.

Finn   You're always fucking right, that's why I fucking hate you.

Julie   Get out from inside that bight!

Finn   Jesus fucking Christ! There you go, right again!

Julie   It's not that I don't hate you too . . .

Finn   Right about the bight!

Julie   . . . but I don't want your blood on my machine when you're minced by the cable.

Finn   *(stepping out from inside cable)*   Ready to fucking go then.

Julie   I'll tell Control.

Finn   So you're getting the fucking inside job a-fucking-gain?

Julie   You're so good on the winch Finn, that . . .

Finn   Fuck off.

They both work at the winch for a few seconds; the ROV rises up and swings out over the sea. **Julie** *feeds its cable out, making sure it's not twisting etc. When it's in position she leaves the winch and goes into the control shack, sits down in front of the video screens, and picks up the phone there.*

Julie (*she dials the phone*)   ROV module to Rig Control. Aye, that time again. Just to let you ken. All clear to launch? Good. Eh, fifty to a hundred metres depth, corrosion check on the north-west leg. Sure. Aye. Bye. (*Shouting out the door.*) They've given us clear Finn. Ready to go?

Finn   Fucking right I'm fucking ready.

He works at the winch while **Julie** *returns to watch the videos. The screen in front of her is represented by a bright light shining in her face. Over the course of the next few lines all other lighting fades away.*

Julie   The raising and lowering, it's the one bit of the job I don't like. I hate it when the ROV's stuck out there in its cage. It's like a dolphin lying on your kitchen table: out of its natural element. But just wait till it gets in the water, then you'll see what it's all about! Dangling about there, swaying and swinging, inching down to the sea – just when I want to get zooming on, on and under the water, aye, that's where me and the ROV should be.

Finn   Okay Julie, ready to drop the fucker.

Julie   This is what it's all about, where you get to grips with the splash zone. (*She puts her hands out to the screen light.*) This is where life gets worth living.

Finn   It's factory work, fuck all else: maintaining and training and checking and trimming: the fact that you're half-way to Norway makes fuck all difference most of the time.

Julie   (*she picks up the screen light. It is a portable lamp with a narrow intense beam. For the moment, it still illuminates her head and hands*)   Union Street looks narrow to the likes of me, it's a single-track back-of-beyond dead-end compared to where I drive. Up and down the North Sea. I drive up and down and east and west and north and south. And I don't drive a Ford or a Datsun or a Beamer. I don't drive a tractor or a bus or a bike. I drive an ROV: remotely operated vehicle.

Finn   (*looking over the edge*)   She's in the fucking water!

The sea has been lying flat beneath them. Now it starts to rise in waves around **Julie** *and* **Finn**. *As the ROV goes through the splash zone, the sea whips up in a frenzy of blue and white.*

Julie   And we're through the swell and the waves: welcome to my world. (*She stands up, moving the lamp so its beam is shining out in front of her.*) Five metres, ten, fifteen. Down a bit more then I'll let off the clamps, release the rams – eighteen, nineteen, twenty – and *out* we go, out of the cage into freedom, freedom! (*She leaves her seat and wanders around inside the sea, the light beaming out through the waves.*) Where the water's over deep for divers, the ROV goes twice as deep. And in my head, and on the screens, I go scouting with it. Headlights on in the dark black depths, and I see things that no one's seen, the floor of the sea, the rocks and the sand, the fish and the weed and the reefs and the wrecks. I've eyes as sharp as a shark's, see landshifts under pipelines or cracks in concrete platforms through water dark as squid ink. In control, in front of the monitors, the joystick and the instrument panels; I'm the one in the driving seat.

The blue of the sea begins to be replaced by black. By the end of **Julie***'s lines, she is completely surrounded by swirling dark waters. Likewise, faint noises of the sea – gurgling water, winds, foghorns and hooters, sonar beeps – fade in, get louder and louder, till by the end of the speech they are almost drowning her out. Through it all she works with great concentration.*

Julie   Half a ton, six feet long, half a million quid! One thousand miles by five hundred miles by three thousand metres of the world's coldest, blackest, stormiest water and it's mine to wander in! Julie Allardyce, twenty-two, eighteen grand a year! To boldly go where no Julie's gone before: down and down and down and down and down and down and down . . .

The black swirls viciously around **Julie***, hiding her completely: blackout.*

4   In dreams

The sea noises mix with and gradually change into general storm noises: waves crashing, wind howling, the rig creaking. Lights up inside the smoko shack, where the deck workers are sheltering, **Grant** *paces up and down.* **Julie** *stares into space.* **David** *and* **Finn** *play cards.*

Grant   Jesus Christ, this weather!

Nobody responds.

Grant   Do you know how much this is costing us?

Finn   It's not costing me anything.

Grant   It's costing the company though – fucking millions! – and anything that costs the company costs us all in the long run.

Finn   Bollocks.

Grant   (*looks out a window*)   I reckon the wind's dropping a bit lads.

An enormous gust of wind shakes the shack, and water smashes against the window.

David   If you ever leave the oil, Mr Grant, don't go for a job as a weather forcaster.

Grant   See in Saudi? You don't get weather like this out there!

Finn   Aye, and you don't get a fucking drink either, so fuck that for a game of soldiers.

Grant   Anybody has drink out *here* is fucked, and don't you forget it, Finlay. (*Glances at* **Julie**.) And another thing that should be banned: women. No more women working offshore!

David   There's only about twenty as it is, for fuck's sake.

Grant Ah, that's the way it used to be, when we still had our heads screwed on. But nowadays they're popping up left right and centre.

Finn I wish one would pop up in my bunk.

Grant Exactly; they come offshore and they start stirring things up. We're meant to be doing a job of work out here, but you start bringing women into it and straight away men's minds get distracted – am I not right Mitchell? – and before you know it there's ill discipline and mistakes being made and rows breaking out: some men just can't handle having women close by, eh Mitchell?

David *looks completely blank.*

Grant Before you know it the whole rig's just in an uproar.

Finn *and* **David** *look at each other, then over at* **Julie**, *who is sitting still, in silence, apparently not hearing at all what the others are saying.*

Finn Hey, Julie.

Julie Eh?

David Cheer up Julie.

Finn Julie's always fucking cheerful.

Julie Aye, I am, but I just . . . had something nagging at me.

David Aye, it was Mr Grant . . .

Finn Do you hear the uproar you're causing out here. It's a fucking disgrace girl! The whole North Sea's whipped up into a frenzy of ill discipline and rows cause of you!

Julie What shite are you talking now, Finn?

Finn It's not me Julie, it's Mr Ops Controller here, he was giving us a wee educational lecture while rain stopped play. Is that not right Mr Grant?

Grant Another thing is, can you tell me, has it ever been *scientifically proved* that women can do the job as well as men?

David Has it been proved that they can't?

Grant Ah, but innocent till proved guilty Mitchell! Men have been innocently going about their lives for thousands of years – taking the *man*'s share of the hard work – and all of a sudden women start saying that they can work just as hard. Well, fuck me with a drill pipe, could they not just've left things the way they were? Mark my words, the day'll soon come when women are banned to the beach.

Finn In your dreams, Grant . . .

Julie (*claps her hands, turns to* **Finn**, *suddenly full of energy*) That's it Finn, a dream! It was a dream!

Finn What?

Julie I had these pictures going through my head, but I couldn't understand them. It was nagging at me: was that a film I saw? did it happen to me sometime? was it a story I read? But no, now I ken, it was a dream! And I never dream! Usually I just come straight awake as soon as the alarm goes, ken, awake and straight into the business of the day. I haven't bothered with dreams for years. But last night I had one. It was so real! Christ, it's hard to believe that's all it was. I really thought I was out on the deck there, at the side of the moonpool.

David Well, you were out there yesterday.

Julie Aye, but this was different, cause yesterday Finn was working with me. In my dream I was all alone, just me and the ROV. It wasn't behaving just right, so I'd opened a front pod and had my hand inside it, working away, checking the circuit boards. Then suddenly something gripped my hand. Inside the pod something had a hold of my fingers and was trying to pull them in. I snatch my hand away, but it comes just an inch then gets gripped again, and now something sharp's biting my skin. My skin's tearing, more the more I pull away, and under the skin the bones are being squeezed till they crush. I bang my free hand on the side of the ROV and yell with the pain. But no one's around to help me: the deck's empty of folk.

Grant Where were you Finlay? You should've been there as well.

Julie But there *was* a voice, a voice murmuring something . . . I looked around, my hand tearing and crushing inside the pod as I jerked this way and that. No one in sight, but still the voice.

ROV (*a voice over the tannoy*) Feed me, I'm hungry, feed me.

Julie My hand's being mangled. I try to scream out, but the voice speaks again.

ROV Feed me, I'm hungry, feed me.

Julie I stare at the ROV. 'Let me go,' I say. 'You can't eat me.' And for a second there's silence, and I think, My God, I'm going mad, talking to a machine! Then the voice comes again.

ROV Feed me, I'm hungry, feed me.

Julie 'You can't eat me, you'd be lost without me, wouldn't know where to go, wouldn't know how to get there. You can't eat me, let me go!'

ROV But I'm hungry, you wouldn't let me starve would you? You're supposed to look after me, but now you're letting me starve! Feed me!

Julie And its teeth close tighter on my flesh and bone. 'You can't eat me now, I'm getting married theday.' Cause suddenly I mind I'm meant to be at the kirk, at my wedding, not out on the rig; already I'm hell of a late. 'Let me go thenow, and I'll come back later and feed you.'

ROV I'll be *really* hungry by then. (*It laughs.*) But okay Julie, it's a deal, come back later and feed me well and I'll let you go just now.

Julie 'Thanks,' I say, and go to pull my hand out, but just as I do there's a stabbing pain, and a grinding noise, a tearing, riving agony, and my hand comes away, gouting with blood, and the ROV's making clanking chewing noises and laughing away to itself. I lift my hand up before my eyes, and then I scream out loud. 'The wedding's off! Call off the marriage! I'll never get married now!'

ROV Why's that, Julie?

Julie And I stare at my hand, my left hand, the hand with one finger eaten away, the third finger on my left hand, ripped off inside the ROV's mouth. Nowhere to put the ring!

Julie *ends up with her supposedly mutilated hand held up in front of her. She stares at it in horror. The story has been told so convincingly that everyone else is staring at her hand too. After a couple of seconds,* **Finn** *breaks the tension.*

Finn Do you want an elastoplast for that?

David Jesus, what a nightmare.

Grant Hold on a minute, what's all this about a wedding?

Julie I'm *glad* I don't usually dream! Better off without them!

Grant No, just cause any change of circumstances should be reported to the company, and I don't recall reading that you were getting married.

David What?

Grant And who are you getting married to Julie? Anybody we know? I mean this could be important.

Julie Eh, Mr Grant . . . it was a dream.

Grant Is that all? No plans even?

Julie Who do you think I am? Nostrajulius, predicting the future in my sleep?

David Aye, good question though Julie: what the fuck does it *mean*, eh?

Finn It means she's been reading too much Stephen fucking King again.

Grant See what I mean lads? Women: they're off in a fucking dream world! And we trust her with company ROVs that cost millions of quid! The whole production relies on her sometimes, and she's away in a dream world!

Julie I was asleep in my cabin at the time.

Finn (*laughs*) Ach, excuses!

Grant (*looks outside*) The weather's definitely turning: on deck, you work-shy cunts.

The others groan, but follow him out as he opens the door of the shack. Immediately they are battered by a raging gale, and torrents of blue and black water wash around and above them, swallowing them completely. Mixed in with the wind and water noises is a foghorn, blasting away: short short long, short short long.

5   From The Crow's Nest

A brightly lit stair. **Julie** *is standing at the door of her friend* **Angela**'s *flat in one of the Seaton blocks. She reaches out and presses the doorbell, a foghorn sounds. The door opens.*

Angela   Julie!

Julie   That's a hell of a funny doorbell you've got!

Angela   Mental, eh? The old guy that lived here afore me was a sailor, ken?

Julie   Well, he got a good view of the sea, I suppose.

Angela   God aye. If you go out on the balcony on a windy night you get spray off the beach on your face.

Julie   Nah!

Angela   Aye!

Julie   Thirteen floors up?

Angela   Aye! The old guy had a nameplate on the door, 'The Crow's Nest', but I took it down. Didn't want anybody calling me an old bird!

Julie   So, Angela, can I come in? Or do you entertain your pals on the doormat these days?

Angela   No, no, come in. But shh! Quiet in the lobby, or you'll wake him up.

Julie (*pausing on the point of entering*)   Wake who?

Angela   Derek! Who else?

Julie   For a second I thought you'd maybe taken Crazy Colin back.

Angela   No chance. He doesn't even ken where I'm living these days, and he's not going to find out.

Julie   What do you tell Derek?

Angela   He asked me once where his daddy was, and I says he was dead. Well, I said he was in heaven.

Julie   Colin Birse in heaven? That's a good one!

Angela   Stranger things've happened . . . maybe.

Julie   Aye, they have, and I've got one to tell you thenow.

They go into the living-room of **Angela**'s *flat.* **Julie** *sits on the settee, looks around;* **Angela** *clears up toys and books from the floor, slings them into a box.*

Julie   So, settling in okay are you?

Angela   Settling in? I've been here near a year!

Julie   Christ, is it that long?

Angela   Aye, it's that long.

Julie   Well, I . . . hey, *you* could've given *me* a ring too!

Angela   Ach, you and your high-flying lifestyle . . . I thought you'd given up on the likes of me: work-shy doley scroungers.

Julie   Don't be daft. I've just, I don't ken, I never seem to have time and . . . I did send you a Christmas card.

Angela   Oh aye, and thanks for Derek's presents: he loved that book where you pressed the buttons and it made the noise of a helicopter and a fire engine and that.

Julie   Did you tell him I was coming?

Angela   No. He'd just've wanted to bide up and see you, he'd've been up for hours. Me and you'd never've got a chance to talk.

Julie   Do you think he'd mind who I was?

Angela   Oh definitely: his Aunty Julie. Something reminds him whiles, and he asks after you.

Julie   Aunty Julie!

Angela   It's funny, he doesn't call his real aunties Aunty, he just calls them by their names. It's only you gets the honour of Aunty.

Julie   Maybe cause they're younger, like.

Angela   Maybe.

Julie   Though I suppose they're . . .

Angela   Carrie's fifteen and Lauren's sixteen.

Julie   Is that right? Still, that is hell of a young.

Angela   Just kids.

Julie   You couldn't've told me that when I was sixteen. 'Just a kid!'

Angela   Ha! You thought you were the last word.

Julie   What? So did you!

Angela   Aye, but I *was* the last word, that's the difference.

Both laugh.

Julie   Aye, you were a bad lot Angie-baby. A glue sniffer. My daddy told me about folk like you.

Angela   Mind that time I got you to spray that graffiti outside the science block? 'Sandra Tait is a blowjob!'

Julie   Hih. I never even kent what a blowjob was!

Angela   Did you not?

Julie   I thought it was something to do with hairdressing.

Both laugh.

Angela   Here, Julie.

Julie   What?

Angela   What *is* a blowjob?

Both laugh.

Julie   If you don't ken by now . . .

Both   . . . you never will.

Angela   Aye, but think about it, eh Julie? What if we had known then what we know now?

Julie   This is it, I did know then! Like when we were about ten and we all hated loons, just couldn't stand them, and everybody was saying how they were never going to get married and that. I mind you saying you'd never have nothing to do with men as long as you lived!

Angela   I should've listened to myself, eh?

Julie   But all the time folk were saying this, and I was kind of going along with it, I was really thinking, no, everybody does get married and I'm not going to be left out; I don't ken *why* they get married, but whatever it is changes and makes them, well, that'll happen to me as well I bet! I kent then that that would happen to me. And now it has: I'm getting married.

Angela   You were so *logical* about everything, Julie! Such a *sensible* bitch! But . . . hold on! What did you just say?

Julie   Eh . . . aye. That's what I was wanting to tell you.

Angela   Wooo! So who is the lucky bugger?

Julie   What do you mean who is it – it's David of course! Do you think I'd go out with him for two and a half year, then marry some other body all of a sudden? Terrible waste of effort!

Angela   What does your brother think?

Drew *wanders across the stage singing the start of the classic Strathdon ballad, 'Drumallochie'.*
Angela *and* **Julie** *don't see him. The feeling should be quite ghostly; there could be a fiddle playing softly behind him.*

Drew
'Twas on a chill November's night when fruits and flowers were gone
One evening as I wandered forth upon the banks of Don
I overheard a fair maid and sweetly thus sang she
'My love he's far from Sinnahard and from Drumallochie'

Drew *whistles or hums a few more bars as he wanders off, then back to the women as if nothing has happened.*

Julie (*surprised at her question*)   Drew? Who cares! Damn all to do with him! Why?

Angela *avoids answering the question by getting up and wandering out the glass door at the end of the room.*

Julie   Where are you going?

Angela   It's a fine night, I fancied a seat on the balcony.

Julie (*following her*)   There's no seats out here . . .

Angela   Not *in* the balcony, *on* it.

The two of them sit on the ledge. **Angela** *is calm, gazes out over the lights of the city, but* **Julie** *peers anxiously down for a while, before speaking again.*

Julie   We're going to see David's ma and da the morn. Tell them the good news.

Angela   How do you get on with them?

Julie   Better than you get on with yours.

Angela   Well, that's not saying much.

Julie (*thinks*)   They must like to see Derek though?

Angela   Oh aye, they're all over him! They forget all the weeks they spent persuading me to kill him.

Julie   What?

Angela   To have an abortion.

Julie (*pause*)   Aye, they did, didn't they. Still, it's a while ago now.

Angela   Aye. (*Pause.*) He starts school next year.

Julie   You're joking.

Angela   No, really.

Julie   Jesus Christ.

Angela   No, it's good though.

Julie   Aye, it's just . . .

Angela   I'll have a lot more time, ken.

Julie   Aye, it's good. It's just – starting school! – Christ, *we* were at school just the other day!

Angela   Then I'm going to try and get into the college, get some highers. Second time lucky!

Julie   It's unbelievable that you could leave school, have a kid, and before you know it your *own* kid's starting school!

Angela   Course I'd've saved myself a lot of trouble if I'd got them five year ago.

Julie   Ho! Too right! You spent more time slagging me off for being a swot than you did doing any work!

Angela   Course, would I be any better off? I mean if I'd got highers and a job and got married and all that, I'd probably be just *starting* to think about having a kid now. Instead here I am, four years ahead of the game!

Julie   That's one way of looking at it I suppose.

Angela   Aye, my way. There's times I feel like jumping off that balcony, but on the whole I'm really happy the way it's ended up. But then I'd nothing to lose – except Colin. And a lot of bruises. Aye, losing him turned out to be the best thing I ever did. That's the difference atween me and you: you've a lot to lose.

Julie   Aye I have: I've everything! My job. My car. My flat. Aye that's another thing: we were kids just the other day, and now I look round and I've all this stuff, adult stuff attached to me! It's scary sometimes.

Angela   The more you have, the more you have to lose, eh?

Julie   I had to fight to get my training, then to get my job, and now I'm fighting to keep it! Well, I'm keeping my mouth shut to keep it.

Angela   Christ, that must be a struggle for you!

Julie   You're not allowed to be a couple offshore, you see. We had a few fights over it, like, but I think he's seen sense now: after we're married David'll hand in his notice and . . . try and find work on the beach.

Angela   What, like deckchair attendant?

Julie   Eh? Oh! No!

Laughter. **Angela** *jumps up again.*

Julie   Where are you going now?

Angela   The view's so good here, I bet it's even better from the top.

Julie   (*going after her*)   The top of what?

Angela   (*running upstairs now*)   The roof! Come on!

The two of them run up many flights of stairs and onto the flat roof of the block. They go and sit on the edge, legs dangling into twenty floors of space, looking out at the sea.

Angela   So. You must be really happy, Julie.

Julie   What do you mean?

Angela   I was just thinking: you must be really *happy*.

Julie   Like I say, I've got everything I ever wanted.

Angela   Aye. (*Looking at* **Julie**, *doubtful for a moment.*) But . . . are you happy?

Julie   I don't know what you're getting at.

Angela   Well, I haven't got anything that I wanted – I never got to art school, never went out on the ran-dan with Shane MacGowan, never got to travel round the world like I wanted to – but I'm happy. Things've turned out exactly the way I *didn't* want them, but I'm happy. You're the opposite of me, Julie, you've got everything you wanted when you were sixteen – qualifications, money, a good job, your own flat in the middle of town, a good man that's marrying you – everything!

Julie   Aye, there you go: your question's answered.

Angela   But it's not.

Julie   Eh?

Angela   You've got it all, but are you happy with it?

Julie   I never thought about it like that, I never stopped to think about it at all really. I just . . . I just took it for granted. But *am* I happy? Christ, I've no idea!

Angela   I mean I'm not saying you're not . . .

Julie   I ken.

Angela   I was just asking cause I haven't seen you for ages and I wondered . . .

Julie   Aye.

Angela   I mean you probably are.

Julie   Aye. Probably. I'll have to think about it.

Angela   (*after a second's silence to let* **Julie** *think*)   So what's your life going to be like once you're married then?

Julie   I don't know. The same as just now, I suppose, except I'll have a ring on my finger. And we'll spend every night thegether instead of just most nights.

Angela   When you get married Julie . . . you're not just marrying a man, you're marrying a whole life.

Julie   Nah, not me: I've already got a life.

Angela It's like having a baby. You're not just giving birth to a wee greeting and shitting machine, you're giving birth to your *own life* for the next . . . five years . . . twenty years! They don't tell you that, but that's what you find out: the baby changes your whole life. I mean I ken you must've thought about it, you must be pretty sure that this is the man you want, this is the *life* you want, but . . . I just thought I'd mention it.

Julie Aye. Thanks. (*Pause.*) Christ, it's a long way down, isn't it?

6 Bonnie Ythanside

Drew *yanks at* **Julie**'s *arm and pulls her off the balcony ledge and into an argument. They are on the Allardyce farm, Ythanbanks, near Woodhead of Fyvie. The argument starts off being a friendly one, with their fighting being an affectionate brother/sister thing, but after a while there does seem to be real anger bubbling just under the surface, coming out into the open, even.*

Drew What are you like, Julie, coming out here and telling me you're getting married? What are you like for fuck's sake?

Julie Like a sister, I suppose.

Drew Damn the bit.

Julie I don't ken why you're so put out by me getting married . . .

Drew I'm not!

Julie . . . unless it's cause you've never managed it.

Drew Listen, you peenge, there's women queuing up to be the wife on this farm!

Julie Aye, the farm's a good catch. Just a shame you come along with it.

Drew Oh aye, it's all coming out now!

Julie What?

Drew You're out here after the farm! 'A good catch' is it? My arse!

Julie What are you talking about Drew?

Drew This was decided years ago: two hundred acre, there's only a living for one of us here, and it makes sense for it to be me.

Julie (*pause*) I ken that was decided.

Drew I tell you, the living here is a thin one: no way could it support the both of us – let alone . . . somebody else as well.

Julie I've got a job, so has David.

Drew Well keep a hold of them, cause I've got the farm.

Julie I'm not needing to work here.

Drew Too much work for not enough pay, eh?

Julie I just don't fancy it.

Drew You've gone awful sappy, quine. That oil's made you soft, I reckon.

Julie Shows how little you ken about working offshore.

Drew I ken this: you don't impress me Julie.

Julie Do you think that's why I do it?

Drew Maybe.

Julie *takes a swing at* **Drew**. *He dodges it. She tries to hit him again, and this time he has to parry the blow. They circle around, each trying to get a grip or land a blow on the other, till after a few seconds they make a lunge for each other, miss, and* **Drew** *disappears.* **Julie** *is immediately back in conversation with* **David**, *as if nothing had happened.*

David Tell me about it then. I can see it gets to you.

Julie Eh?

David You're always so happy on the way out here, but as soon as we arrive you start getting edgey.

Julie Edgy?

David Aye. What is it – Drew? You always seem to be getting at each other.

Julie That's just kidding though; there's nothing in it.

David Is there not?

Julie Me and Drew . . . we always mess around like that. We get on fine though, always have. When we were kids, right, we had these bunk beds – him up on top, me down below – and it was a brilliant laugh. We'd tell each other stories half the night, things we'd heard on the school bus, or from my granny and granda in Fyvie. We'd just take bits of their stories and add our own bits on when we couldn't remember something. It was great.

David I always wished I had a brother for stuff like that. Or a sister even. Christ, even a dog would've been something! But we lived in this wee flat so . . .

Julie I mind we used to pretend the bunk beds were a ship. We'd hang blankets over the sides and there I'd be working away down in the boiler rooms of the bottom bunk, shovelling coal into the furnaces behind the pillow. And Drew'd be up top, on the bridge, with the compass and the tea tray for a steering wheel. (*Pause.*) I always wanted to be the one up top, steering the ship, but I never got to be. Only boys got to do that. Quines had to stay down in the galleys: galley slaves!

David Where would you have steered for if you'd been captain?

Julie Ach, I don't ken. Nowhere. It was just wanting to be steering was the important bit, not where I was going.

Out of nowhere, **Drew** *jumps on top of* **Julie**, *and they fight again, more seriously this time. They roll around in front of* **David**, *but he doesn't see them. Then the fight suddenly stops again.*

David I always wished I could have a brother or a sister, just for things like that. I missed all that stuff.

Julie You always got on well with your folks though.

David Well, I had to, in a way, I mean it was just me and them in the house. Usually I couldn't bring my pals from school home even, cause my dad was on nights at the printers', and he was asleep all through the day when I wanted to be playing. The main thing when I was a kid was keeping quiet.

Julie Not much wonder you grew up weird!

David Strong but silent, you mean?

Julie Aye, weird.

David And by the time my dad left the printers' I was already started offshore, so . . . (*He shrugs.*) To be honest I'm glad I was, cause I reckon he was even worse for a while after that.

Julie Till you got him the job with security.

David For a year or so he was a nightmare, my mum said. And he'd have to be really bad afore she'd complain.

Julie It's amazing what folk put up with, out of habit just.

Julie *sees* **Drew** *coming, and jumps up to meet the attack. After a few blows, they reach a stalemate, their hands around each other's throat, and they argue instead:*

Julie You always hated me working offshore, cause I earned more siller than you. You can't stand that, a woman showing you up.

Drew Nobody's showing me up. I do good honest work here.

Julie And the work me and David do isn't honest, is that what you're saying?

Drew Maybe.

Julie I'll tell you, Andrew, you don't ken what work is! Honest or dishonest, it's work I've been doing, work that puts pounds in the bank. All you've earned is subsidies, EurofuckingDisney money!

Drew Come on, out with it.

Julie With what?

Drew With what you really want to say. Come on you bastard, say it.

Back to the quiet chat, though **Julie** *is clearly getting more worked up now:*

David Okay, you used to get on so well with him, but when did you fall out?

Julie We never did! We get on fine.

David Julie, anybody can see you just rub each other up the wrong way. What went wrong?

Julie   Nothing went wrong! (*Pause.*) It's just, I suppose, things did start to change atween us around the time that, well, when they found the first tumour in my dad's gut. I was twelve, Drew was about fourteen. From then on he changed, he didn't want anything to do with me after that. He just started hanging around my dad all the time, not even speaking to me.

David   I suppose that's natural, really. I mean if he thought your dad was away to, eh, to die, maybe, I suppose he would've wanted to spend time with him.

Julie   It was three and a half years afore he died.

David   But nobody could've known how long . . .

Julie   It wasn't that Drew wanted to spend time with him, just for the being with him. It was like Drew started copying him, trying to turn into him. Wearing his old bunnets at the age of fourteen for God's sake!

David   I suppose he kent then – sooner than he wanted, maybe – that he'd have to take over the running of Ythanbanks.

Julie (*furious*)   Aye, that's what *he* decided. *He* decided then that *he* would take over, that he would farm the place when dad died. And how about me? He decided I wouldn't get a look in! He decided it was going to be his, he'd have it all himself, there was no place for me there. He decided I'd have to bugger off away from our land and work at something else, only come back for an afternoon once a month and even then not be allowed to have a say in the running of the place. And why? Cause I was handless? Cause I didn't ken about farming? No! Just cause I was a quine and he was a loon, that was all it was, that's what disqualified me from working on the land.

David (*he is shocked; this is the first time there's been such an outburst of bad feeling from* **Julie**) Julie, calm down.

Julie   Calm down? He decided all this when I was bloody twelve. And I never got to say a word about it. That was it. Twelve. Finished. Chucked off the land. Chucked off my own land.

Drew *appears again, and* **Julie** *leaps up to face him. They are both tense, ready to fight, but instead are shouting:*

Drew   Come on, say it.

Julie   No.

Drew   Out with it.

Julie   No, I don't want to.

Drew   Come on, you bastard.

Julie (*with a new ferocity*)   Okay, I want it, I want this land, this is *my* land, not just yours, it belonged to my father and mother, and to my father's mother and father afore, and it's not something that can be taken away from me – even by you. It's inside me. This earth, me, I want it, I need it. See? See, you bugger? It's inside me. It is me. I belong here, this is my home, let me back – let me work here!

Drew (*pause*) Farming's changed, Julie. It's always changing, I ken that, but this past few year it's been quick change, ken? Hard to keep up with. And they're not changes for the better. (*He looks around.*) There's not work for you here. There's nothing for you here.

Julie There is work. Look around! I can see it!

Drew There is work, but there's no money. There's not a living on this land for you any more.

Julie Aye but, no, no . . . look, I told you already, I don't want to work here, I've got a good job, I like my job, the pay's great and . . .

Drew Will you make up your mind then? First you want to come here, then you don't; you swan it over me for years cause you're working in the oil, and now you're turning round and saying . . .

Julie I don't ken what I want. I want Ythanbanks. I know this place so I want to be here, I want to be somewhere I know.

Drew You don't ken this place any more, Julie. You left, and you can't come back.

Julie But I have come back, I'm here!

Drew See that river down there quine? It's still the Ythan, same as when we were bairns; doesn't mean it's the same water flowing by that we used to guddle in.

Julie (*after a pause for thought*) Mind, we used to aye be piling up boulders and bits of wood and that, trying to build dams across the river.

Drew They never worked though.

Julie They aye got washed away.

Drew It's a fact quine. You've got to face up to facts.

7 Facts are chiels that winna ding

From various parts of the stage, and all around the theatre, the rest of the cast troop on. Their arrival is preceded by a tremendously loud rattling and banging, for they are carrying or wearing various oil drums, canisters, and petrol tins, which they beat with drumsticks. They also drum on objects and surfaces all around the stage. Out of the racket emerges a regular rhythm, and under the rhythm a chanting begins to be heard:

Drummers Face the facts, face the facts, face the facts, face the facts . . .

The drummers form a circle around the stage, and their speed and loudness increase. Suddenly there is a very brief pause, long enough for **Julie** *to shout:*

Julie Whose facts?

Five seconds' more drumming, then another brief pause:

Drew Facts are facts!

The drummers restart immediately, and from their positions marking time at the edge of the stage start to spiral in, getting closer and closer to **Julie** *and* **Drew** *standing in the middle of the stage. Their chant has changed:*

Drummers Facts are chiels that winna ding, facts are chiels that winna ding . . .

The drummers are in a close circle around **Drew** *and* **Julie***, drumming right in their faces. After a few seconds of this,* **Julie** *leaps forward and breaks through the circle.*

Julie Show me!

The drummers immediately stop drumming and start shouting out the following facts and figures, competing with each other to get them over to **Julie** *and to the audience. Divide the lines up between individuals and groups as appropriate. The whole lot should be put over quickly – in about thirty seconds – with much overlapping, and often conflicting messages being given simultaneously. It's the overall battery of information that's important, not the successful transmission of any one 'fact'.*

Drummers Farming's been our heartblood for five thousand years.
Farming earns four hundred million pounds a year for the North-East.
Five thousand years!
That's a tenth of all our income.
Oil's been around for twenty.
The number of hired farm workers has fallen by more than a third over the last twenty years.
There's a record number of farmers going bust.
More farmers kill themselves than any other profession.
Over sixty per cent of the cattle slaughtered in the region are born elsewhere.
The government pay farmers not to grow crops: they call it set-aside, I call it lunacy.
Consumption of beef's at a hundred-year low.
Production of oil seed rape's at an all-time high.
Farms are getting bigger.
Farms are getting fewer.
The small farms are being swallowed up.
The small farmers's getting squeezed out.
Farmers are turning over faster than ever before.
Farmers from outside the area are taking over more than ever before.
Farming's the heartblood of the North-East.
Has been for thousands of years.
Will be for thousands more.
Oil's been around for twenty.
Oil's about to run out.

Julie Stop.

The drummers freeze.

Julie Half of these facts is wrong! 'Oil's been around for twenty'? Oil's been here for three hundred million years!

Drew But you know what they mean.

Julie Aye, but that's not the facts, that's just opinions. Come on, let's hear the other side of the story.

The drummers start shouting out again, oil facts this time. Possibly some of them could be communicated by other means – e.g. slides, sandwich-boards, banners, back-projection, passing notes amongst the audience – as well as shouting.

Drummers Oil is three hundred million years old.
It's the power that drives the whole world.
It's keeping the whole British economy afloat.
Oil is a bituminous liquid resulting from the decomposition of marine or land plants, and perhaps also of some non-nitrogenous animal tissues.
Oil is money.
Actually, North Sea oil is only about one hundred and forty million years old, i.e. it was largely formed during the Jurassic Period. Funnily enough, Steven Spielberg has yet to make a film about it, perhaps because decomposing vegetable matter would be hard to market as a cuddly toy or a lunch-box.
Oil is Scotland's ticket to prosperous independence.
Oil is the only reason Scotland hasn't been allowed to break away.
Oil is going to come out of the North Sea for at least sixty more years.
Oil is going to finish in sixty years and then we'll get our independence
Eh . . .
Oil is god.
Oil is power.
Oil is the devil.
Oil is the biggest of the world's big industries.
Oil is measured in barrels of exactly forty-two gallons; the figure was established in 1482 by King Edward IV of England as the standard size for transporting and trading in herring, at that time the most valuable commodity exported from the North Sea.
Oil is all around this town, like the flood all around the ark of Noah; after the black flood ebbs, will Aberdeen be left high and dry?
Oil is used to light the fuels of hell; I beg all concerned to cease further drilling forthwith, lest the flames of Satan's realm should be quenched for lack of fuel, and the sinners of the centuries escape their rightful torture.
Oil is a non-renewable energy resource.
Oil is the preserved urine of whales.
Oil is the blood of the living planet, the seas its perspiration, the grass and trees its hair, the hills pimples on the face of the earth.
Oil is John D. Rockefeller.
Oil is Armand Hammer.
Oil is Samuel Samuels, Henri Deterding, John Paul Getty, Calouste Gulbenkian, Josef Stalin, Saddam Hussein, Buckskin Joe, Red Adair, Ronnie MacDonald . . .
Oil is me.
Oil is you.

By this time the shouting should have been orchestrated into a peak of noise and quite likely confusion.

(*It doesn't matter if there's confusion, in fact it's desirable.*) *At its peak, the noise is cut clean off, and* **Julie** *speaks.*

Julie I wish I'd never asked now.

Drummers Facts!

Julie That wasn't any help, it just confused things more!

Drummers Face the facts!

Julie You made it seem like oil and farming were opposites, were enemies, like it was a competition between the two of them!

Drummers Facts!

Julie But that's not right, it's simplistic, it's a distortion: it makes the facts into lies!

Drummers Face the facts!

Julie Forget the facts! What about real life?

Instant blackout and instant launch into the – totally contrasting – next scene.

8 Happy families

The Mitchell family living-room. Very cosy. It is some time after the news of the proposal has been broken, and cheery chat continues. **David***'s mother* **Barbara** *leads the conversation, with* **Julie***'s backing, and despite disruption from* **David** *and his father* **John***, who has his own say direct to the audience.*

Barbara (*getting up from the tea-table*) I suppose I better do the dishes then.

Julie Sit down Mrs Mitchell. Me and David'll do them in a minute.

David (*mutters*) Speak for yourself.

John You'll have to watch this one, son!

David That's okay, I like watching her.

Julie You're so romantic, dear.

John Takes after his old man.

Barbara Ha, you're joking! (*To* **Julie**.) Did I ever tell you how *we* got married?

David At the point of a shotgun, was it not?

John Oi!

Barbara No, I mean how your father proposed to me.

John *and* **David** Not that old story!

Julie What is it? Is it a good one?

Barbara Well . . .

John She's lying.

Barbara I haven't told her yet! How do you ken I was going to lie?

John Your lips were moving.

David Dear oh dear!

Barbara I will ignore his insults, as always. He wasn't always so bold, you see Julie.

Julie Was he not?

Barbara No, he was right quiet! See when he first came up from down south? He never opened his mouth.

David And now you don't get the chance, eh!

Julie Wheesht!

John (*direct to audience. This speech, and* **John**'s *other direct addresses, should overlap with the other characters' speeches following them*) I wouldn't say I resent it. That's too strong. I mean it does piss me off a bittie – excuse my language – or at least it did, aye it did piss me off. But not now. Now I'm over it. I'm grateful to him. Hih, of course I am. (*Pause.*) But still it doesn't seem quite right to me, my own laddie having to provide me with a job. Ken?

Barbara We started going out when we were real young, you see Julie, younger than you even, I was just out of the school in fact, and we kept company for, oh, years; I mean things did move slower in those days if you know what I mean . . .

David I thought this was the swinging sixties?

John The sixties didn't begin till 1975 in Aberdeen, son, and even then they weren't very swinging.

Barbara . . . but even by those standards he was a slow mover. All the way through his apprenticeship we went out.

Julie At the printers'?

John Aye, any time she'd gone in a huff and wouldn't let me touch her, she'd say she was feart of me leaving big inky-black handprints on her dress for the neighbours to see. Call me a slow mover!

Barbara You and your pawing!

David Ma, you'll make me puke!

Julie (*frowning at* **David** *to shut up*) So what happened next?

Barbara Well, we were out walking about the Duthie Park one night, and we'd been all through the winter gardens and never a word from him. All those cactuses made his mouth dry, he said.

John (*direct to audience again*) I mean it should really be the other way round, ken? That's how you picture it. Providing for your kid, bringing them up, getting them through school. And then, when they leave, you maybe have a word in the ear of somebody at your work, get the boy a start. But: twenty-four year in that printshop, and then one night I find I'm not printing the morning paper, I'm printing redundancy notices, and one of them's mine! So I couldn't get him a start; he had to get me one!

Barbara   It was a fine summer's night, the flowers were all out in the park and the stars in the sky, and there were couples sitting about on the grass kissing. And somebody had a radio with them and as we passed it was playing a love song. And I turned to him and I said, John, we've been going out thegether a fair long time now. Ihm-hm, he says. Five years I make it. That's me. Here's him: Five years? Ihm-hm. Well John, I said, Do you not think it's about time we was getting married? (*Pause.*) Ihm-hm, he says, and then he walks on. I follow after him, but for ten minutes he doesn't speak a word. I grab his arm, Here, Johnny, I said, You're not saying much for somebody that's just . . . proposed marriage. No Barbara, he says, That's just it: I've said over much already!

Laughter.

John   Aye, and maybe I had.

Julie   So that is how it happened then?

John   No! There's not a word of truth in the whole damn . . . Ach, that's it, I'm away out. Come on David, I'll buy you a dram (*Turning to audience.*) So I wouldn't say I resent David getting me the job. I mean it was me who got myself the job, really. Okay, he fixed up the interview and that, cause the company likes different folk in a family working for it. But it was me who actually did the bloody interview. Not that they asked much. I mean, security guard, what are they going to ask you? Ever pocketed any major oil installations? No? You're in! (*Pause.*) It wouldn't've been like that a few years ago, that's all I'm saying. New technology put me out of a job, and it's the new technology that David works with. Of course he got me a job. It's the way the world is these days: totally buggered.

Barbara   See this Julie? It's started already.

David   Mother, shut your face.

Julie   I could come too.

David   I thought you were volunteering to do the dishes?

Julie   Aye, but if you help as well they'll be done in no time and I could . . . aye, and your mum too . . . we could all go out for a drink.

John   Come on *David*, the whisky's evaporating while we speak. (*To audience.*) Twenty year ago it wouldn't've happened, that's all I'm saying. The whole town's been turned upside down, and a lot of folk like me with it. (*As he leaves, ignoring his wife.*) You have to hold on to what you can.

David   (*shrugs in what is meant to be an apology*)   See you later.

Julie   See you.

She goes to kiss him, despite obviously being pissed off; he tries to avoid her, but she gets him.

Barbara   Hoi, you're not married yet.

John   That's well seen.

Laughter.

The two men come forwards, out of the house. They are still laughing. Then **John** *stops, and grabs* **David** *by the elbow. Simultaneously,* **Barbara** *grabs* **Julie** *by the elbow inside the house.*

John/Barbara   Wait. I've just one thing to say to you.

David/Julie   What's that?

John/Barbara   Don't get married.

9   Lover's leap

Birdsong, flowing water, sunshine through the leaves. The River Ythan flows along the front of the stage. The far bank is steep and rocky, a small cliff; tufts of vegetation grow out of the front of it, and there is a small ruined building at the top. **David** *and* **Julie** *are near the bottom, climbing slowly upwards. They keep moving throughout the scene, right out above the audience if possible.* **Julie** *knows the handholds, leads the way.*

David   Are you sure about this?

Julie   Trust me. I did it hundreds of times when I was a kid.

David   Aye, but you were young and swack then. You're an old stiffie these days.

Julie   If only I could say the same about you.

David   I heard that. What did you say?

Julie   I said okay, I'll give up the Grolsch and the Jack Daniel's and the Bloody Marys and the Buds and the wine and the peach schnapps, I'll go back to ginger beer and milk with a drop of tea the morn. If you do too.

David   It's funny, I suddenly can't hear you any more.

Julie   Your lugs are good for that, eh?

David   As I was saying, I suddenly can't hear you any more.

Julie   (*pause*)   You used to hear everything I said. You used to come closer if you couldn't hear me right.

David   (*indicating that they're on different bits of the cliff*)   Well I can't come closer to you now, can I.

Julie   You never can, these days.

David   Well, I don't need to any more, cause I ken what you're going to say, don't I. It was different when we first went out, we didn't ken each other: everything you said was new and out of the blue. But now I've heard it all afore, I know what you're going to say afore *you* do even. I don't need to listen to you any more.

Julie   That's terrible.

David   I kent you were going to say that.

Julie   No, but seriously. You have to keep listening, otherwise, otherwise . . . Christ, we might as well all be talking to ourselves.

David   Look at my mum and dad. They haven't really listened to each other for twenty-five year, and they still get on fine. It's not a problem.

Julie   Well I think it is, if . . .

David   Which is more than I can say for this fucking cliff. I'm stuck!

Julie (*looking over at his pitch*)   You just have to get over to the left a bit, use your knees to kind of grip onto the rock and then just stretch.

David (*he does what she said*)   And me with all my new Benetton gear on, fuck! What is it we're supposed to be looking at anyroad?

Julie   This is Lovers' Leap. It's out of an old story. There's a ruin on top, you'll see it when we get there. Me and Drew used to call it The Castle when we were wee, but it's not really that.

David   What is it, a pigsty or something?

Julie   No, it was some kind of watchtower but . . . (*They should be getting near the top by this time.*) The story is, there was this lassie, right, the laird's daughter, and she was really in love with this young guy. The miller. But her old man wouldn't let them see each other, cause he was just a peasant, and she would inherit all the land for miles around. Well one day the lassie goes to her father and says, Cut me out of your will, father, for I want to get married and live with the man I love. Fine, says the father, for the Laird of Fetterlear's coming over to see's the morn, and I've promised he can have you for a wife. Never, says the daughter, he's an old scrunty man, and anyway, it's the miller I love: I'm eloping! But afore she can run, her father grabs her and drags her away and shuts her up in the tower at the top of this cliff. And there you'll stay till the morn's morn, he laughs, when you'll marry the Laird of Fetterlear! And now I'm away to run that miller off my land once and for all. The lassie looks out of her window, down at the rocks and the river way below. What am I going to do? she cries . . .

Drew (*appearing through the trees at the bottom of the cliff*)   Jump!

David   Jesus Christ man, you just about had me off there!

Julie   What do you want, you big galoot?

Drew   Hope you've a head for heights, Davy.

David   Ach, this is nothing. Offshore there's a hundred things worse than this.

Drew   Aye, like all that five-star grub you have to eat: must be terrible for you.

David   No, like hanging upside down from a girder in a force ten gale. I've done that. When it's your job you have to. (*He tries to do a bit of climbing, but then gets nervous and stops.*)

Julie   What are you needing anyway, you gype?

Drew   Ach, it doesn't matter.

Julie   No, what?

Drew   Mind that old cottar house up by the forestry plantation?

Julie   Where dad let old Wattie bide?

Drew   Aye, I've been meaning to demolish it for ages, just to get that corner of the park clear. I was needing you to come and give's a hand to take the windows and the rickle of furniture out first.

Julie   We could help you later on.

Drew   Nah, it's okay, David told me about how you had to get back to town early and that.

Julie   Eh?

David   That's right. Maybe some other time.

Drew   Och aye, there's no hurry. Next time you're out maybe. (*He leaves.*) If you're not back by four I'll send for the mountain rescue.

Julie   What's going on? We were meant to bide till the morn's morn, try and get on better terms with my brother.

David   Ach, what's the point?

Julie   What?

David   He's like you: makes up his mind like that (*Snaps fingers.*) then he's stubborn as a pig stuck in a pipe.

Julie   So?

David   It was just making you miserable being here, I could tell, so I thought it'd be better if we headed back to town.

Julie   For God's sake! Thanks for deciding for me!

David   We're getting married, you'd better get used to it.

Julie   I'll make up my own mind when I leave here, I don't need you telling me! I like Ythanbanks, it still feels like home, though everybody says it's not. I don't need you dragging me away after five minutes.

David   What's the point of staying? You just play the same old games with Drew, you don't really talk.

Julie   (*sarcastically*)   Not like *we* talk, eh?

David   Aye, exactly.

Julie   Well I don't ken if we do any more.

David   I booked a table at that Chinese Olympic place for thenight. We can talk there.

Julie   Typical! You're always deciding things for the both of us, and not even asking me about them!

David   I could cancel it.

Julie   That's not the point!

David Christ woman, you're never happy! You're pissed off cause I don't talk to you, and then the one time I specially arrange it so we *can* have a good long talk – you're pissed off at me for doing that too! I can't win!

They start climbing the cliff again here, but there's no pleasure in it any more, they just have to do it.

Julie This isn't about winners and losers.

David That's funny, you were keen enough to win that argument about who was going to stay offshore.

Julie That's cause it wasn't a proper argument, it was just ridiculous. Of course it has to be me stays offshore: I've got the training, the prospects, the big wages.

David The ovaries.

Julie *What?*

David But I'm just a roustabout, eh? Just a North Sea scaffie?

Julie Look, you ken only one of us can work on the rig after this so-called marriage . . .

David Okay, but only one of us can have babies.

Julie (*pause*) What's that supposed to mean?

David Well, you say *now* that you like your work offshore . . .

Julie I do. (*She scrambles up onto the top of the cliff.*)

David You say it makes sense for me to give up the one stab at a decent paying job I have, it makes sense for me to be back on the sites at a hundred quid a week or something . . .

Julie You could get something better than that!

David You say these things now, but what's going to happen when you fall pregnant? Will you still want to go back offshore after that? The ROV joystick in one hand and jiggling the pram in the other?

Julie I don't believe you're saying this.

David Ken what I think? Drew chucked you off the farm, and now you're getting your revenge on him by chucking me off the rigs!

Julie You self-centred two-faced macho shithead!

David It's like my dad says: you can't win with a woman, cause once they're beaten they just start calling you names. And after that . . . it's bursting out greeting. Give me a hand up will you.

She does, he reaches the top, looks around.

Julie I've never heard you speak such rubbish.

David Well you should've listened better.

Julie Aye, I think I should.

David   So this is it, is it? The famous Lovers' Leap. We climbed all that way just to see this pile of shit.

Julie   Aye this is it, this is where we've got to. And the lassie in the old story threw herself off here, plunged to her death on the rocks below, rather than marry someone she didn't love.

David   But this is 1993, things don't happen like that any more.

Julie   No; now we're the lovers, and *this* is the leap. (*She goes to the edge of the cliff and climbs all the way down with amazing skill in about five seconds flat.*)

David   Julie, come back, come back when I tell you! How do I get fucking down from here? Come back!

But she is already walking away along the bank of the river.

10   Danger

Back offshore. **Grant** *is sitting in the smoko shack, looking at a newspaper.* **Julie** *is just along from him, having a cup of tea; she looks preoccupied, morose almost, but it's impossible to ignore someone for ever in such a small space.*

Julie   I heard some guy got killed yesterday over at Delta.

Grant   Aye, I heard that too.

Julie   A big swell caught the supply ship and he was crushed atween two containers.

Grant   (*shrugs*)   Ah well, life goes on.

Julie   His doesn't.

Grant   (*shrugs again*)   His doesn't. But mine does.

From out of nowhere (the top of the cliff from the last scene, actually), **David** *swings in on a winch, high up. As the rope stops swinging, he climbs up a few metres, takes out a hammer from his belt, and starts battering at a rusty bit of panel there.* **Grant** *looks up from where he is sitting, and shouts out an order above the rising sea and wind noise.*

Grant   Not there Mitchell! Higher up!

Julie   Did you say something there?

Grant   When you come down to it, the North Sea's not really that dangerous a place to work.

Julie   Really?

Grant   I mean you're more at risk on a building site, or on a farm! How many teuchters get drowned in slurry tanks or crushed under tipping tractors every year?

Julie   Well, too many. Any's too many.

Grant   And how about the stress? Farmers've got the highest suicide rate for any job there is! That's a fact! Out in the so-called peaceful countryside. But listen to this:

Aberdeen has the lowest suicide rate for any city in the whole of Britain. Why? Cause so many Aberdonians have good well-paid jobs in the oil industry. Don't talk to them about danger and death: this is the life!

Wind and sea noises fill the theatre. **David** *has got a grinder and is working on the corroded metal with it. Sparks go flying all around.*

Grant (*leaping to his feet*)   I hope you've got a hot-work permit for that, Mitchell.

David   What?

Grant   Have you got a permit?

David   For the grinder? Aye. Have you got a permit for sending me up here in this wind?

Grant (*quietly*)   I don't need one.

David   What?

Grant   No slacking now. I'm needing that sealed and painted before the shift ends.

David *shouts something, but the wind drowns him out.* **Grant** *returns to his newspaper.* **Julie** *leans over and taps the page he's reading.*

Julie   So was there anything in there about the death at Delta?

Grant   You're joking!

Julie   The usual whitewash.

Grant   Rubbish! It's just, well, what's the point in getting folk back on the beach all worried? One death in the paper and they get the idea it's Russian roulette out here. You see, it doesn't make the papers when there's *no* incidents for weeks on end.

Julie   Aye Mr Grant, you're a good company man.

Grant   I'm just an ops controller, I'm no company man.

Julie   Yet!

Grant   Keep going Julie, flattery'll get you everywhere.

Julie (*pauses for a second to show she's ignoring his innuendo*)   You have to admit, you're a man that usually takes the company line.

Grant   I make up my own mind, based on the things I see – and how much I'm getting paid when I see them.

Back to **David** *on the rope. He is swaying about now in the increasingly strong wind, but still trying to paint the bit of metal he's working on.*

Grant   Hoi, you missed a bit!

David   What?

Grant   Be more careful, you missed a bit!

David   I can't hear you.

Grant   What?

David   I'm chucking this in. The wind's too strong. The paint's getting blown all over the shop.

Grant   I told you Mitchell, that has to be finished this shift. Stay where you are till I tell you.

David   Permission to plunge to my death, sir?

*But **Grant** is back in the smoko again.*

Julie   So offshore isn't a dangerous place to work then?

Grant   There's only about twenty folk a year get killed offshore. On average. I mean some years the figure is higher . . .

Julie   Like 1988.

Grant   Eh, aye.

Julie   It was twenty a minute for a while there.

*Pause. **Finn** walks in.*

Finn   I've just been watching a stoater of a film. You should've seen it Julie.

Grant   Nah, Julie's been too busy organising a new sit-in.

Finn   What?

Grant   Sit on my face, I said, Fine! But don't get fucking political with me.

Julie   He's talking shite.

Grant   Nah, she just about had me signing up for the OILC!

Julie   It's lies Finn: I was thinking aloud, that's all. You ken me, I just like to get on with my work – though half the time some bastard's trying to stop you. Hih, I mind this science teacher I had at the school. I'd been choosing my highers, see, and he calls me in: 'Miss Allardyce, I see you've opted for higher physics and chemistry.' 'Aye. Are my marks not good enough?' 'Oh there's no problem there, it's just . . . would you not be better off studying biology? I always think it's a much more *feminine* science.'

Finn   What's that got to do with safety stuff?

Julie   Everything.

Grant   Nothing.

Finn   Here's what I think: I think there's a lot of bullshitters on the beach that don't give a toss about us working out here. They drive about in their cars, they switch on their central heating, they fry up their bacon and beans – and the thought of folk in the middle of the North Sea drilling up the oil and gas they're using, it never enters their head. And then one day a chopper ditches, or there's a gas leak, or a platform comes adrift in a gale, and, oh dear me, suddenly they're up in fucking arms, getting themselves in a fuck of a state, shooting their mouths off! And why? Cause they feel fucking guilty! Cause ninety-nine per cent of the time they don't even think of us. Cause a hundred per cent of the time they're gobbling up the stuff we produce – they're keeping us out here! Fuck them!

Julie   Aye, serve them right if we all die! Three cheers for chocolate fireguards!

Grant   Keep things in perspective, I say. Okay, a couple dozen folk offshore get killed; but how many people are killed in road accidents in the same time? Thousands!

Julie   So what are you saying, we should all give up our cars?

Grant   No, just folk on the beach: before they start lecturing us about oil-deaths, *they* should give up *their* cars.

Julie   That'll never happen.

Finn   Aye, and just as well, or we'd be out of a job.

Grant   And talking of jobs, I'm away for a crap.

Finn   You should check out the video. *Driller Thriller*, it's called. I thought it was about a toolpusher that goes psycho and batters everybody to death with a pipe joint. But nah, it was a dentist who put all these women patients under the gas, then laid the reclining chair out and put fillings in all kinds of strange places!

Grant *has left by this time, and* **Julie** *isn't listening, so* **Finn** *shuts up.*

Julie (*she should start saying this before* **Finn** *finishes his last speech*)   The problem is, you can't measure grief; you can't pour it out like a gallon of petrol, or a barrel of crude. It's infinite. One mother whose bairn dies suffers all the grief there is. Not less grief if it's a one off and not one in twenty, or one in a thousand. Any amount of death means the same thing: absolute grief. All the grief there is. Too much.

Finn   For fuck's sake Julie, cheer up, give us a smile. The women in the film all had great smiles – course, it was about a dentist.

Julie   Finn, I don't like that crap, it's not realistic.

Finn   Aye, exactly, that's what's so good about it! Come on: you're not bad looking when you smile, you know.

Julie   What?

Finn   Tell you what, come back to my bunk and I'll act out the plot of the film for you.

Julie   You act it out? What did you say it was, *The Muppet Movie*?

Finn   No, it was one of those Dutch imports, know what I mean?

Julie   One of those! *The Incredible Shrinking Man*, then?

Finn   Christ, have you got a problem Julie Allardyce?

Julie   Aye, I'm surrounded by arseholes and pricks.

Finn   So was the girl in the film.

Julie   Fuck off.

Finn Christ, you have to watch yourself in this place: you're in danger of getting your head bitten off at any fucking moment.

Julie *gets up to leave, but just then* **David** *staggers in, soaking wet, windswept, covered in flakes of rusty metal and paint splashes. He slumps into a seat.*

Julie Jesus, they didn't have you out in this shit did they?

David Half-way out the flare boom.

Julie (*putting her hand on his shoulder*) You're having a hard time of it these days, eh? Stuck up crumbling cliffs, or dangling off the platform in a raging gale!

David (*putting his hand on top of hers*) I didn't ken you cared.

Julie Despite everything, I do.

She looks him in the eye, but then breaks away and leaves the room. **Finn** *stares after her in amazement.*

Finn Fuck's sake! One minute she's ripping my throat out, next she's treating you like her bosom buddy. What's your fucking secret?

David My secret? Oh! Eh . . . I'll tell you when you're a bittie older Finn.

11 Away and play with your joystick, Grant

We are in the darkened ROV control module. **Julie** *is looking at the videos, etc.* **Grant** *sidles up behind her. (Again the screen is represented by a portable light. During the course of the scene,* **Julie** *shines it on herself, or in* **Grant***'s face or groin at appropriate moments.)*

Grant Wedlock is a padlock, Julie.

Julie What?

Grant Wedlock is a padlock. It's a song.

Julie I never heard it.

Grant That would explain it then.

Julie (*facing him*) Explain what?

Grant Why you're being stupid enough to get married to that no-hoper Mitchell.

Julie (*hiding her anger by turning away*) I don't ken what you're talking about.

Grant You must think I'm thick as shit.

Julie I wouldn't say you were as thick as it . . .

Grant (*he seizes the light, and shines it in her face*) I've got eyes, you know. I can see what's going on. You're lucky I haven't reported the pair of youse yet. (**Julie** *ignores him, so he continues, moving the beam of light up and down her body.*) I thought we could maybe come to some kind of an arrangement. I'll keep quiet about you and Mitchell, if you . . . well . . . we could sort out the details later on.

Julie (*taking the light back*) I could report you for that. Sexual harrassment.

Grant   And if you did, I'd have to explain to the company why we were on that subject in the first place. It'd be a shame, cause you're good at your job, eh?

Julie   Aye.

Grant   You like it, eh?

Julie   Aye.

Grant   More than you like Mitchell, or about the same?

Julie (*looking him in the eye*)   Me and David Mitchell are friends, nothing more. And me and you have to work together, and there's never going to be more to it than that. Okay?

Grant (*starting to leave*)   Wedlock is a padlock, Julie . . . but if you ever want it opened, remember me: I'm the man with the key to fit your lock.

Julie (*under her breath, but viciously*)   Away and play with your joystick.

Grant (*coming back in, angry*)   What was that Allardyce?

Julie   I was just thinking it's funny how some ROV operators call their machines 'she'. 'I'm just going to put her into the moonpool,' they say. 'She's a bad tempered bitch theday.' I never understood it.

Grant   So what do you call yours then, 'big boy'?

Julie   No, I don't call it he or she or anything. It's just a lump of metal, a lump of metal with a lot of clever stuff inside it, but nothing more. It's not a person I'm steering around down there, it's just a lump of machinery. But that's it, you see! Most of the other ROV pilots I've met, they wish it was a person they were controlling. They're out here a fortnight at a time, and meanwhile, what's their wife or their girlfriend getting up to onshore? The old North Sea widow syndrome! You ken what I'm talking about Mr Grant! So these guys get out here and they grab the joystick and they waggle it about like fucking crazy bastards, and all the time they're shouting, 'Come on you bitch, do what you're told!' and 'Christ she's a sluggish hoor this one!' and I just sit here and . . . laugh. It's pathetic, Mr Grant, pathetic.

Grant (*checks watch*)   I don't have the time for this Allardyce.

Julie   Pity.

Grant *leaves, slamming the door.* **Julie** *smiles and turns back to her work.*

12   Navigator

Back onshore. It is the last night of **David** *and* **Julie***'s last onshore fortnight unmarried. In the morning they'll go offshore for a fortnight, and at the end of that they'll be getting married. So both are out with their friends, celebrating. Meanwhile,* **Drew** *is looking after* **Derek***; we don't see him, but from somewhere up in the darkness, his voice emerges, singing a lullaby.*

Drew
There once was a troop of Irish dragoons
Came marching down through Fyvie O

And the captain's fell in love with a very bonnie lass
And her name it was called pretty Peggy O

He hums for a bit, starts making up his own words:

Peggy was bad, she didn't like her dad
And she lived by herself in a castle O
When the soldier came her way, she told him he could stay
And his name it was called Captain Andrew O . . .

Lights up on **Julie** *and* **Angela** *marching along Aberdeen beach, singing, and drinking from bottles of beer.*

Julie *and* **Angela**
Now there's many a bonnie lass in the Howe of Auchterless
There's many a bonnie lass in the Garioch O
There's many a bonnie Jean in the town of Aberdeen
But the flower of them all is in Fyvie O

Julie   It's funny, I hated this when they made us sing it at the school . . .

Angela   I hated everything they made us do at the school.

Julie   . . . but I quite like it now. Or at least I don't like it, but I understand what it's about.

Angela   Except I keep imagining the mannie Urquhart, his beard sticking out over the top of the piano, pounding away.

Julie   'Give it some oomph, girls!'

Angela   He always liked you, eh, Urquhart?

Julie   He always gave me the creeps, the old perv. On the way out of the class he'd put his arm around my shoulder and say, 'And here is the bonnie lass herself!'

Angela   Jandies!

Julie   Some things never change.

Angela   But there was a few teachers at the school that liked you, eh? And you liked them . . .

Julie   Well, I went along with them I suppose. But just to get what I wanted in the end.

Angela   It was always me that was the rebel, me that hated the world, that wanted to smash the place up. I wanted to throw acid in everybody's face. But you were all for the world and getting on in it, and all for people and getting on with them. Me, I painted my bedroom black and grew my fringe down over my eyes. So I wouldn't have to look at anybody, and nobody could see me.

Julie   That's the next verse! It's
'Come down the stair pretty Peggy my dear
Come down the stair pretty Peggy O
Come down the stair, comb back your yellow hair
Take a last farewell of your daddy O'

Angela (*while* **Julie** *is singing, so that only the audience hears*)   But here we are a few years later and it's all different, it's the opposite. I've got Derek, and I love him. I worry about the future and what the world's going to be like for him. I want it to be a nice place for when he's growing up. But you, you Julie Allardyce, you're digging tons of black poison out of the seabed, and you don't give a damn: you're painting the *world* black.

Julie   What are you saying Ange?

Angela   Och, I was just thinking about Derek.

Julie   Who's babysitting thenight anyroad?

Angela   It's . . . hih. Nobody you'd ken.

Angela *and* **Julie** *wander off. From above them as they go, comes the sound of* **Drew** *softly whistling a verse of the song. Then he's drowned out as* **David** *and* **Finn** *come breenging on, cans in hand.* (*Remember:* **Finn** *doesn't know about the marriage yet, or about* **David** *and* **Julie**'s *relationship at all.*)

Finn   Once I've paid up my fucking house, you'll not catch me offshore. I'll jack that in and never go near the fucking sea.

David   It wouldn't be so bad if you could move around a bit. Follow the sun, ken? It's just being stuck in the one place that's the bastard.

Finn   Ah-ha! (*Starts to change direction, then stops and carries on as before.*) Ach, it's just the seamen's mission. I thought it was a fucking bar.

David   I ken: I'll get myself a boat! A boat with a bunk bed and a wee cooker and everything. Just the ticket. Then head off into the wild blue yonder: point the nose of the thing for the equator and cheerio!

Finn   Where the fuck's that pub from last time? What's it called? The Schooner . . .

David (*pushing open a shopdoor. They are in a ship's chandler's*)   Quick, in here . . . (*Pointing at wall behind* **Chandler**.) I want some of those.

Chandler   Charts?

David   Aye.

Chandler   Where of?

David   The Sargasso Sea. Zanzibar, North-West Iceland, Honolulu, the Great Barrier Reef, Van Dieman's Land, the Amazon Basin, Timbuctoo, Montego Bay . . .

Chandler   We only stock British coastal charts.

David   You're joking?

Chandler   Sorry.

Finn   Call yourself a fucking . . . a fucking . . .

Chandler   Ship's chandler.

Finn   Aye, well . . .

David   Never mind Finn, forget it. (*To* **Chandler**.) Here, do a bit of navigating for us pal: how do we get to the Schooner Bar?

Back with **Julie** *and* **Angela**.

Julie   But 'A soldier's wife I never shall be
A soldier shall never enjoy me O
For I never do intend to go to a foreign land
So I never shall marry a soldier O'

Angela   Oh 'A soldier's wife you never shall be
For you'll be the captain's lady O
And the regiments shall stand with their hats into their hands
And they'll bow in the presence of my Peggy O'

Julie   Bollocks!

Angela   What?

Julie   All this shite about bowing regiments! I don't believe a word of it! Typical men's lies trying to get into your pants!

Angela   Do you think it?

Julie   Christ aye: especially coming from a squaddy for God's sake!

Angela   But does he not die of a broken heart in the end, the soldier?

Julie   Ach, that's just another lie made up by the mannie writing the song to get into the pants of whoever he was singing it till!

Angela   You're just bitter and twisted Julie Allardyce.

Julie   No, I'm just being realistic. You've been away from men over long Angie, you're forgetting what they're like.

Angela   Who says I've been away from men?

Julie   Well you never said anything to me about any man!

Angela   I have my reasons.

Julie   Secrets, eh? It's David: you've been having a mad affair with him behind my back!

Angela   No!

Julie   That's a shame.

Angela   Eh? What way is that to talk when you're a fortnight off getting married to him? I thought it was meant to be the happiest day of your life!

Julie   Och, I don't know. I suppose every couple has their arguments, eh? I mean it's a stressful time! But still . . .

Angela   What's the problem, not enough sex?

Julie   (*changing the subject*)   The colonel he cries, 'Now mount boys mount . . .'

Angela   It is not enough sex!

Julie No, it's not that, it's . . . hey, don't change the subject. If you haven't been seeing David, who is it that's such a big secret?

Angela Och . . . You don't ken him.

Drew *sings from the darkness again, quietly, tenderly.*

Drew
Now there's many a bonnie lass in the Howe of Auchterless
There's many a bonnie lass in the Garioch O
There's many a bonnie Jean in the town of Aberdeen
But the flower of them all is in Seaton O

Back with the lads. **Finn** *standing still,* **David** *walking slowly in circles around him, drinking.*

Finn Tell you what, David. If you're wanting a life on the ocean wave, you could get a job on one of the standby boats.

David Oh Jesus.

Finn They'd let you into that no bother: half of their crews make roustabouts seem like brain surgeons!

David Wise the head.

Finn What?

David That has to be the worst fucking job in oil. You're on for a month at a time, spewing your ring with seasickness the whole time!

Finn You were the one who wanted onto a fucking boat.

David Aye, but going somewhere, that's the whole fucking point, not just bumping round and round a fucking platform for a month at a time! I was needing to be moving somewhere, not just sticking in one place. (*Drinks.*) Anyway, I've changed my mind. I'll stay working where I am but, but, go on more fucking holidays! (*Drinks again.*) Christ, on the standbys you're not even *in* one place, you're just going round and round a place, bobbing up and down. It's like driving round and round the Mounthoolie roundabout for a month – throwing up in a galeforce wind!

Finn The only boat I'm interested in is steamboats. Come on give me the fucking bottle.

David (*passes the whisky over*) You'll fucking damage yourself pal.

Finn Aye, but in approximately (*Checks watch.*) ten hours' time we'll be starting another shift of enforced fucking sobriety, so within a fortnight I'll be totally healthy again.

David Just in time to come back onshore and get wrecked again.

Finn Exactly. Now pass me the fucking whisky.

David I already did.

Finn Oh aye!

Both laugh.

Back with the women, drunker than ever now.

Angela   But the colonel he cries 'Now mount boys mount'

Julie   And the captain replies 'Oh tarry O
Oh gang nae awa for another day or twa
Till we see if this bonnie lass will marry O'

Angela *and* **Julie**
It was early next morning that we rode away
And oh but our captain was sorry O
The drums they did beat over the bonnie braes of Gight
And the band played 'The Lowlands of Fyvie O'

Long ere we won into old Meldrum town
It's we had our captain to carry O
And long ere we came into bonnie Aberdeen
It's we had our captain to bury O

Both burst into mostly fake tears and sobs of sorrow, which quickly change to mostly real laughter. They drink some more beer and calm down.

Angela   Do you think that really happened?

Julie   It's just a song   Do you think 'Bohemian Rhapsody' really happened?

Both of them think for a while, mouth the words to themselves.

Angela   Suppose not, eh?

Julie   Nah.

Angela   But do you think anybody could ever love somebody else that much?

Julie   Nah.

Angela (*presses quiz-show buzzer*)   Wehhhh! That was the wrong answer Miss Allardyce. The right answer was, 'Yes Magnus, if my David left me, of a broken heart I would surely die.'

Julie (*thinks*)   I would be sad for a while.

Angela   Sad?

Julie   I mean I've got used to having him around: you have your job, and your car, and your place to bide – and you have your man to take back to the place you bide. Aye, I'd miss him.

Angela   There must be more to it than that though! (**Julie** *shrugs*.) Like, a minute after leaving him, you're already thinking about the next time you'll meet? Like, when you're with him, you seem to be seeing funny things going on all around – walking down Union Street and the faces of the folk passing by just constantly make the pair of you burst out laughing? Or suddenly you start noticing what a fine-looking place Aberdeen is – wow, you say, look at the sun on the side of that flats, it's like they're made of solid gold!

Julie   I don't know about that.

Angela   Like you have twice as many baths as usual! You wash the dishes after your tea in case he comes round. Your bed, that always seemed just the right size for you to stretch out in, well, now it feels like it's way too big and empty . . . when he's not in it with you . . .

Julie   Angela, who is this guy you're seeing?

Angela   It's your brother, Drew.

Faint light up on **Drew**, *sitting up high, looking happy.*

Drew   And her name it was called pretty Angie O.

In a bar.

David   To be honest Finn . . . well.

Finn   What?

David   There's something I have to tell you.

Finn   You can't be pregnant, we were always so careful!

David   Fuck off.

Finn   What then?

David   Well . . . it's my round I think.

Finn   I know whose round it is; it's mine. Sit down!

David   Oh fuck, maybe I shouldn't, I mean . . . it's kind of secret.

Finn   You can trust me with a secret! Come on, tell! You can trust me. Anyway, if you don't tell me I'll break your arm.

David   Okay, okay. But I'm only telling you cause . . .

Finn   . . . cause we're mates. I know, you don't have to . . .

David   . . . cause I'm blootered.

Finn   You cunt!

David   But I will tell you. It's this. I'm not going to be sailing away anywhere.

Finn   How?

David   I'm well and truly stuck in the one place. Settled down in one place, you might say.

Finn   Eh?

David   I'm getting married.

Finn   What!

David   Aye!

Finn   You fucking dirty dog!

David   Aye well. That's me.

Finn   You kept that quiet you dog, you fucking dark horse! Christ, you never even mentioned you were shagging anybody! Any time the subject came up you always kept your gob shut – I was beginning to think you were the North Sea's first queer roustabout. And now this!

David   Hih, aye.

Finn   So who is the poor unfortunate then? When am I going to meet her?

David   You ken her.

Finn   Eh?

David   It's Julie.

Finn   Julie?

David   Julie Allardyce. That you work with.

Finn   (*after a pause*)   Fuck's sake. Julie Allardyce. Does that mean I can't think about her when I have a wank any more?

David   Ahhh, you fucking foul bastard . . .

Finn   Here, I knew her before you did, in fact it was me that fucking introduced her to you, so don't get fucking possessive about her all of a sudden.

David   Just fuck off and buy me a drink will you? It's my fucking stag night after all.

Finn   Christ, so it is, fucking magic! Oblivion here we come!

David   I'll drink to that.

Back with the women.

Julie   Drew?

Angela   Aye.

Julie   You are joking Angela?

Angela   No.

Julie   Jesus Christ. (*Realisation.*) And it's him that's babysitting for you now, eh?

Angela   Aye.

Julie *strides off across the stage, her face set in fury; she is rushing back to* **Angela**'s *flat.* **Angela** *runs along, trying to keep up with her, trying to calm her down.*

Angela   I mean I ken it's a big surprise for you – God, *I* was surprised!

Julie   Surprised? Is that what you call it?

Angela   What would you call it?

Julie   How about insane? No? Off your fucking head? Or was it just drunk and desperate?

Angela   Julie! Don't be like that! He's great: a good laugh, gets on with Derek really well . . .

Julie   You need your head looked at, quine. (*Shakes her head.*) Are you sure it is Drew? I mean – handy with the bairn, good to get on with? – it doesn't sound like my brother to me.

Angela   I was saying to Andrew just the other day, me and him always hated each other when we were bairns. I'd come round to visit you, and he'd always be hanging around, ken. A real dangleberry! We used to think he was a wee shite.

Julie   But he's changed: he's a big shite now.

Angela   Nah, but once you get talking to him Julie, he's a really nice guy: you've no idea. He listens to what I'm saying, ken, and he thinks about it, I can see him thinking about it. He doesn't just come out with what he believes and that's the end of it: he listens, and he thinks it over.

Julie   I don't believe this.

Angela   It's true. It was years since I'd seen him, then I bumped into him one day up town. He gave me a lift home, and then we got talking and . . .

Julie   Spare me the details Ange!

Angela   I think he's maybe lonely out at Ythanbanks all by himself.

Julie   Don't make me greet!

Angela   He told me you'd been having rows.

Julie   Did he? I suppose he says I started them all.

Angela   No. He says the two of you are alike. You have these really definite ideas about what you want, what you're doing with your life, and you want the whole world to fit in with your plans. And that's okay till you meet somebody else who's got different ideas, different plans – like when you get talking to Drew – cause then BANG! Big collisions!

Julie (*sarcastically*)   You're fairly getting to be an expert on the Allardyce psychology, Angela. I'm impressed.

They have arrived outside **Angela**'s *block of flats.* **Julie** *stops, looks at* **Angela** *for a second, throws back her head and shouts up at the sky.*

Julie   Andrew Allardyce, show your face!

Angela   He'll never hear you.

Julie   Come down you traitorous bastard!

Angela   Julie, I have to live here.

Julie   You can't hide for ever, Allardyce.

Drew *steps out onto the balcony high above, and peers down at them.*

Drew   Wheesht quine, you'll wake the bairn.

Julie   I won't be quiet, I'm having this out with you: come down here!

Drew   I can't just leave Derek.

Julie   Right, that's it. (*She pushes open the door to the flats and runs in.*)

Angela   The lift's out of order, you'll have to . . .

But **Julie** *is gone.*

Angela (*shouts up to* **Drew**, *then rushes after* **Julie**)   I don't want a punch-up in my flat Drew, come down and meet her half-way.

Drew   I'm always trying to do that, but . . . God's sake

Angela *has disappeared.* **Drew** *goes inside, and soon all three of them are sprinting back and forth, up and down the stairs. The sound of their feet thumping on the concrete of the stairwell echoes thunderously.* **Julie** *suddenly stops, and whips round to face* **Angela**, *who is right behind her.*

Julie   You'll be moving out to Ythanbanks to bide next.

Angela   We have been talking about that actually.

Julie (*clutching her head in her hand*)   Aaaaaaaarrrrrrrggggggghhhhhhh!!!!!!!

Drew (*arriving from above*)   What the fuck's going on?

Julie   I'll tell you: I've been stabbed in the back by my brother and my best friend of twenty year!

Drew   What are you talking about quine?

Julie   What a way to spend my hen night!

Angela   I thought you'd be happy for us, Julie.

Julie   Happy? How can I be happy when I'm burning up inside? I'm burning, roasting, there's a flare in my chest. I'm burning with anger or hatred or jealousy or SOMETHING! I can't stand it, cool me down!

Angela *holds out a bottle of beer and she grabs it, takes a long drink, then flings the bottle away.*

Julie   What am I drinking – petrol?

Drew (*putting a hand on her shoulder*)   What's got into you Julie?

Julie   Fuel's got into me, fuel for burning! All my life I've been filling up, more and more stuff piling up inside me – my dad and the farm and the work and the shite from the bears and David, *David* – it all piles up, and the pressure builds up, and the temperature too till the stuff you started with's gone, and what you have left is fuel! Crude! Oil's building up, till you're ready to burst, building and filling till . . . one day . . . something gets you, something drills down into your heart and BLOWOUT! BLOWOUT! The fuel's jetting out, it's blowing like a gusher, and it's burning, burning, full of fuel – and I'm burning!

The scene ends with this shout that is almost a scream.

13   Burnt out

On the balcony of **Angela***'s flat, shortly after the big row on the staircase.* **Drew** *stares out over the sea;* **Angela** *comes out from the living-room, shutting the door quietly behind her.*

Angela   She's asleep.

Drew   How about Derek?

Angela   You ken what he's like: if the flats tumbled down into the sea he'd just yawn and roll over.

Drew   Hih. (*Pause.*) Was she drunk?

Angela   Can you not tell the difference atween somebody blazing with jealousy and somebody bleezing drunk?

Drew   I've never seen her like that afore.

Angela (*embraces him*)   She's never seen you like *this* afore, that's the problem.

Drew   Do you think it?

Angela   It must've been a shock to her.

Drew   I thought she'd like it, ken, her brother and her best friend getting involved; it's kind of like a jigsaw, all the pieces fitting thegether.

Angela   Aye, but she feels like she's the piece left over, the bit that doesn't fit in anywhere . . .

Drew   Her and David, surely they fit thegether . . .

A noise comes up to them from the street below. It is **Finn** *and* **David** *singing drunkenly as they stagger along the road.*

Finn *and* **David**
There once was a troop of Texas tycoons
Came driving down through Fyvie O
And they used their expertise to explore the cold North Sea
And the whole of the countryside went crazy O

Oh who can resist the feel of siller in his fist
Who doesn't want work and wages O
Let the others go to hell, I'm doing fine myself
And the oil's going to keep us rich for ages O

They wander off down the road. Back to the balcony.

Angela I'm not sure. Some of the things Julie was saying, I reckon there's trouble brewing there.

Drew Trouble's never far away from Julie.

Angela You're joking! Julie's the least troublesome person I ever kent! I was the one who was always in the shit at school. I was the one that 'got into trouble' with a psycho from Mintlaw. Julie was no trouble at all: always in the top class, straight into that training scheme, passed all the exams, two years offshore being great at her job, and to cap it all she's engaged to this nice-seeming guy who's also earning stacks of cash, who's also got his foot in the door of the whole oil thing.

Drew So what's her problem then? What was all the bawling about?

Angela Her problem is, me and you, we don't have any of that things, but we're still really happy; but Julie, she's got it all, and . . .

Drew . . . she doesn't like it.

Angela Is it not obvious?

Drew To you maybe: you're getting awfully good at working out the thoughts of the Allardyce clan!

Angela (*remembering* **Julie** *said just this earlier on*) You're quite like her really, you know. Exactly like her, except you're the exact opposite. Ken?

Drew You're like her too: speak a terrible hease of shite sometimes.

Angela And you say the nicest things . . . (*They kiss.*) Better go and wake her up, I suppose; she'll want to get her stuff thegether for going offshore the morn. (*She opens the door to the lounge.*)

Drew You do it, you're better at that kind of thing.

Angela   God aye, I'm the Red Adair of emotional blowouts. You ken who Red Adair is, eh?

Drew   Michty aye. (*Pause.*) Used to dance with Ginger Rogers.

14   Survival suits

Early morning. In a departure lounge at Dyce heliport. **Julie**, **David**, **Finn** *and* **Grant** *are struggling into survival suits, along with various other workers about to fly offshore. They all look hungover;* **Julie** *is also approaching an emotional all-time low, and seems distant from the others' wisecracking.*

Julie   One day I'll find a suit that fits me. (*The one she's putting on is much too big.*)

David   Once they'd fished you out of the sea they'd need another half hour to winch you out of the survival suit.

Finn   'Survival' suits! Who are they trying to kid? You'd be better off wearing a dinner jacket and white fucking dickie. At least when they hauled you out of the sea in a block of ice you'd look the part: a fucking penguin. (*He does a penguin walk, then falls down onto a chair.*)

Julie   Who gets the dead man's seat theday then? I'd take it, but I can't, I'm not a man.

Finn   I'll have it, I'll have it. The way my head feels this morning, violent death would be a fucking blessing.

Grant   I'm sure that could be arranged, Finlay.

Voice over PA   Flight 126, 126. The departure of this flight will be delayed by four minutes.

David   Oh shit . . .

Voice   Sorry, that reads forty minutes.

Everybody   Oh shit . . .

Voice   This is due to a helicopter crew shortage. Thankyou.

Finn   No, thank*you*.

Grant   (*as everybody sits down, unzips their suits etc.*)   So chopper captains get hangovers as well.

David   Aye, I saw him last night outside the Schooner, chucking up into his pilot's hat.

Finn   No, that was me with your baseball cap.

David   Makes a change from all of us chucking up in the back of his chopper . . .

Grant   Typical Aberdeen helicopter company, though. Too tight to hire a spare pilot, eh!

Julie   Ha ha.

Grant   Here, that reminds me. Did you hear about the Aberdonian toolpusher? His wife wanted to see what it was like flying offshore, so he has a word with the pilot. Here man, I'll slip you a ten . . . a five . . . three quid if you'll give the wife a hurl. Ach, she can come for nothing, says the pilot, just as long as you sit in the back there and don't interrupt me. Keep quiet and it's a freebie! Well, an hour and a half later they touch down up at one of the Brents. I'm amazed, says the pilot, you came the whole way and never said a word. Aye, says the Aberdonian, it was right hard to keep quiet, especially when we went through that bittie turbulence and the wife fell out of the machine!

Finn   Here's a good one, right. Fred fae Fitty goes and visits Frankie fae Froghall one Saturday morning, and arrives just in time to see him giving each of his five wee kids a fifty pence bit. Pocket-money time, says Frankie. Five times fifty pence every week of the year! says Fred. That's a hell of an amount of siller by Christmas! Extravagance, man! Ah but, says Frankie, I told them the electricity meter's a piggy bank: the bairns keep us in heat and light all year round!

David   Here, this is slander, you bastards!

Grant   Ah, we've touched a nerve I think!

Julie   It's not slander.

Grant   Ah-ha lover boy! *She* has spoken!

Julie   It's downright racist, that's what it is.

Finn   Away and shite!

Grant   Right, there was this Aberdonian working in a shipyard down on the Clyde . . .

David   Christ, this must be an old story.

Grant   And he gets part of his anatomy cut off by a circular saw.

Julie   (*sarcastically*)   Ha ha ha.

Grant   No, it's his hand, his hand gets cut off. Anyway, the man's about to be rushed to hospital, when the ambulance driver says, Quick, get the sawn-off hand, and we'll maybe be able to sew it back on again. So all the guys in the yard, they start searching for the hand, but they can't find it anywhere, it's lost amongst all the scrap and shite on the floor. And the ambulance driver shrugs, and he's just about to piss off, when one of the guy's mates says, Hold on, I've got an idea: once an Aberdonian, always a bloody Aberdonian. And he takes a ten pence piece out of his pocket and drops it on the floor. Tinkle, tinkle tinkle . . . And out scuttles the hand, snatches up the money, and grips on tight all the way to the hospital.

David   That's enough you bastards. I'll show you some *real* Aberdonian culture: the Dance of the Randy Roughneck.

David *starts singing the 'Stripper' tune, with different voices for different instruments etc. He uses this to accompany a comic dance/strip, during which he peels off his survival suit, with teasing looks over his shoulders, pulling up and down of zips etc.* **Finn** *and* **Grant** *join in singing and clapping; they cheer and shout ('Get them off' etc.) at particularly raunchy moments.* **Grant** *in particular tries to involve*

Julie, *by nudging her, tugging at her zips. She gets increasingly pissed off. Just as* **David** *strips the survival suit off completely, there is an announcement:*

Voice over PA   Attention, attention. Flight 126 is now departing. Please board immediately.

Julie   Thank fuck for that!

Finn   Too right: another thirty seconds and he'd've been down to his Ys!

Grant   Christ, you were pretty fucking sexy there Mitchell, I'm telling you. I'd go for him, wouldn't you Julie?

Julie   No, I don't think I would.

15   Accident

A sunny day out on the rig deck. The green light burns steadily. There is the noise of pulleys, motors, wind, generators. **Julie** *and* **Finn** *are hauling the ROV on board after a job, with* **Julie** *watching the videos as before,* **Finn** *handling the cable etc.* **David** *is nearby, working at some tedious task;* **Grant** *is around somewhere too. There is a fairly long period of nothing happening, just to establish the routine everyday nature of the work in progress. After a while, the ROV rises past the edge of the deck, swings a bit, then stops, the cable loose on the deck beneath it.* **Finn** *manipulates the controls for a few seconds, but nothing happens.*

Julie   What's the problem?

Finn   What?

Julie   Why've you stopped?

Finn   It's not me that's fucking stopped.

Julie   Is there a jam?

Finn   I reckon it's the fucking docking device.

Julie   A failure?

Finn   I don't fucking know; it just fucking stopped.

Julie   Let me have a look.

Grant (*pausing as he passes*)   What's up?

Finn   Some kind of fucking jam.

Julie (*examining the winch, from a safe position*)   Maybe the bullet's at an angle and the dogs . . .

Grant   Come on, we can't fuck about, we need to get this bastard out the road afore the supply ship arrives.

Julie You think we like it hanging around? There's a jam in the docking device, we're trying to clear it now!

Grant A jam? you should've said! Roustabout, get over here.

David What's going on?

Grant We need a bit of manpower here, we've got a cable jammed. Get up there and give it a yank will you?

Julie Don't go inside the bight . . .

Grant (**David** *pauses, so he gives him a shove, and spits at* **Julie**:) Here, you might tell him what to do in the fucking bedroom, but not on my fucking deck, okay?

David Hey . . .

Grant We have to get this cleared! Do it! Now!

David *shrugs, goes over to the ROV, and gives a big tug on its cable. Obviously this does some good, for the motor starts again; but something fails to grip, and the ROV falls a few feet instead of rising. This makes the slack cable tighten suddenly, trapping* **David**'s *hand and yanking him up into the air. It happens in an instant.* **David** *screams. All of this very fast and confused and noisy.*

Finn Fuck! Davy!

He runs towards him, then back to the winch controls. The light starts flashing yellow, indicating an alert.

Grant What the fuck's going on?

Finn She's jammed again, the bastard fucking . . .

Grant Mitchell, you stupid cunt!

Julie David! Get him down! (*Runs over and lifts his feet in her arms, trying to take some of the weight off his hand.*)

Finn Grant, get a fucking ladder.

Grant Allardyce, get a ladder here: we have to get this clear . . .

Julie (*taking no notice*) Finn, we have to slacken the cable.

Finn There's only one way to do that: drop her over the side.

Julie Jesus Christ! (*Thinks for a split second, clenched fists to her forehead, but there's only one possible answer for her.*) Go on, ditch the bastard.

Finn Eh . . . are you sure?

Grant (*having found it himself*) Here, stand on this ladder.

Julie He can't stand anywhere, he's fucking unconscious. Finn, cut the umbilical!

Finn I can't ditch her, I hardly got the chance to fly her yet!

Julie Ditch it!

Grant   Stop! We'll take the weight off his hand with the ladder, then figure out some way to . . .

Julie   The cable is cutting his hand off!

Finn   Jesus Christ . . . Grant, you're a witness to this, I don't want to do it, but . . . (*He goes over towards the nearby workshop container.*)

Grant (*blocking* **Finn***'s way*)   That's half a million quids' worth of company property!

Julie   It's that or David's hand.

Grant   Just give me a few minutes to think this over.

Finn   I mean I don't want to lose my contract . . .

Grant   Aye: now *you* wise the fucking head Allardyce.

Julie (*she runs over and knocks* **Grant** *away from the front of the container*)   Right, don't bother yourself Finlay, I'll fucking ditch the bastard.

She grabs a grinder out of the workshop container and starts to cut through the main umbilical cable with it. A shower of sparks flies everywhere. **Grant** *watches, appalled, from the deck.* **Finn** *goes over and supports* **David***.*

Grant   You need a hot work permit for that, for God's sake.

Julie   I don't believe you!

Grant (*getting to his feet, trying to stop her working*)   But this is a serious risk to the whole installation here! Every time a grinder is used you need to obtain a . . .

Finn   Enough Grant, shut your face and help me.

Grant (*goes to help* **Finn***, but is still snarling at* **Julie**)   You know you'll never work offshore again?

Julie   Me or David?

The cable is cut. The ROV falls away. **Finn** *lowers* **David** *to the ground.*

Grant   In fact you'll be run off on the next free seat.

Julie   In that case, Grant . . . (*On the way over towards* **David***, pauses for a second and punches him in the face as hard as she can.*) Finn, get onto the fucking medic, will you, and the radio room for a chopper.

Finn (*runs off, shouting into his radio*)   Medivac! Medivac!

Grant   You're finished out here, Julie Allardyce.

Julie   Thank Christ! I'm finished out here! I'm finished!

Immediately cut into full blast helicopter noise, pitch darkness.

16 No mercy dash

Darkness. Helicopter noise. Lights up on **David** *lying on a stretcher in the back of the chopper.* **Julie** *is sitting beside him. The sound of drumming starts to emerge from under the engine noise, gradually getting louder. The rest of the cast march onto the stage, beating on oil drums and petrol cans, and walls and objects they pass. Their faces are expressionless, hard hats are pulled down over their eyes but the drumming is savage.* **Julie** *watches them for a while, till* **David** *tugs her sleeve, pulls her down towards him, and speaks.*

David Thanks for being there for me Julie. What an idiot, eh? If it hadn't been for you, aye, and Finn as well I suppose, where would I be now? Grant would've left me hanging there till the seagulls picked my een out. No: he'd've ditched me over the edge to save the machine! So thanks, Julie. Specially cause . . . I ken what the ROV meant to you, but you chose me.

He falls silent for a spell. **Julie** *looks at the drummers again. They are now marching in a line, no longer beating on random objects; now they are drumming on the hard hat of the person walking in front of them. Signs of weariness or pain are starting to show on their faces.*

David What's going to happen to me now, eh? This won't do much for my typing speed, will it? Anyway, the hand's still there so who cares. It's good you're here to look after me; as long as you love me I'll be okay.

Julie This is it David . . .

David Aye, this is what's really important.

Julie No, what I mean is, I don't love you.

The drummers, who have taken over from the engine noise completely by this time, fall silent.

David What?

Julie I don't love you David. We better finish. No sense in fooling ourselves. It's over.

David Julie, what do you mean?

Julie Do you think I wouldn't've chose Finn over the ROV? Do you think I wouldn't've chose *Grant*? Fuck's sake! I chose you because you're a human being and the ROV's a lump of metal. That's why I chose you. I didn't choose you cause I love you.

David Julie . . .

Julie Cause I don't love you any more.

The drummers start up again, but this time not with a complex clattering; this time they beat out a slow, steady, simple heartbeat rhythm. **Julie** *talks over the top of them, getting up from her seat and striding about the stage, doubling up or leaping about as the emotions of what she's saying dictate.*

Julie You fall in love, or you dive into love. Either way it's a splash zone. For six months or a year you're battered about, tossed this way and that – you're up on the peaks and down in the troughs – but all the time it's raging, it's whirling, it's a wild wild time.

A force ten time! You're carried along, rushed along, so fast you can't breathe, and there's spray on your face and wind at your back and sun in your eyes. Like that time we went surfing up at the Broch! And it feels so wild, you want it to last for ever, but it's scary as well cause you're not in control. 'See that sea down there? It's a big bad bastard and for now it's tossing us this way and that and we're surfing along and laughing, but any split-second the big old bastard sea could change its mood and break us instead, come crashing down on our heads, big lumps of water crashing and smashing . . .' But there's no time to worry about that even, cause for now you're still being swept along, swept along on top of the waves! Only you're not.

You look around, and something's changed, a year's passed and you're not up amongst the surf and the sky any more, you're cruising along through the depths. You've started to sink, and you never noticed! Everything's calm, everything's smooth, everything's clear – but dark. Down you go, deeper and deeper, still moving forward, but down. From the clear blue water just under the splash zone, down and down to the dark green depths, down and down – and still it's calm and peaceful, no turbulence reaches you now – down to the black, down to the black deeps of the sea. Of love. Deep love. Calm love. Dead love! There's all this weight above you, and it's crushing down upon you. You can't see where you're going, for you're too far away from the outside world – up there, the sun, the waves – you're floating blind through the dark. And after a while it doesn't matter you're blind, cause you're not moving anywhere anyway, you've sunk to a stop, you've rooted in the mud, the mud of the seabed, the mud of the sexbed, the habit of the sex. You're stuck, you're fucking stuck, and by the time you realise, you're almost too late, there's almost no chance whatsoever of escape.

You start to notice the others, the others that mean you're not alone, you're not special, you're not unusual even! Oh no, no: there's others, all around. All around you, stuck in the mud, you hear their mumbles, their jokes, their pet names, their petty rows and hypocritical reconciliations – you see their tight lips and their white-lying eyes and their same old hug, same old handhold, same old kiss or same old sitting at opposite ends of the sofa, rolling to the outside edges of the bed, one in the pub, one in the kitchen, one with the kids, one with the mates, one in the strums, one in a rage, one in tears, one in torment, the other in torment, both in torment and boredom and hatred and torment and self-hatred and . . . that's . . . it . . . till . . . you . . . die.

Unless you break free. Kick your feet free. Get out of that mud. Quick, before it reaches your mouth! Before it reaches your brain . . . While there's still a chance, break free! 'Come back, look out,' the others say, 'what you're doing's dangerous! Never hear of the bends? Decompression sickness? If you break free of the mud and shoot away up, your blood'll boil into bubbles, your heart'll burst, you'll be dead by the time you get back to the air – if the air still exists up there!'

But I don't care, you tell them. That's what I'm saying now: I don't care! I'm going back up, I'm breaking free, I'm heading back up to the air and the light and wild surf. And I'm leaving you David, I'm leaving you, and it breaks my heart, cause I did love you. I loved you, and that's what got us *into* these depths, and the only way out of the depths is to say it, say it, say it: I don't love you, I'm leaving, it's over.

17   Drumallochie

Sudden change from the noise of the flight to gentle fiddle music. We're at Dyce heliport. **Julie** *helps* **David** *down from the helicopter, but as soon as his feet touch the ground his mother and father grab him, shoving* **Julie** *aside.* **David** *does nothing to stop this. Then* **Drew** *appears and leads* **Julie** *away. He sings the whole of the song that he started in scene 5, again with suitable fiddle accompaniment.* **Julie** *seems numb at first, then joins in, singing verse 3 and verse 5. During the course of the song they move away from the heliport; by the end they are back at Ythanbanks.*

Drew
'Twas on a chill November's night when fruits and flowers were gone
One evening as I wandered forth upon the banks of Don
I overheard a fair maid and sweetly thus sang she
'My love he's far from Sinnahard and from Drumallochie'

I said 'My pretty fair maid, you're walking here alone
Lamenting for some absent one upon the banks of Don
Come tell the reason of your grief, come tell it all to me
And why you sigh for Sinnahard and for Drumallochie'

Julie
'Oh Peter was my true love's name upon the banks of Don
He was as fine a young man as e'er the sun shone on
But the cruel wars of Scotland they have parted him from me
And now he's far from Sinnahard and from Drumallochie'

Drew
I said 'My pretty fair maid, come give to me your hand
For on the bonnie banks of Spey I have both house and land
And I will share it all with you if you will be my bride
And you'll forsake the bonnie lad that lived upon Donside'

Julie
Says she 'Kind sir, your offer's good but I must it deny
And for the sake of my true love alone I'll live and die
And for the space of seven years jet black shall cover me
For him who lived at Sinnahard near by Drumallochie'

Drew
But since my love was weeping I could no longer stand
I clasped her in my arm and said 'Oh Betsy know your man
Behold your faithful Peter now he's free from every care
And on the bonnie banks of Don we've met to part no more'

Julie *and* **Drew**
'Aye, on the bonnie banks of Don we've met to part no more'

The fiddle continues for a short time, blending in with birdsong, the sound of the Ythan etc. **Julie** *and* **Drew** *come to a halt.*

Julie   I loved it when granny and granda sang that.

Drew They're real places, you ken, Sinnahard and Drumallochie, up by Kildrummy, that's what's so good about it.

Julie I don't know what's so good about it, but . . . Drew, ken Wattie's cottar house up in the lee of the plantation?

Drew Aye.

Julie Did you knock it down yet?

Drew No, I never got round to emptying it even. Do you want to give's a hand to do that the now?

Julie Not exactly.

The fiddle starts up again, while **Julie** *and* **Drew** *walk on. They enter the old house, shoving the door open, coughing at the dust.*

Drew The power's off at the mains.

Julie Open those shutters, will you?

Drew *opens the shutters, and bright light comes pouring in through the window, leading into the next scene.*

18 A wedding

The Wedding March blasts out on a grand organ. Arched doors at the back of the stage are flung open, and the music gets even louder as people spill out of the kirk. In the middle of the steer is a bride in a big white dress and a groom in a kilt get-up. The lights behind them are so bright that they are more or less silhouetted, and for a while we can't make out who they are. Folk throw confetti over the happy couple, and flashes go off as photos are taken. Everybody is laughing and cheering and shouting. Now the lights from the kirk dim, and we can see that it is **Drew** *and* **Angela** *that have been getting married. They are surrounded by the whole cast, including* **Julie** *and* **David**.

The rig lights start to come up, and also the lights for the river and trees at Ythanbanks. Gradually the cast splits up into separate groups, with **David** *and* **Finn** *and* **Grant** *back on the rig, going through the docking dogs routine that* **Julie** *and* **Finn** *did early on. Elsewhere there are drummers drumming, somebody climbing the Lover's Leap cliff, somebody else playing 'The Bonnie Lass o'Fyvie' on a fiddle.* **Drew** *and* **Angela** *pass from one group to the next getting congratulations from each one.*

Only **Julie** *is by herself. She also passes from one group of folk to the next, but she doesn't interact with them, just looks at them and moves on. When she has visited each group, she comes up to the front of the stage and sings, her voice rising clear above the clashing noises and music behind her.*

Julie
Now there's many a bonnie lass in the Howe of Auchterless
There's many a bonnie lass in the Garioch O
There's many a bonnie Jean in the town of Aberdeen
But the flower of them all bides at Fyvie O

Blackout.

Julie Allardyce

In the spring of 1993, Paul Pinson asked me if I would be interested in writing a play to be co-produced by Boilerhouse and the Lemon Tree. For a few years I had been concentrating on fiction, but I was happy to accept his offer and write for the stage again. This was partly because of Boilerhouse's high reputation as a dynamic young theatre company, and partly because of the Lemon Tree's equally high reputation as a dynamic young venue. But the thing that really got me excited about the commission was that it allowed me to write about the north-east, and for north-east actors; most importantly, it meant the play would have a decent run of performances in the area's capital, Aberdeen. None of my previous plays had stayed in Aberdeenshire for more than a few nights before moving on, so I was keen to make the most of this opportunity to create something specifically for the place I come from.

Initially, we discussed my writing a play about the impact of the oil industry on the north-east. Before long the emphasis, quite rightly, shifted: this was to be a play about the *people* of the north-east, not about 'impact' or any other abstract notion. But I certainly couldn't ignore the oil: I knew from my own experience – and that of my friends and family – that everyone who lives within fifty miles of Aberdeen has their lives affected by the oil every day, whether they like to admit it or not. I felt this to be particularly true of folk of my own age group, whose birth coincided with the discovery of North Sea oil, who have grown up alongside the industry, and whose notion of their identity is far less fixed and certain than that of their immediate ancestors.

My first task in writing the script was to find a character who was typical or representative of this oil generation – somebody born in the mid-sixties or later, who had no personal memory of the pre-oil days, who had been brought up surrounded by, and often taking for granted, the high-tech multinational-capitalist culture that comes along with the oil companies. But somebody who was not *so* far removed from traditional work and life of the north-east that they couldn't feel the pull of the old ways in their bones from time to time. In his trilogy of novels, *A Scots Quair*, set in the Mearns to the south of Aberdeen, Lewis Grassic Gibbon created such a character for the years around the first world war: Chris Guthrie. That is one of the great books of the century, and my own much less ambitious and inspired effort can only suffer by comparison with it. But I feel I should mention Gibbon, because I'm sure his example had a lot to do with the way I came to imagine *my* central character, Julie Allardyce.

While I'm owning up to influences, I should mention a less obvious but probably more important one: Kasimir Malevich, the Ukrainian Suprematist painter. An exhibition of avant-garde art from the years around the Russian Revolution visited Edinburgh in the summer of 1993, and I was immediately excited by the work of Malevich and his contemporaries, especially Liubov Popova and Olga Rosanova. I was very struck by Malevich's pictures, such as *Suprematist Painting: Aeroplane Flying* and *Black Square and Red Square* (both 1915); I loved their clean, sharp lines, and the way the different rectangles and crosses and circles of bright colour floated apart from each other: untouching, but in harmony.

As I wrote *Julie Allardyce*, I found myself attempting to create a dramatic equivalent of a Suprematist painting. Different scenes emerged in different styles – naturalism, folktale-telling, stand-up comedy, Brechtian epic, *son-et-lumière*, bothy nicht . . . you spot them.

My feeling was that life in the north-east these days is fragmented, with bits of old traditional local culture, bits of culture from Europe, Japan, America; there's people born in all parts of the globe settled there, and locals going off to work and live in the Middle East and Texas; there's folk who think oil has been a curse on the way of life in the area, others who think oil saved the north-east from becoming an economic disaster area. I believed it would be fitting to imitate this kaleidescope of experience in the very form of the play. More than that: I thought I would be ignoring the reality of life in the area if I didn't attempt to write a drama of contrasting – but ultimately harmonious – scenes, textures, styles.

I wanted the styles of acting to change from scene to scene. I wanted the lighting to drench each scene in different bright colours, or in darkness. I wanted a soundtrack of delicate fiddle music and brutal industrial noise. I wanted a set of big, bold geometric shapes, echoing both the paintings of Malevich and also the (strangely Suprematist) sights to be seen around Aberdeen harbour: huge blue cranes with yellow jibs, bright red support vessels and orange lifeboats, enormous rectangular sheds along the quays, ferries in blue, white and orange with ten-foot-high lettering on their sides, squads of circular tanks for oil and gas storage. And the green links, the yellow beach, the grey sea and the black black oil.

That's what I thought I wanted, but the director, designer and cast ended up making the play look and feel quite different from how I'd imagined it. They all had a lot of creative input into how *Julie Allardyce* was staged, and I'd like to thank them here for their hard work. I'm sure their efforts had a lot to do with the play's popular success at the Lemon Tree, and with the way it touched many members of the audience at a deep level. Nonetheless, this script is closer to my original vision of the play, and reinstates several scenes that were cut in that production; it also includes a small amount of new material.

Despite the play's venue-specific origins, I hope that someday it will be performed somewhere other than Aberdeen. One thing I came to feel during the writing and production of *Julie Allardyce* was that Julie's problems and dilemmas are, after all, far from unique to the north-east: they crop up everywhere that people are learning to be themselves.

Duncan McLean
August 1994

Duncan McLean was born in Aberdeenshire in 1964. In the mid eighties he was a member of the Merry Mac Fun Co., a cooperative based in Edinburgh, which toured cabaret, street theatre and melodramatic comedies to venues throughout the central belt and the highlands and islands of Scotland. The plays he wrote for the Fun Co. were *The Randan* (1985), *Sharny Dubs* (1986) and *The Country Doctor* (1987). In 1989 two one-act plays were performed at the Pilton Triangle Arts Centre in Edinburgh: *Four Goblin Hamburgers in Gravy* and *Two Young Fuckers*. For the past few years he has been writing fiction. His first book of stories, *Bucket of Tongues*, won a Somerset Maugham Award in 1993; his first novel, *Blackden*, was published by Secker & Warburg in 1994; forthcoming is another novel, *Bunkerman*. He lives in Orkney, where he is working on a non-fiction book about Bob Wills and his Texas Playboys.

Methuen Modern Plays

include work by

Jean Anouilh
John Arden
Margaretta D'Arcy
Peter Barnes
Brendan Behan
Edward Bond
Bertolt Brecht
Howard Brenton
Simon Burke
Jim Cartwright
Caryl Churchill
Noël Coward
Sarah Daniels
Nick Dear
Shelagh Delaney
David Edgar
Dario Fo
Michael Frayn
Paul Godfrey
John Guare
Peter Handke
Declan Hughes
Terry Johnson
Kaufman & Hart
Barrie Keeffe

Larry Kramer
Stephen Lowe
Doug Lucie
John McGrath
David Mamet
Arthur Miller
Mtwa, Ngema & Simon
Tom Murphy
Peter Nichols
Joe Orton
Louise Page
Luigi Pirandello
Stephen Poliakoff
Franca Rame
Philip Ridley
David Rudkin
Willy Russell
Jean-Paul Sartre
Sam Shepard
Wole Soyinka
C. P. Taylor
Theatre Workshop
Sue Townsend
Timberlake Wertenbaker
Victoria Wood

Methuen World Classics

Aeschylus (two volumes)
Jean Anouilh
John Arden (two volumes)
Arden & D'Arcy
Aristophanes (two volumes)
Aristophanes & Menander
Peter Barnes (two volumes)
Brendan Behan
Aphra Behn
Edward Bond (four volumes)
Bertolt Brecht
  (four volumes)
Howard Brenton
  (two volumes)
Büchner
Bulgakov
Calderón
Anton Chekhov
Caryl Churchill
  (two volumes)
Noël Coward (five volumes)
Sarah Daniels (two volumes)
Eduardo De Filippo
David Edgar (three volumes)
Euripides (three volumes)
Dario Fo (two volumes)
Michael Frayn (two volumes)
Max Frisch
Gorky
Harley Granville Barker
  (two volumes)
Henrik Ibsen (six volumes)
Terry Johnson

Lorca (three volumes)
David Mamet
Marivaux
Mustapha Matura
David Mercer
  (two volumes)
Arthur Miller
  (four volumes)
Anthony Minghella
Molière
Tom Murphy
  (three volumes)
Peter Nichols
  (two volumes)
Clifford Odets
Joe Orton
Louise Page
A. W. Pinero
Luigi Pirandello
Stephen Poliakoff
  (two volumes)
Terence Rattigan
Ntozake Shange
Sophocles (two volumes)
Wole Soyinka
David Storey
  (two volumes)
August Strindberg
  (three volumes)
J. M. Synge
Ramón del Valle-Inclán
Frank Wedekind
Oscar Wilde